Teacher's
Edition
→ *Level 4* ←

→ *Program Authors* ←

Carl Bereiter, Ph.D.

Sandra N. Kaplan, Ed.D.

Michael Pressley, Ph.D.

*A Division of The **McGraw·Hill** Companies*

Columbus, Ohio

www.sra4kids.com

SRA/McGraw-Hill

*A Division of The **McGraw·Hill** Companies*

Send all inquiries to:
SRA/McGraw-Hill
8787 Orion Place
Columbus, OH 43240-4027

Printed in the United States of America.

ISBN 0-07-572499-5

2 3 4 5 6 7 8 9 QPD 07 06 05 04 03

Table of Contents

UNIT 1 Risks and Consequences

Good-by Violet

   a fantasy by Roald Dahl ✦ *illustrated by* Doris Ettlinger

Thinking Skills:

Determining Cause and Effect	Identifying Synonyms	Evaluating Risks and Consequences
Identifying Cause-and-Effect Relationships	Drawing Conclusions	Redesigning Ideas
Adding to Expanding Vocabulary	Extrapolating Information	Summarizing Opinions
	Determining Motivation	Evaluating a Character's Actions
	Evaluating Actions	Formulating Questions
	Making Inferences	

Mella: Young Friend of the Python

   a legend from Zimbabwe retold by Marianna Mayer

   illustrated by Shelley Johnson

Thinking Skills:

Identifying Main Events	Judging Circumstances	Identifying Elements of a Legend
Sequencing Main Events	Proving with Observation	Making Connections
Comprehending Poetic Devices	Determining Character Traits	Summarizing Concepts
Understanding Author's Purpose	Evaluating a Character's Thoughts and Actions	Evaluating Relationships
Proving with Examples		Determining Relevance

Behind Rebel Lines: The Incredible Story of Emma

   historical fiction by Seymour Reit ✦ *illustrated by* Meg Aubrey

Thinking Skills:

Identifying Unfamiliar Words	Proving with Examples	Judging Character
Defining Unfamiliar Words	Evaluating a Character's Actions and Behavior	Determining Purpose
Determining Character Traits	Recalling Details	Redesigning an Identity
Drawing Conclusions	Evaluating Actions through Persuasive Writing	Extrapolating Information
		Formulating Questions
		Comparing Perceptions

UNIT 2 Dollars and Sense . . 20A

UNIT 3 From Mystery to Medicine

Communication 74A

UNIT 6 A Changing America 94A

Cultivating a Lifelong Love of Learning

UNIT 5

Storytelling

The universe is made of stories, not atoms.
—Muriel Rukeyser—

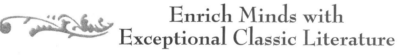

Enrich Minds with Exceptional Classic Literature

Open Court Classics contains an unmatched collection of selections including essays, poems, myths, and fables for children in Levels 2–6. From the heartwarming tale of sisterly love in Louisa May Alcott's *Little Women*, to the fantasy of Margery Williams's *The Velveteen Rabbit*, the literature in **Open Court Classics** provides students with a challenging array of literary themes and genres.

Provide Quality
Literature with a Purpose

Each unit of ***Open Court Classics*** explores a comprehensive, interesting theme and encourages students to develop higher-order thinking skills in the evaluation of their reading.

The wide variety of literature in ***Open Court Classics*** shares common goals: it spurs new thoughts, challenges old notions, and helps students develop new levels of understanding.

Shaping a New Generation of Literary Minds

Hurt No Living Thing

by Christina Rossetti
illustrated by Jim Effler

Hurt no living thing:
  Ladybird, nor butterfly,
Nor moth with dusty wing,
  Nor cricket chirping cheerily,
Nor grasshopper so light of leap,
  Nor dancing gnat, nor beetle fat,
Nor harmless worms that creep.

109

Student Anthology, Level 2

Challenge Students through Literature

Kipling. Plath. Alcott. Whitman. Orwell. Frost. Their classic writings have influenced generations of young readers. **Open Court Classics** gives students the opportunity to read these and many more treasured authors. This helps students develop a foundation of literary awareness that can serve as a springboard for a lifelong love of learning.

Open Court Classics will challenge students to improve their higher-order thinking skills, language skills, and reading comprehension, while giving them the chance to read some of the finest examples of literature available for young people.

Enhance Students' Critical Thinking Skills

Open Court Classics can be used as a supplemental reading program for enhancing any curriculum for advanced students. Flexibly designed with lessons that encourage independent study, ***Open Court Classics*** is easily adaptable for both the teacher's and students' needs. Students well-suited for the program include those who have the following traits:

- A wide-ranging core of general knowledge
- Extensive vocabulary, sharp memory, and the ability to readily use abstract reasoning
- The ability to produce new ideas by bringing together elements usually thought of as independent or dissimilar
- Keen interest or skill in problem solving
- Motivation to work independently

> "Using a broad definition of giftedness, a school system could expect to identify 10% to 15% or more of its student population as gifted and talented."
>
> *–Council for Exceptional Children*

 **Implement the Program with Ease**

Each level of ***Open Court Classics*** contains three simple components: the ***Teacher's Edition***, the ***Student Anthology***, and the ***Responding to Literature*** workbook. Differentiating instruction has never been easier than with ***Open Court Classics***. Workbook lessons have been designed to allow for as much or as little teacher involvement as desired. Students can work on lessons independently or in small groups.

Creating Independent Learners

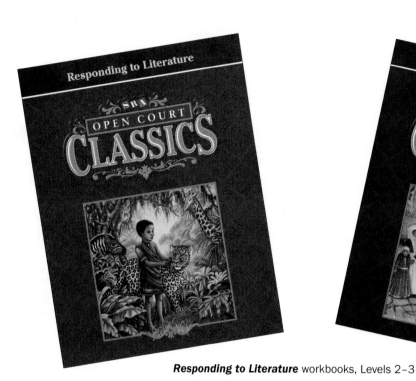

Responding to Literature workbooks, Levels 2–3

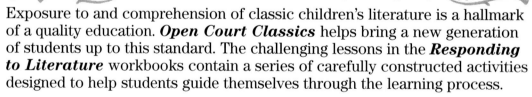 Build Knowledge through Inquiry

Exposure to and comprehension of classic children's literature is a hallmark of a quality education. ***Open Court Classics*** helps bring a new generation of students up to this standard. The challenging lessons in the ***Responding to Literature*** workbooks contain a series of carefully constructed activities designed to help students guide themselves through the learning process.

The activities focus heavily on independent inquiry and investigation. Students continually evaluate their findings to assess new questions that arise. This circular learning process helps students to build continually upon their foundation of knowledge.

Responding to Literature workbooks, Levels 4–6

Foster Character Building

In recent years, many states have begun programs that teach students the basics of character. ***Open Court Classics*** includes character-building concepts within each unit that help foster and reinforce positive personality traits and behaviors.

By encouraging students to evaluate the characters, themes, and situations found in their reading with activities such as What Would You Do?, students begin to refine their understanding of how personality traits guide actions and consequences. Character-building concepts help students to better understand key character traits such as kindness, respect, trustworthiness, and responsibility.

Taking Advantage of Built-In Teacher Support

Workbook activities encourage students to find answers and think critically.

Useful teacher support helps guide students through activities.

The Next Step takes students beyond the activity to further writing or research.

UNIT 4
Robinson Crusoe
Lesson 3

Objective
Students will think critically about items necessary for their survival.

Thinking Skills
✦ Prioritizing personal needs
✦ Judging basic necessities
✦ Distinguishing essentials from nonessentials

Activity
Ask students what basic necessities they need to survive for one day. Then have students imagine that they are in a situation similar to Crusoe's and must prioritize the supplies necessary for survival. Encourage students to think about the importance of companionship. Point out that in addition to the supplies Crusoe took from the ship, he retrieved two cats and a dog to keep him company.

The Next Step
Have students conduct research to identify different kinds of survival kits, such as wilderness or natural disaster survival kits. Then have students investigate the contents of each survival kit, such as a flashlight, compass, and water bottle, and the emergency situation for which each kit is intended. You might also suggest that students create a survival kit for their home or classroom based on the needs of the area in which they live.

58   **Unit 4 Survival ✦ Robinson Crusoe**

Name_____ Date_____

UNIT 4 Survival • *Robinson Crusoe*

What Would You Do?
The morning after Robinson Crusoe washes ashore, he returns to his ship looking for supplies. Because the small raft he built cannot carry much weight, he must carefully choose what to take. The items he selects are food, clothing, and tools.

Imagine that, like Crusoe, you have only three boxes to fill with supplies. You do not know how long you will be stranded or what you will find on the island. If you could take whatever you want from your home, what would you choose to help you survive? Choose a category label for each box, such as *Food* or *Clothing*. Then choose the items that will go in it. Explain why you chose each item. **Possible answers below:**

Box 1 Category: Clothing

Items: Shoes to protect my feet; long pants to protect my legs from sharp rocks; a coat to wear if it is cold.

Box 2 Category: Gear

Items: A flashlight to see in the dark; a net to catch fish.

Box 3 Category: First-aid Kit

Items: Bandages to cover scratches or cuts; sunscreen to protect my skin.

When your list is complete, meet with a classmate to discuss and compare items.

58   Robinson Crusoe ✦ Open Court Classics

Responding to Literature p. 58

Teacher Tip As students complete the assigned *Responding to Literature* pages, be sure they progress with recognizing information needs related to the topics of their knowledge-building projects.

The open, flexible instructional plan in **Open Court Classics** makes it easy for teachers to have as much or as little involvement as they want in their students' daily activities. Options for different instructional tactics are included in each lesson so that teachers can guide the lesson in a variety of ways.

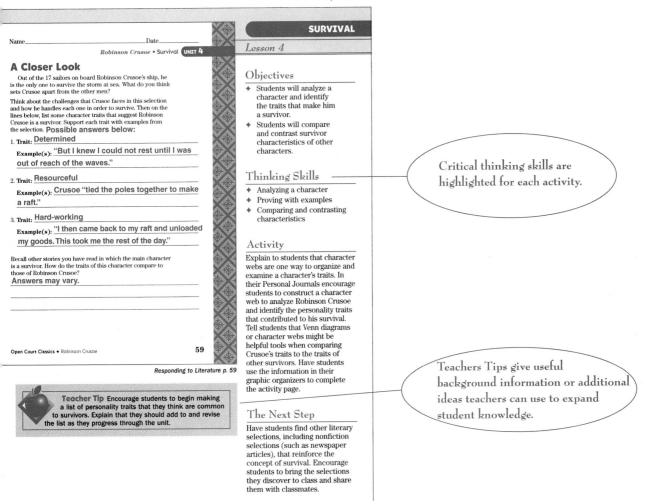

Name_____ Date_____

Robinson Crusoe • Survival **UNIT 4**

A Closer Look

Out of the 17 sailors on board Robinson Crusoe's ship, he is the only one to survive the storm at sea. What do you think sets Crusoe apart from the other men?

Think about the challenges that Crusoe faces in this selection and how he handles each one in order to survive. Then on the lines below, list some character traits that suggest Robinson Crusoe is a survivor. Support each trait with examples from the selection. **Possible answers below:**

1. **Trait:** Determined

   Example(s): "But I knew I could not rest until I was out of reach of the waves."

2. **Trait:** Resourceful

   Example(s): Crusoe "tied the poles together to make a raft."

3. **Trait:** Hard-working

   Example(s): "I then came back to my raft and unloaded my goods. This took me the rest of the day."

Recall other stories you have read in which the main character is a survivor. How do the traits of this character compare to those of Robinson Crusoe?
Answers may vary.

Open Court Classics ✦ Robinson Crusoe   **59**

Responding to Literature p. 59

Teacher Tip Encourage students to begin making a list of personality traits that they think are common to survivors. Explain that they should add to and revise the list as they progress through the unit.

SURVIVAL

Lesson 4

Objectives

✦ Students will analyze a character and identify the traits that make him a survivor.
✦ Students will compare and contrast survivor characteristics of other characters.

Thinking Skills

✦ Analyzing a character
✦ Proving with examples
✦ Comparing and contrasting characteristics

Activity

Explain to students that character webs are one way to organize and examine a character's traits. In their Personal Journals encourage students to construct a character web to analyze Robinson Crusoe and identify the personality traits that contributed to his survival. Tell students that Venn diagrams or character webs might be helpful tools when comparing Crusoe's traits to the traits of other survivors. Have students use the information in their graphic organizers to complete the activity page.

The Next Step

Have students find other literary selections, including nonfiction selections (such as newspaper articles), that reinforce the concept of survival. Encourage students to bring the selections they discover to class and share them with classmates.

Unit 4 Survival ✦ **Robinson Crusoe**   **59**

Critical thinking skills are highlighted for each activity.

Teachers Tips give useful background information or additional ideas teachers can use to expand student knowledge.

Students explore each unit through a series of three to four lessons and use their findings from each lesson to help prepare their comprehensive, knowledge-building projects. The projects, presented to the class at the end of the unit, offer students a chance to demonstrate the skills and knowledge they have developed relating to each unit theme. Depending on the number of selections in the unit, students will spend about six weeks on each unit.

Simple assessment tools are built into each unit. In the Appendix of each ***Teacher's Edition***, teachers will find the scope and sequence and explanations of the assessment rubrics.

Putting the Components to Use

Student Anthologies **(Levels 2–6)**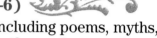

Contain collections of classic stories including poems, myths, and fables. Each unit is organized by a theme that matches those found in *Open Court Reading*.

Responding to Literature **Workbooks (Levels 2–6)**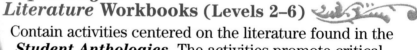

Contain activities centered on the literature found in the ***Student Anthologies***. The activities promote critical thinking skills and independent learning through inquiry and investigation.

Teacher's Editions **(Levels 2–6)**

Provide all the information needed for each lesson. Easy-to-use and well organized, the instruction in the ***Teacher's Editions*** is designed to foster independent student learning. Informal assessment tools are included for each lesson.

 Support for Teaching

Professional tools and additional resources for the program can be found at the SRA Web site, www.sra4kids.com.

 # Written by Trusted and Experienced Authors

Carl Bereiter, Ph.D.

An accomplished author, researcher, and professor, Dr. Bereiter has published extensively on teaching and learning. He serves as Professor at the Centre for Applied Cognitive Science, Ontario Institute for Studies in Education.

- Invented CSILE (Computer Supported Intentional Learning Environments), the first networked collaborative learning environment in schools, with Dr. Marlene Scardamalia. The current version, *Knowledge Forum®*, is in use in 12 countries.
- Coauthor of *Surpassing Ourselves: An Inquiry into the Nature and Implications of Expertise*
- Author of *Education and Mind of the Knowledge Age*
- One of 100 people honored in the Routledge Great Thinkers in Education
- Member of the National Academy of Education

Michael Pressley, Ph.D.

Honored by the National Reading Conference as the 2000 recipient of the Oscar Causey Award for career contributions to reading research, Dr. Pressley was recently inducted into the International Reading Association's Hall of Fame. Currently Dr. Pressley is Professor of Teacher Education, Literacy, and Educational Psychology at Michigan State University.

- Editor of *Journal of Educational Psychology*
- Author of *Reading Instruction That Works: The Case for Balanced Teaching* and coauthor of *Learning to Read: Lessons from Exemplary First-Grade Classrooms*
- An expert in comprehension instruction and in the ethnographic study of the elementary classroom experience
- Author of more than 250 scientific articles

Sandra N. Kaplan, Ed.D.

An expert in the field of gifted education, Dr. Kaplan currently serves as Associate Clinical Professor in the Rossier School of Education at the University of Southern California.

- Coauthor of *Lessons from the Middle: High End Learning for Middle School Students* and *The Gifted Emergent English Language Learner*
- Executive Committee Member of the World Council on the Gifted
- Past President of the National Association of the Gifted
- Author of more than 40 articles and books on gifted education

 # Reviewers

Catherine Brighton
Associate Professor
Charlottesville, VA

Julie Canzone
Teacher
Inglewood, CA

Kim Dodds
Teacher
Corona del Mar, CA

Ellen Edmonds
Director of Early Childhood
Charlotte, NC

Olga Lentine
Magnet Coordinator
Los Angeles, CA

Martha Scherpelz
Teacher, Gifted and Talented
Dublin, OH

Margaret Shandorf
Resource Teacher
West Palm Beach, FL

Pat Thurman
Coordinator, Gifted and
Talented Education
Santa Ana, CA

Frances Weissenberger
Teacher
Los Angeles, CA

Kristin Worden
Teacher
Los Angeles, CA

First weigh the considerations,
then take the risks.
—Helmuth von Moltke—

Unit Goals

- To extend understanding of what motivates people to take risks
- To identify the elements of a fantasy
- To read a legend and recognize its characteristic elements
- To discuss the risks and consequences associated with trust
- To evaluate the authenticity of a work of historical fiction
- To investigate risks and consequences faced by workers in a variety of professions

Introduction

Many of the choices that we make involve taking risks. Whether the consequences are positive or negative, taking risks helps us learn about ourselves and others. This is demonstrated by the selections in this unit, which feature three main characters with very different reasons for taking risks. Selection 1 is "Good-by Violet" on page 12; Selection 2 is "Mella: Young Friend of the Python" on page 22; and Selection 3 is "Behind Rebel Lines: The Incredible Story of Emma Edmonds, Civil War Spy" on page 30. Reading and discussing these selections will encourage students to consider various motivations for and consequences of taking risks.

Unit Discussion

To help students begin thinking about the unit theme, ask them to share what they already know about risks and consequences. Invite students to tell the class about their personal experiences or about stories they have read that relate to risks and consequences. Continue the discussion by asking questions such as the following:

✦ What are some reasons that people take risks?

✦ What does the quotation in the unit opener mean to you?

✦ What are some possible consequences of *not* taking a risk?

Knowledge-Building Project

In this unit students will investigate careers that involve risk taking. Tell students that while nearly every worker faces risks at some point in his or her career, there are some professions in which workers must deal with risks on a regular basis. Have students brainstorm a list of professions that they feel are especially risky. Fire fighting and law enforcement are likely to appear on students' lists of risky professions. If students have difficulty naming other careers, encourage them to consider jobs in such fields as medicine, finance, entertainment, sports, and the military. For each profession on the list, students should note what they perceive to be some of the associated risks and possible consequences. Remind them that throughout the unit they should return to this list to review the items that they have already recorded and to add new ideas. As students proceed through the unit, they will learn more about the risks and consequences of a particular profession and will interview someone who works in that field. As part of the Unit Wrap-Up, students will present the results of their research in writing or on videocassette.

> **Teacher Tip**
> As an alternative to the outlined project, students might want to investigate an entrepreneur and write a mock interview. Interview questions and answers formulated by students should focus on the risks and consequences involved as the entrepreneur began his or her business venture.

	Unit 1 Project Overview
Unit Overview	Students begin their investigations by brainstorming a list of jobs that are associated with risk taking.
Selection 1	Students select a profession for investigation and begin their research.
Selection 2	Students formulate interview questions.
Selection 3	Students interview a person who works in the selected profession and make final preparations for their presentations.
Unit Wrap-Up	Students present the results of their research.

Good-by Violet

Student Anthology pp. 12–21

Selection Goals

- To recognize that a fantasy is an imaginary story that includes characters, settings, and events that do not exist or occur in the real world
- To understand the selection's appeal to readers
- To understand how this selection relates to risks and consequences

Selection Summary

This selection is an excerpt from Roald Dahl's classic fantasy book *Charlie and the Chocolate Factory*. As one of five lucky children touring Willy Wonka's chocolate factory, Violet Beauregarde gets to see how Wonka's candies are made. However, when she does not do as she is told, she has to face some surprising consequences.

Genre: Fantasy

Share with students some of the elements of a fantasy, which include

- ✦ people, animals, or objects that do things they cannot do in the real world.

- ✦ creatures and settings that do not exist in the real world.

- ✦ events that could not happen in the real world.

⇢ *Part 1* ⇠
Building Background

Activate Prior Knowledge

✦ Ask students to share information or ideas they have about the book *Charlie and the Chocolate Factory* or the movie *Willy Wonka and the Chocolate Factory*, which was based on the book.

✦ Have students discuss what it would be like to visit a candy factory. Encourage them to talk about whether they think it would be challenging to control their behavior in such a place.

✦ Ask students to share stories about a time when they did not weigh the possible outcomes before taking a risk, and their actions resulted in a humorous or interesting consequence.

Background Information

✦ This work of fantasy does have some basis in reality. Roald Dahl attended a school located near a chocolate factory in Derbyshire, England. The factory was Cadbury's, a famous chocolate maker in England, and students at the school were often invited to test new types of candy bars.

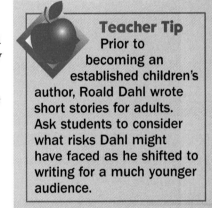

Teacher Tip
Prior to becoming an established children's author, Roald Dahl wrote short stories for adults. Ask students to consider what risks Dahl might have faced as he shifted to writing for a much younger audience.

✦ Dahl once remarked that if he had not had children of his own, he would not have been capable of writing books for children. Dahl made a deliberate effort to view the world through children's eyes, which is one of the reasons he has been called the most successful children's author in the world. Dahl was able to capture and portray children's hopes, fears, and dreams in entertaining stories.

✦ Several of Dahl's children's books have been made into feature films. The films include *Willy Wonka and the Chocolate Factory*, *James and the Giant Peach*, and *Matilda*. Each of these works contains elements of fantasy, which Dahl frequently used.

Previewing the Literature

Browse the Selection

✦ Ask volunteers to read aloud the title, the name of the author, and the name of the illustrator. Then have students browse the first page or two of the selection to look for clues that tell them something about the selection or to look for anything that catches their attention, such as challenging or unfamiliar words. Remind students not to browse the entire selection to avoid ruining any surprises that might occur at the end.

✦ Note on the board those things students mention as a result of their browsing and any questions they have about the selection.

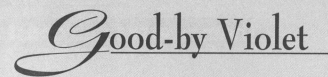

Set Purposes for Reading

As they read, have students focus on how Dahl uses dialogue to move the selection along, his vivid descriptions of people and events, and his use of humor.

Expanding Vocabulary

Students can use a variety of skills, such as context clues, word structure, and apposition, to determine the meanings of words. They can apply these skills while reading to clarify other challenging words. The words listed below can be found in the Glossary of the *Student Anthology.* Page numbers indicate where the words can be found in the selection.

spellbound, p. 16 Held by another as if under an incantation, or spell.

gaping, p. 16 Staring at in amazement.

peculiar, p. 18 Strange; unusual.

Have students bring in a spiral notebook or three-ring binder to use as a Personal Journal and divide it into at least four sections. Add any new sections that you and your students find useful.

✦ **Vocabulary Words**—for selection vocabulary words and definitions

✦ **Writing**—for workbook assignments or knowledge-building projects

✦ **Research Notes**—for notes taken on their knowledge-building projects

✦ **Selection Questions**—for any questions they have about the selection

⋄ Part 2 ⋄

Reading the Selection

Read

✦ Have students silently read *Student Anthology* pages 12–21, stopping at the end of each page if they have any questions or need clarification.

✦ Encourage students to use visualizing or any other comprehension strategies that might help them read the selection.

Discuss

The following discussion suggestions can be carried out on different days, depending upon how much time you allot to each selection.

✦ Have students discuss their general reactions to the selection.

✦ Ask students how this selection relates to the theme.

✦ Encourage students to review the questions they listed on the board before reading to see if the selection answered their questions.

✦ Have students review the elements of a fantasy. Then have them discuss those elements of "Good-by Violet" that are not possible or do not exist in real life.

✦ Have students discuss what they learned about Violet Beauregarde from the speech and actions of her parents.

✦ Have students discuss whether the consequences of Violet's actions were appropriate or too harsh.

After students have discussed the selection, choose from ***Responding to Literature*** pages 2–7, and ask students to complete the assigned pages.

✧ Part 3 ✦
Knowledge-Building Project

Have students review their lists and begin to think about which profession they would like to investigate. If students are having difficulty generating a list of professions, suggest that they use resources such as university course books or the yellow pages for ideas. You might also suggest that students conduct preliminary research on several of the professions to determine which one they find appealing. This initial investigation could lead to new discoveries that take their research in a different direction. Encourage students to be open to such changes in this early stage of their investigations.

Once students select a profession to investigate, they should conduct research to discover more about the work and the risks involved. Literature produced by professional organizations might be especially helpful. In their Personal Journals have students make a list of questions that they have about the career they have chosen to investigate. Students might inquire about the job description, motivations for entering the field, the education and/or training required, the work environment, and risks encountered.

By the end of the next selection, each student should have prepared a list of interview questions to ask someone who works in the career being investigated.

> **Assessment**
> Use the Research Rubrics: Recognizing Information Needs on Appendix page 148 of the *Teacher's Edition* to assess how well students identify relevant sources. Discuss with students the rubrics that will be used to evaluate their projects.

UNIT 1

Good-by Violet
Lesson 1

Objective

Students will learn to identify cause-and-effect relationships.

Thinking Skills

✦ Determining cause and effect
✦ Identifying cause-and-effect relationships

Activity

Suggest that students think about cause-and-effect relationships associated with characters other than Violet. Then have students review the selection to identify examples of cause-and-effect relationships. Encourage them to display the information in a graphic organizer that illustrates the causes and corresponding effects.

The Next Step

Have students discuss why they think writers create cause-and-effect relationships in stories. Ask them to compare causes and effects with risks and consequences. You might also suggest that students brainstorm several cause-and-effect situations they might experience during a day at school, a day with friends, and so on.

Name_____ Date_____

Getting Started

This excerpt from *Charlie and the Chocolate Factory* shows how certain *causes*, or actions, lead to certain *effects*, or results. These are called *cause-and-effect relationships* in all stories. For example, a cause might be Charlie finding a dollar bill. An effect of this is Charlie buying a candy bar with a Golden Ticket.

Refer to the selection and identify other cause-and-effect relationships. Then in the space below or in your Personal Journal, create a graphic organizer to organize this information and show the connections among events.

Possible graphic organizer and answers below:

Cause	Effect
Charlie Bucket finds a dollar bill.	He buys a Wonka candy bar.
Charlie finds a Golden Ticket in the candy wrapper.	He gets to visit Willy Wonka's chocolate factory.
Wonka invented a gum meal.	Cooking and kitchens are no longer necessary.
Violet ignores Wonka's warnings.	She chews the new gum.
Violet turns into a blueberry.	She is rolled to the Juicing Room.

2   Good-by Violet ✦ Open Court Classics

Responding to Literature p. 2

Teacher Tip Explain to students that one cause might have many effects, or several causes might result in a single effect. To illustrate this point, have students identify at least two effects for one of the causes they identified and at least two causes for one of the effects.

Name_____ Date_____

I Can Do It, Too

How do authors, such as Roald Dahl, use words to create a sense of excitement in a story? Instead of repeating the same words, Dahl uses *synonyms*, which are different words that mean the same thing. What words did you find in the selection that gave you a sense of excitement as you read?

Look back at the selection and list these words below. Then find another word in the selection that has a similar meaning. Finally, think of a synonym to go with the synonym pairs from the selection. **Possible answers below:**

Synonym Pairs		My Synonym
1. amazing	fascinating	astonishing
2. terrific	marvelous	stupendous
3. watching	staring	observing
4. absolutely	utterly	completely
5. screamed	screeched	bellowed
6. enormous	gigantic	massive
7. minute	instant	moment
8. yelled	shouted	exclaimed

Extra Effort: Write an antonym for each synonym pair listed. Then think about the techniques used by authors to create excitement in other stories you have read. How do the techniques used by these authors compare to the techniques used by Dahl in "Good-by Violet"?

Open Court Classics ✦ Good-by Violet   **3**

Responding to Literature p. 3

Teacher Tip Comprehension Strategies Ask students whether they visualized as they read the selection. Discuss how visualizing helps readers better understand what they read.

Assessment Use the Informal Comprehension Strategies Rubrics: Visualizing on Appendix page 145 of the *Teacher's Edition* to assess how well students visualize.

Objective

Students will increase their vocabularies and learn to identify synonyms.

Thinking Skills

✦ Adding to expanding vocabulary
✦ Identifying synonyms

Activity

Ask students why an author might include synonyms in his or her writing. Encourage students to describe how synonyms might make a selection more interesting to read. Then have students identify pairs of synonyms from the selection. Ask students to think of another synonym for each pair. Encourage students to discuss the slightly different meanings of the synonyms and how they might change what readers feel and think.

The Next Step

Explain that tone conveys the mood, such as serious or humorous, of a selection. Then have students read another selection by Roald Dahl and compare its tone with "Good-by Violet." How do the levels of energy and excitement compare in the two pieces? Ask students to identify the techniques Dahl uses to set the tone for each selection.

Objective

Students will think and write creatively to extend the author's ideas.

Thinking Skills

◆ Drawing conclusions
◆ Extrapolating information

Activity

Have students think about what might happen to Violet in the Juicing Room and about different ways this selection could have ended. Encourage students to list ideas for both an additional paragraph and an alternative ending before choosing which they will write. Suggest that students draw an illustration to accompany their work. Allow time for students to share their completed work with the rest of the class.

The Next Step

Encourage students to consider the risks they took when writing their additional paragraphs, or when writing their alternative endings. Have students think about different consequences that could result from their risks. Ask them to consider which involves a greater risk—writing or sharing your writing with others. Then encourage students to compare their risks to the risks an author like Dahl might take when writing an ending. What consequences might occur?

Name_____ Date_____

Just Imagine

Roald Dahl ends the selection with the Oompa-Loompas taking Violet to the Juicing Room. However, Dahl does not give any clues about what is going to happen next. What do you think will happen to Violet in the Juicing Room? How would you have ended the selection?

Use the lines below to begin planning and organizing your ideas. Then in your Personal Journal, write a paragraph describing what happens to Violet in the Juicing Room, or write an alternative ending to the excerpt. When you have finished drafting, revising, and editing, read your paragraph or alternative ending to the class.

Ideas may vary.

_____

_____

_____

_____

_____

_____

_____

_____

_____

See Appendix pages 128–129 for writing a description and Appendix pages 133–134 for writing a paragraph.

4   Good-by Violet ◆ **Open Court Classics**

Responding to Literature p. 4

Teacher Tip For this activity, encourage students to incorporate in their own writing the techniques that Dahl uses. It might be helpful for students to list some elements of Dahl's style—for example, use of dialogue, humor, and words that create a sense of energy and excitement—before getting started.

Name_____ Date_____

Lesson 4

Life Lessons

In this selection, how is Violet's lack of respect or value for adults implied by the author? Review the selection and look for ways in which Dahl provides the readers with some clues about how Violet might have become this way. Look closely at the characters of Mr. and Mrs. Beauregarde. What did you think about the two characters as you read? How did their actions play a role in Violet's dilemma?

In the space below, create a web to analyze the characters of Mr. and Mrs. Beauregarde. Then in your Personal Journal, write a persuasive paragraph explaining how they influenced Violet. When you have finished, answer the question below.

Possible character web:

passive
They let Violet chew the gum.

encouraging
(Mr. and Mrs. Beauregarde)
They cheered for Violet.

accusing
They blamed Wonka.

How did this story affect your ideas about how children should communicate with adults?
Answers may vary.

_____

See Appendix pages 120–121 for persuasive writing and Appendix pages 133–134 for writing a paragraph.

Open Court Classics ✦ Good-by Violet   **5**

Responding to Literature p. 5

Objective

Students will learn to analyze characters and write a persuasive paragraph to support their analyses.

Thinking Skills

✦ Determining motivation
✦ Evaluating actions
✦ Making inferences

Activity

Have students review the selection to examine the speech and actions of Violet's parents. As students create a character web to analyze Mr. and Mrs. Beauregarde, they should form opinions about whether these two characters influence Violet's decision to take a risk. Remind students that in persuasive writing, the writer's opinion should be clearly stated and supported with evidence from the text.

The Next Step

Have students form two teams to debate the issue of whether or not Violet's parents are partially responsible for what happens to her. Have several students act as judges to determine which team's arguments are more convincing.

Teacher Tip **Writing** Explain that in order for a persuasive paragraph to be convincing, the writer must have a clear purpose. Encourage students to generate ideas and organize their thoughts so their purposes are clear before they begin to write their paragraphs.

Assessment Use the Getting Ideas Writing Rubric on Appendix page 146 of the *Teacher's Edition* to assess how well students generate and evaluate ideas.

Good-by Violet
Lesson 5

Objectives

✦ Students will write a press release from the perspective of Willy Wonka to promote an invention.
✦ Students will consider the risks and consequences associated with creating a new candy or improving an existing candy.

Thinking Skills

✦ Evaluating risks and consequences
✦ Redesigning ideas

Activity

Ask students to consider the risks and consequences associated with inventing something new. You might ask students to recall a time they tried a new product. How might their responses have affected the inventor and his or her invention? Then have students write a press release from the perspective of Willy Wonka to describe a newly invented candy. Encourage students to share their press releases with the rest of the class.

The Next Step

Have students conduct research to find out how some popular candy bars and other sweets got their names.

Name_____ Date_____

Think like an Inventor

The setting of this selection is the Inventing Room of Willy Wonka's magical factory, where he makes delightful treats with interesting names. Who could resist a Whipple-Scrumptious Fudgemallow Delight, an Everlasting Gobstopper, or a Scrumdidilyumptious Bar?

As an inventor, Mr. Wonka must take risks in order to create new things or improve existing things. Consider the risk involved when creating a new candy with an unusual taste or flavor. Think about the consequence if people dislike the new candy. Imagine that you are Mr. Willy Wonka. Use the lines below to come up with ideas for your newest, *most* unusual candy. Then in your Personal Journal, write a press release about your new invention. In your press release, explain what risks you had to take and why, and what reactions you expect from consumers.

Ideas may vary.

_____

_____

_____

_____

_____

_____

_____

See Appendix page 135 for writing a press release.

Extra Effort: Think about an invention that affects your life. Investigate the risks the inventor had to take and the consequences that might have occurred. Record what you learned from your research in your Personal Journal; then share your findings with the class.

6   Good-by Violet ✦ Open Court Classics

Responding to Literature p. 6

Teacher Tip Students might enjoy compiling a class cookbook. Encourage them to bring in real recipes for their favorite sweet treats or create recipes for their invented candies.

Teacher Tip As students complete the assigned *Responding to Literature* pages, be sure they continue to recognize information needs as they select a profession to investigate for their projects.

Name_____ Date_____

In My Opinion

In the Inventing Room, everyone gathers around Violet as she chews the newly invented gum. Although Willy Wonka tries many times to warn Violet not to chew the gum, she refuses to listen. The author describes the drastic changes that happen as Violet swells into a giant blueberry.

Consider the risk taken by Violet in this selection. What consequences do you think Violet considered before taking the risk? Summarize your thoughts about Violet's choices and the consequences of her actions on the lines below. Then meet with a partner to discuss your ideas and any new ideas or questions that were raised.

Responses may vary.

_____
_____
_____
_____
_____
_____
_____
_____
_____
_____
_____
_____
_____
_____

Open Court Classics ✦ Good-by Violet   7

Responding to Literature p. 7

Teacher Tip Although students are considering an impossible situation from a humorous selection, remind them to take the activity seriously and give careful thought to their responses.

Assessment Use the *Responding to Literature* pages as an informal assessment of students' ability to understand the selection, identify cause-and-effect relationships, and identify synonyms.

Lesson 6

Objective

Students will practice formulating and evaluating their own opinions.

Thinking Skills

✦ Summarizing opinions
✦ Evaluating a character's actions
✦ Formulating questions

Activity

Ask students to think about a time when their quick actions led to an unexpected situation. Then have students summarize their opinions about Violet's choices and consequences. Have students meet with partners to discuss their opinions about Violet's predicament. During the discussion, encourage students to think about the effects that Violet's choices and the ensuing consequences might have had on the other characters in the selection.

The Next Step

A fable is a short tale that teaches a moral or lesson about life. Have students read some fables to find out more about this genre and its characteristic elements. Then have students rewrite "Good-by Violet" in the form of a fable. Students can write their fables in their Personal Journals.

*M*ella: Young Friend of the Python

MELLA:

Young Friend of the Python

from ***Women Warriors:***
Myths and Legends of Heroic Women

by Marianna Mayer
illustrated by Shelley Johnson

This tale of young Mella's courage and later her
role as tribal leader is based upon the oral history of the
Buhera Ba Rowzi tribe from Zimbabwe.

In a home of reeds and fiber on the edge of the lush green forest, Mella sat upon a grass mat and held her ailing father's frail hand. He had once been the wise, strong leader of the tribe, but now he could barely lift his head. The family had offered prayers and many sacrifices for his recovery. The tribal healers tried to use their magic. They played music from their pipes and drums, but they could not rouse him. Day by day his condition worsened, and as he grew weaker, the family began to prepare for his death. All, that is, except Mella.

22

One night while the villagers were sleeping, Mella walked out into the forest, following the footpath to a clearing. The moon overhead shone like a golden crescent in the black velvet sky. All along the moonlight had been her guide. Now she stopped and looked up at Bomu Rambi, the merciful moon goddess.

Mella called out, "Please, Bomu Rambi, give me some sign to show what I must do to save my father." Suddenly the wind swept through the trees, and the branches gently swayed with the mysterious presence of the goddess. All at once Mella heard the soft words of Bomu Rambi floating toward her on the wind. "You must go to the Python Healer," said the moon goddess. Though the night was warm, Mella shivered. The Python Healer struck terror into the villagers' hearts. His cave stood at the foot of a mountain in the deepest, thickest part of the jungle, and no one dared go there. Some time ago Mella's own brothers had sought him out for their father's sake. But they had fled in horror from the entrance of the python's cave, and returned to the village so terrified that they could not speak of what they had seen.

23

Student Anthology pp. 22–29

Selection Goals

- To recognize the elements of a legend
- To investigate risks and consequences associated with trusting someone

Selection Summary

Mella's father is ill and becoming weaker each day. Determined to help him, Mella seeks advice about what she might do to save her father. Instructed by the moon goddess to visit the dreaded Python Healer, Mella must overcome her fear and take a risk for her father's sake. The risk she takes results in both positive and negative consequences for Mella and her village.

Genre: Legend

Share with students some of the elements of a legend, which include

✦ the story of a hero or heroine.

✦ factual elements, but through countless retellings, the heroes and their actions become exaggerated.

☀ *Part 1* ☀
Building Background

Activate Prior Knowledge

✦ Ask students to share what they know about legends. Invite them to discuss other legends they have read or heard.

✦ Tell students that this selection is from a collection of stories about women warriors. Explain that a warrior is not necessarily a person who fights in military battles. The word *warrior* also means "one who is engaged energetically in an activity, cause, or conflict." With this definition in mind, encourage students to name some people whom they consider to be warriors.

Background Information

✦ The heroine of this selection, Mella, is from Zimbabwe, a country in Africa. Two of Zimbabwe's characteristic features are its forests, which cover nearly half of the country, and its gold, which has been mined since ancient times. Both of these factual elements are included in the selection.

✦ One of the characters in this selection is the moon goddess Bomu Rambi. Point out to students that while gods and goddesses often appear in legends, the subject of a legend is a human hero. This is one difference between legends and myths, in which gods and goddesses can serve as the subject or hero.

✦ Like the Python Healer in this selection, snakes appear in the legends and mythologies of many cultures, including African, Native American, Greek, and Chinese. Snakes have often appeared in these genres as symbols of wisdom or health. They have also been perceived as protectors. Ask students if they can think of any other stories that feature a snake as a main character.

Previewing the Literature

Browse the Selection

✦ Have students browse the first couple of pages of the selection to look for anything that catches their attention, such as challenging or unfamiliar words, clues about how the selection relates to the theme, and familiar elements.

✦ Note on the board those things students mention as a result of their browsing and any questions they have about the selection.

> **Teacher Tip**
> Tell students that good readers keep thinking about questions that come up as they are reading, and they keep coming back to those questions. As they read the selection, encourage students to make notes in their Personal Journals of questions they have and of important information or ideas in the selection.

Set Purposes for Reading

As they read, have students focus on the elements of a legend, ways in which Mella is tested, and how the author uses the sounds of certain words for effect.

Expanding Vocabulary

The words listed below can be found in the Glossary of the **Student Anthology.** Page numbers indicate where the words can be found in the selection.

crescent, p. 23 — A thin, curved shape.

merciful, p. 23 — Showing great kindness or forgiveness beyond expectations.

silhouette, p. 25 — The dark outline of a figure or object. [French, after Étienne de *Silhouette* (1709–1767), French finance minister.]

vapors, p. 27 — Thin steam or smoke that can be seen in the air.

devoured, p. 28 — Ate greedily. [Latin *devorare: de- + vorare,* "to swallow."]

amulet, p. 28 — A charm usually worn around the neck to protect the wearer.

> **Teacher Tip**
> Remind students to use word structure to figure out the meanings of some words, such as *merciful.* Identifying the meanings of the word's parts—the base word *mercy* and the suffix *-ful*—should enable students to define *merciful* as "full of or showing mercy."

❖Part 2❖
Reading the Selection

Read

✦ Have students silently read **Student Anthology** pages 22–29, stopping at the end of each page if they have any questions or need clarification.

✦ Encourage students to use predicting or any other comprehension strategies that might help them read the selection.

Discuss

The following discussion suggestions can be carried out on different days, depending upon how much time you allot to each selection.

✦ Have students discuss their general reactions to the selection.

✦ Ask students what this selection adds to the theme that the other selection did not.

✦ Encourage students to review the questions they listed on the board before reading to see if the selection answered their questions.

✦ Have students review the elements of a legend and discuss which of the elements are included in this selection.

✦ Ask students to discuss the risks Mella and the Python Healer took and the consequences of their risks.

✦ Have students discuss whether they think there is a lesson to be learned from this selection.

After students have discussed the selection, choose from ***Responding to Literature*** pages 8–13, and ask students to complete the assigned pages.

→ *Part 3* ←

Knowledge-Building Project

Students should be researching the profession they chose to investigate. Remind students that during the course of their research, they will not only find answers to their questions, but they also will discover new questions about their subjects. These questions should be recorded in their Personal Journals and included as part of students' investigations of risks and consequences.

The next step is for students to generate a list of interview questions that they would like to ask a worker in the field that they are investigating. Students should use the information gathered from their research to help them formulate relevant, probing questions. Explain to students that while the nature of their investigations will require them to ask some personal questions, they should respect the interviewees' privacy. Have students review and comment on each other's interview questions before they conduct their interviews.

By the end of the next selection, students will have conducted their interviews.

> **Assessment**
> Use the Research Rubrics: Finding Needed Information on Appendix pages 148–149 of the *Teacher's Edition* to assess how well students collect information. Review with students the rubrics that will be used to assess their projects.

UNIT 1

Mella: Young Friend of the Python

Lesson 1

Objective

Students will learn to identify the main events of a selection and to organize the events in a plot diagram.

Thinking Skills

✦ Identifying main events
✦ Sequencing main events

Activity

Explain to students that a plot consists of a problem, or conflict, and the actions that one or more characters take to resolve the problem. Then have students use **Responding to Literature** page 8 to take notes about the chain of events in this selection. Have them use their notes to create a diagram in their Personal Journals that outlines the plot of the selection.

The Next Step

Have students discuss their plot diagrams. Encourage them to compare the formats they created and the information they included in each section of their diagrams.

Name_____ Date_____

Getting Started

The plot of a story is composed of a series of events. The plot usually contains four parts: a beginning, a middle, a climax or high point, and an end. Use the lines below to make notes about the main events in this selection. Then create a plot diagram in your Personal Journal. Remember to tell what happens in the same *sequence*, or order, as the events appear in the story. **Possible answers below:**

Beginning: Mella's father is ill, and she asks the moon goddess for help.

Middle: Mella sets out to find the Python Healer.

Climax: Mella finds the Python Healer and takes him to her sick father.

End: Mella becomes the tribe's leader.

8   Mella: Young Friend of the Python ✦ **Open Court Classics**

Responding to Literature p. 8

Teacher Tip Because this selection includes several exciting events, students might have difficulty deciding which one is the climax. To help them with this task, explain that the climax often occurs shortly before the problem is solved.

Name_____ Date_____

Lesson 2

Mella: Young Friend of the Python • Risks and Consequences **UNIT 1**

Making Sound Decisions

Writers sometimes choose words based on their sounds. Alliteration, assonance, repetition, and onomatopoeia are some techniques that writers use to make their writing interesting to read *and* hear.

Find the definition for each technique listed below. Then look in the story for an example of each technique, and write it below. When looking for examples, read the passages aloud and listen to the sounds of the words. Consider why the author chose these words. **Possible answers below:**

1. **alliteration:** The repetition of a consonant sound at the beginning of words.

   Example: . . . sound of the serpent's hissing . . .

2. **assonance:** The repetition of vowel sounds.

   Example: . . . night as the giant python . . .

3. **repetition:** The use of words (or phrases) more than once.

   Example: . . . drew closer and closer . . .

4. **onomatopoeia:** The use of words that imitate a sound.

   Example: In a hissing whisper . . .

Open Court Classics ✦ Mella: Young Friend of the Python   **9**

Responding to Literature p. 9

Teacher Tip **Writing** Explain to students that internal rhyme, end rhyme, and rhythm are techniques writers use to create feelings through the sounds of words. Encourage students to try to use these techniques.

Assessment Use the Poetry Writing Rubric on Appendix page 146 of the *Teacher's Edition* to assess how well students identify the techniques used in poetry and apply the same techniques in their writing.

Objective

Students will learn to identify the writing techniques of alliteration, assonance, repetition, and onomatopoeia.

Thinking Skills

- ✦ Comprehending poetic devices
- ✦ Understanding author's purpose
- ✦ Proving with examples

Activity

Have students use a reference source to define each of the terms listed. Then have them search the selection for an example of each technique. When students have finished, ask them what effects they think the author hoped to achieve by employing these techniques. Encourage students to describe how the sounds of the words affected their feelings and reactions.

The Next Step

Discuss with students why the sound of language is an especially important element of poetry. Then have students locate poems that provide examples of alliteration, assonance, repetition, and onomatopoeia. Ask students how these techniques create a musical quality. Then have students incorporate these techniques in a poem on a subject of their choice.

Mella: Young Friend of the Python

Lesson 3

Objective

Students will think reflectively and express their ideas through persuasive writing.

Thinking Skills

✦ Judging circumstances
✦ Proving with observation

Activity

Before students begin, ask them to think about a time they demonstrated bravery. Ask students if they were brave for their own sake, or for the sake of someone else. Then have students consider whether Mella's situation is unique or whether people are often brave for the sake of someone they love. Have them express their views in a persuasive paragraph.

The Next Step

Have students research other stories or examine real-life situations from recent news events in which a character or person takes a risk on behalf of someone else. Then ask students to compare Mella's risks and consequences with those of the characters or the situations they researched.

Name_____ Date_____

I Wonder

As Mella makes the journey to the Python Healer's cave, "her thoughts were only of her father, and they gave her courage to go on." If there is some chance that her father's life might be saved, Mella is willing to risk facing great danger.

Consider Mella's situation. Then using your observations of the people around you, judge whether people are often brave for the sake of someone they love. Write your notes below; then in your Personal Journal, write a persuasive paragraph to present to the class, your teacher, or a small group. As you write your persuasive paragraph, be sure to follow the steps of the writing process. Include additional questions you have about courage in your Personal Journal.

Notes may vary.

_____

_____

_____

_____

_____

_____

_____

_____

_____

_____

See Appendix pages 120–121 for persuasive writing and Appendix pages 133–134 for writing a paragraph.

10   Mella: Young Friend of the Python ✦ **Open Court Classics**

Responding to Literature p. 10

Teacher Tip Comprehension Strategies Tell students that making predictions helps readers stay involved by encouraging them to think ahead. Ask students what predictions they made and whether they confirmed or revised their predictions as they read.

Assessment Use the Informal Comprehension Strategies Rubrics: Predicting on Appendix page 145 of the *Teacher's Edition* to assess how well students make and revise predictions based on information in the text.

Name_____ Date_____

Think like a Warrior

The legend of Mella can be found in a collection of stories from *Women Warriors: Myths and Legends of Heroic Women.* What do you think it means to be a warrior? What traits should a warrior possess?

In many different cultures throughout history, groups of warriors have lived by strict codes, or rules for behavior. For example, centuries ago in Japan, there was a class of warriors called *Bushi.* They followed a set of codes that emphasized justice, courage, kindness, politeness, truthfulness, honor, loyalty, and self-control.

On the lines below, generate a set of codes that you think Mella follows. For each code, provide support by writing an example from the story. Then meet with a partner to discuss why the codes Mella follows are important.

Possible answer: Loyalty—Mella demonstrated

loyalty when she overheard the villagers' plan to kill

the Python Healer, and she "ran back to the Python

Healer's cave, ready to give her life if necessary to

save her friend."

_____

_____

_____

_____

Extra Effort: What other stories have you read in which the main character follows strict rules for behavior? What are the consequences of the character's behavior? Record your responses in your Personal Journal.

Responding to Literature p. 11

> **Teacher Tip** As students complete the assigned *Responding to Literature* pages, be sure they continue to find needed information for their knowledge-building projects.

> **Teacher Tip** Encourage students to use various comprehension strategies while reading the selection. Meet with individual students to determine which strategies a student is using while he or she is reading.

Lesson 4

Objective

Students will learn to analyze a character and support their analyses with examples.

Thinking Skills

✦ Determining character traits
✦ Evaluating a character's thoughts and actions

Activity

Emphasize to students that this activity is about virtues and codes of honor, *not* about glamorizing violent behavior. If necessary, explain that virtues and codes of honor are admirable qualities, such as respect, honesty, and truthfulness, that a person aspires to live by. Then have students consider Mella's thoughts and actions and create a list of qualities that might serve as her code of behavior. Students should provide an example in which Mella exhibits each quality they list.

The Next Step

In this activity students learned a little about the *Bushi* warriors of Japan. Have students conduct research to discover more about this group or about the codes of behavior followed by other groups of warriors.

Objective

Students will learn to identify elements of a legend and to make comparisons.

Thinking Skills

✦ Identifying elements of a legend
✦ Making connections

Activity

Have students write about how this selection compares with other legends they have read. Encourage students to create a graphic organizer, such as a Venn diagram, to arrange their information. Suggest that students also use words such as *same*, *like*, and *both* to show how the legends are alike and words such as *different*, *but*, and *than* to show how they are different.

The Next Step

In this selection the moon goddess Bomu Rambi plays an important role. Have students conduct research to find other legends and myths in which the moon is a main character. Ask students to compare the different ways the moon is described and to discuss why they think the moon is an important element of so many stories. Encourage students to investigate stories from a variety of cultures.

Name_____ Date_____

Making Connections

The story of Mella is a *legend*. A legend is a story about a hero that is partly true and partly make-believe. As a legend is retold over time, the hero and the events usually become exaggerated.

Think back to the story of Mella. What are some of the qualities of this story that make it a legend? How does it compare to other legends you have read? Record your ideas on the lines below.

Responses may vary.

_____

_____

_____

_____

_____

_____

_____

_____

_____

_____

_____

Extra Effort: Go to the library and select another legend to read. Bring the legend you select to class and share it with classmates.

12   Mella: Young Friend of the Python ✦ **Open Court Classics**

Responding to Literature p. 12

Teacher Tip To help students identify some aspects of this legend that are based on fact, make available reference materials about Zimbabwe, the country in which this legend is set.

Name_____ Date_____

Mella: Young Friend of the Python • Risks and Consequences **UNIT I**

Life Lessons

   Although her older brothers had been too afraid to enter the Python Healer's cave, Mella finds the courage to go there. In taking the risk of trusting the Python Healer, Mella is rewarded not only with her father's recovery but also with a new friend.

   What do Mella and the Python Healer teach you about trust? Write your thoughts on the lines below. Remember to use examples from the story to support your ideas.

Responses may vary.

_____

_____

_____

_____

_____

_____

_____

_____

_____

_____

Extra Effort: Think about a time when you demonstrated trust. How was it similar to the trust displayed in the story? How was it different? Write your thoughts in your Personal Journal.

Open Court Classics ✦ Mella: Young Friend of the Python   **13**

Responding to Literature p. 13

Teacher Tip Encourage students to record ideas and questions about what they read in their Personal Journals. This type of personal writing can help students reflect on and connect with selections.

Assessment Use the *Responding to Literature* pages as informal assessment of students' understanding of the selection, plot, sound of language, and a genre's elements.

Objective

Students will examine the relationship between two characters and describe its relevance to their own lives.

Thinking Skills

✦ Summarizing concepts
✦ Evaluating relationships
✦ Determining relevance

Activity

Have students consider how Mella's relationship with the Python Healer affects their ideas about trust. Before they begin writing, encourage students to think about examples to include from their lives as well as from the selection. For example, students might describe an unlikely friendship that they have formed.

The Next Step

Have students take a closer look at the Python Healer and write an analysis of this character. Ask students to include information about risks the Python Healer took and the consequences of his choices. Suggest that students also consider how the Python Healer was perceived by the people in the village. Encourage students to use relevant events from the selection to support their analyses of the character.

Behind Rebel Lines

Student Anthology pp. 30–49

Selection Goals

- To recognize that historical fiction is about real events and people but includes some fictional elements, such as dialogue

- To identify risks taken by Emma and to understand the consequences

Selection Summary

In "Behind Rebel Lines: The Incredible Story of Emma Edmonds, Civil War Spy," Seymour Reit tells the true story of a young woman who joins the Union army disguised as a man. Emma's military duties, however, include additional disguises, which she wears on missions as a spy. In this selection Emma goes behind rebel lines and comes away with much to tell.

Genre: Historical Fiction

Share with students some of the elements of historical fiction, which include

- ✦ a story that is set in a particular time and place in the past.

- ✦ details that make the story more realistic.

- ✦ realistic characters that act appropriately for the time in which the story is set.

- ✦ real people and actual events.

☙ Part 1 ☙
Building Background

Activate Prior Knowledge

✦ Ask students to share what they know about historical fiction. Invite them to discuss other selections they have read from this genre.

✦ Ask students to share what they know about the causes of the Civil War and its participants. Explain that people who fought for and sympathized with the Confederate army from the South were called rebels, and people who fought for and sided with the Union army from the North were called Yankees.

✦ Ask students if they have ever worn a costume or a disguise. Discuss whether they think it is challenging to pretend to be someone else.

Background Information

✦ Historians have estimated that approximately 400 to 750 women fought in the Civil War. These women would have had to disguise themselves as men in order to enlist in either the Confederate or the Union army. Emma Edmonds used the name Franklin Thompson to serve the Union army not only as a spy, but as a male nurse, treating wounded soldiers. Edmonds's true identity was revealed after the war, and she later became the only female member of the Grand Army of the Republic, an organization formed by veterans of the Union army.

> **Teacher Tip**
> Students might be curious about how women were able to enlist in the army as men. Explain that at the time of the Civil War, there was no standard physical exam for men enlisting for military service. Recruiters often simply looked for noticeable disabilities, such as poor eyesight or a hearing impairment.

✦ Historical fiction captures the essence of the time in which it is set. To learn about a particular time, writers of historical fiction often study personal journals and letters, newspaper articles, photographs, and art from that period. Seymour Reit used Edmonds's published memoirs, information from the National Archives, and United States Army records.

✦ Edmonds's experiences are also recounted in her autobiography *Nurse and Spy in the Union Army*.

Previewing the Literature
Browse the Selection

✦ Have a volunteer read aloud the title of the selection and the names of the author and illustrator. Then have students browse the first two pages of the selection for ideas about what this selection has to do with taking risks.

✦ Note on the board those things students mention as a result of their browsing and any questions they have about the selection.

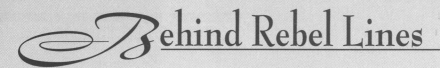
Set Purposes for Reading

Encourage students to set purposes for reading this selection. Suggest that students consider the following questions as they read: Who is taking risks? What are the reasons for taking risks? What might the consequences be?

Expanding Vocabulary

The words listed below can be found in the Glossary of the **Student Anthology.** Page numbers indicate where the words can be found in the selection.

chaplain, p. 30   A clergy member who leads services and counseling for a military unit. [Medieval Latin, *chapel.*]

rummaged, p. 33   To have looked for something by moving things around.

matron, p. 33   A dignified married woman.

vigil, p. 36   The act of keeping watch over. [Late Latin *vigilia,* from Latin, "wakefulness, watch," from *vigil,* "awake."]

delirium, p. 39   A state of confusion caused by a high fever. [Latin *delirare,* "to be crazy."]

morbid, p. 40   Frightful or awful. [Latin *morbus,* "disease."]

bedraggled, p. 42   Wet and dirty as if trailed through mud.

tethered, p. 49   To have fastened or held an animal in place with a rope or chain.

✦ *Part 2* ✦

Reading the Selection

Read

✦ Have students silently read **Student Anthology** pages 30–49, stopping at the end of each page if they have any questions or need clarification.

✦ Encourage students to use monitoring and clarifying or any other comprehension strategies that might help them read the selection.

Discuss

The following discussion suggestions can be carried out on different days, depending upon how much time you allot to each selection.

✦ Have students discuss their general reactions to the selection.

✦ Ask students what this selection adds to the theme that the other selections do not.

✦ Encourage students to review the questions they listed on the board before reading to see if the selection answered their questions.

✦ Have students review the elements of historical fiction. Then have them discuss whether the author created dialogue that is authentic and believable.

✦ Have students discuss how Emma Edmonds weighed everyday concerns against larger issues of the war.

After students have discussed the selection, choose from *Responding to Literature* pages 14–19, and ask students to complete the assigned pages.

→Part 3←
Knowledge-Building Project

At this point in their investigations, students should have a final list of interview questions designed to help them investigate the risks and consequences associated with a particular career. Students should make arrangements to interview someone who performs that job. If students are unable to meet with the interviewee in person, encourage them to consider alternatives, such as a telephone or e-mail interview. You might also suggest that students record the interview on an audiocassette for more accurate notes.

Before students conduct their interviews, they should have some idea of how they plan to present the results of their investigations. A biography or photo-essay would be appropriate for written presentations. Preparing a videocassette is another option. Students should consider special plans they need to make and materials they need to gather for their presentations. For example, they might request copies of photos from the interviewee or permission to take photos during the interview.

By the end of this selection, students should be ready to present their information.

Teacher Tip Tell students that if they plan to record the interview on videocassette, they should get the interviewee's permission in advance. Also remind them that regardless of how the interview is conducted, it is courteous to send a thank-you note to show appreciation for the interviewee's time and help.

Assessment Use the Research Rubrics: Communicating Research Progress and Results on Appendix page 149 of the *Teacher's Edition* to assess how well students present their findings. Share with students the rubrics that will be used to evaluate them on their projects.

Objectives

✦ Students will identify unfamiliar words common to a specific time in history.

✦ Students will use a dictionary to define unfamiliar words.

Thinking Skills

✦ Identifying unfamiliar words

✦ Defining unfamiliar words

Activity

Have students reread the selection and look for words related to the Civil War era that are unfamiliar to them. Then have students use a dictionary to define those words. After students complete the activity, ask them whether the use of these words made the setting of this selection more realistic.

The Next Step

Have students work in pairs to write a conversation between two Civil War soldiers. The dialogue should incorporate words from the students' lists. Encourage the partners to perform their dialogue for the rest of the class.

Name_____ Date_____

Getting Started

Imagine that you were sent back in time to the Civil War. As you walk around an army's campsite, you overhear the soldiers' conversations. What new words do you hear? How can you better understand everything the soldiers are saying?

In historical fiction, authors often use words from the time and region in which the story takes place. As a result, some of the words' meanings may be new to readers.

Reread the selection and look for words related to the Civil War era. List the words below; then use a dictionary to find each word's meaning. Meet with a classmate to compare words and meanings.

Possible answers below:

1. **adjutant:** An assistant to a commanding officer.

2. **caisson:** A two-wheeled vehicle pulled by horses. Usually carried artillery or coffins.

3. **contraband:** An escaped slave during the Civil War.

4. **gallant:** A noble person. A person who does not retreat in battle.

5. **shaver:** A small child.

6. **picket:** A soldier sent to warn of an enemy's approach.

14   Behind Rebel Lines ✦ **Open Court Classics**

Responding to Literature p. 14

Teacher Tip **Comprehension Strategies** Ask students whether they monitored their understanding of the text. Have them tell how they clarified words and phrases they did not understand as they read the selection.

Assessment Use the Informal Comprehension Strategies Rubrics: Monitoring and Clarifying on Appendix page 144 of the *Teacher's Edition* to assess how well students recognize and define unfamiliar vocabulary.

Lesson 2

Quite a Character

Many adjectives could be used to describe Emma Edmonds. What adjectives would you use to describe Emma? Write them below. Then write some examples from the selection to support your ideas.

Possible answers below:

Adjectives used to describe Emma: caring, determined, and intelligent

Ways that Emma shows she is

1. caring : **Emma keeps a vigil over Allen Hall.**

2. determined : **Emma leaves the abandoned house to carry out her assignments.**

3. intelligent : **Emma memorizes the Confederate army's secret plans instead of writing them down.**

Extra Effort: Which adjectives that describe Emma could also be used to describe Mella from "Mella: Young Friend of the Python"? If these same adjectives were used to describe someone you know or a real person about whom you have read, who would that person be? Record your ideas in your Personal Journal.

Open Court Classics ✦ Behind Rebel Lines   **15**

Responding to Literature p. 15

Objective

Students will learn to analyze and describe a character.

Thinking Skills

✦ Determining character traits
✦ Drawing conclusions
✦ Proving with examples

Activity

Discuss with students the remarkable courage Emma showed to enlist in the Union army, to maintain her disguise as a man, and to wear additional disguises to spy on the Confederate army. Then have students write adjectives that they think best describe Emma and provide an example from the selection in which Emma exhibits those qualities.

The Next Step

Have students write an essay in which they compare and contrast Mella, from the previous selection, and Emma Edmonds. Remind students that a Venn diagram is a helpful tool for comparing and contrasting two related subjects.

Teacher Tip Tell students that the feeling a word creates or the meaning it suggests is called *connotation*. A word can have a positive, negative, or neutral connotation. Use the words *gaze* (positive), *glare* (negative), and *look* (neutral) as examples. Then have students consider the connotation of each word they used to describe Emma.

Objective

Students will learn to evaluate a character's behavior.

Thinking Skills

✦ Evaluating a character's actions and behavior
✦ Recalling details
✦ Proving with examples

Activity

Have students list three ways in which Emma Edmonds gains people's trust in this selection. Then have them list other qualities they think a spy should possess. Encourage students to share their responses with a partner when they are finished.

The Next Step

Have students conduct research to discover more about some real-life spies. In the course of their research, ask students to note any particularly daring risks or interesting consequences they uncover. Allow time for students to share these findings with the rest of the class.

Name_____ Date_____

Think like an Undercover Agent

An *undercover agent*, or spy, is a person who secretly gets information from people. One of the most important things a spy does to get this information is to make people trust him or her.

In this selection, Emma Edmonds is a successful spy because she is able to gain people's trust. Think about how Emma accomplishes this. What does she do to make herself seem trustworthy? List three ways Emma makes people trust her. Then complete the rest of the page.

Possible answers below:

Ways Emma (Bridget O'Shea) gains people's trust:

1. **Emma joins in the singing with the women at the Confederate camp.**

2. **She returns Allen Hall's watch to Major McKee.**

3. **Emma leads the Confederate soldiers to the abandoned house.**

What other character traits do you think would be important for a spy to have? Justify your choices with examples from the story.
Answers may vary.

_____

_____

_____

16

Responding to Literature p. 16

Teacher Tip As students complete the assigned *Responding to Literature* pages, be sure they progress with the necessary preparations for their knowledge-building project presentations.

Name_____Date_____

Behind Rebel Lines • Risks and Consequences **UNIT 1**

In My Opinion

Soon after Emma Edmonds begins her secret mission as Bridget O'Shea, she finds a Confederate soldier, Allen Hall, who is near death. After Hall dies, Emma deliveres his gold watch to Major McKee, as Hall had requested. While at the camp, she discovers some secret plans. How do you feel about Emma using Hall's death to spy on the Confederate army? Should a spy do whatever it takes to complete a mission?

In the form of a persuasive paragraph, write your thoughts about Emma's actions on the lines below. You can use your Personal Journal to develop a plan before you begin writing. When you have finished, exchange papers with a classmate and complete the rest of the page.

My Opinion
Persuasive paragraphs may vary.

_____

_____

_____

_____

_____

My Partner's Comments (How did this persuasive paragraph affect your own opinion?)
Comments may vary.

_____

_____

See Appendix pages 120–121 for persuasive writing and Appendix pages 133–134 for writing a paragraph.

Open Court Classics ✦ Behind Rebel Lines   **17**

Responding to Literature p. 17

Objective

Students will formulate and defend their opinions through persuasive writing.

Thinking Skills

✦ Evaluating actions through persuasive writing
✦ Judging character

Activity

In their Personal Journals, encourage students to generate a list of ideas for both sides of the argument before choosing a perspective to use in their paragraphs. Then have students consider the questions posed to them and write a thoughtful response in the form of a persuasive paragraph.

The Next Step

Have students write a journal entry from Emma Edmonds's perspective in their Personal Journals. Students should write about what Emma learned from the risks she took—not in terms of the information she collected as a spy, but what she learned about herself, others, and the world around her.

Teacher Tip **Writing** Tell students to present the points of the argument in a persuasive paragraph in order of importance. Tell students that a persuasive paragraph should leave readers with the most convincing point fresh in their minds.

Assessment Use the Persuasive Writing Rubric on Appendix page 146 of the *Teacher's Edition* to assess how well students organize and present their points.

Objective

Students will formulate a purpose and new identity for Emma's next mission and then design a costume appropriate to the mission and the period in which the selection is set.

Thinking Skills

✦ Determining purpose
✦ Redesigning an identity

Activity

Discuss with students missions or assignments that might have occurred during the Civil War. Then have students determine a purpose for Emma's next mission and create an identity for her to use, complete with personal information. Encourage students to research the style of dress during the Civil War before creating an authentic costume for Emma. Suggest that students use books available in the classroom or use the Internet to find this information.

The Next Step

Emma Edmonds's success as a spy was due in part to her creativity. She relied on this skill when designing disguises and, once behind enemy lines, when devising ways to obtain information. Have students consider and discuss the ways in which risk-takers must use and rely on their creativity, sometimes as a matter of life and death.

Name_____ Date_____

UNIT 1 Risks and Consequences • *Behind Rebel Lines*

I Can Do It, Too

In her role as a spy for the Union army, Emma Edmonds wears many disguises. She becomes an escaped male slave named "Cuff," an Irish peddler named "Bridget O'Shea," an African American woman working as a laundress, and a young, southern man named "Charles Mayberry."

Imagine that Emma has another secret mission, and it is your job to create her next disguise. Before you formulate Emma's new identity, clarify the purpose of her mission. Then fill in the information below, and design a costume for Emma to wear. Look at reference materials to learn about 1860s styles of dress to create an authentic costume.

Answers may vary.

Purpose of Mission: _____

_____

Name: _____

Age: _____

Occupation: _____

Place of Birth: _____

In your Personal Journal sketch the outfit that you created for Emma's new identity.

18   Behind Rebel Lines ✦ Open Court Classics

Responding to Literature p. 18

Teacher Tip Consider contacting a Civil War reenactment group, which might be available to give a presentation to students dressed in authentic Civil War attire.

Assessment Use the *Responding to Literature* pages as an informal assessment of students' understanding of the selection, unfamiliar words, and character analyses.

Name_____ Date_____

Lesson 6

Going Deep

In her autobiography *Nurse and Spy in the Union Army,* Emma Edmonds stated she was thankful that she "was free and could go forward and work, and was not obliged to stay at home and weep." At a time when most women worked at home, Emma and hundreds of other females enlisted in the army. Disguised as men, women were expected to perform as any other soldier.

Knowing the risks involved, why do you think these women made the choice to go to war?

Answers may vary.

_____

_____

_____

_____

_____

_____

_____

_____

Now meet with a partner to compare ideas of why women joined the army. Record additional questions that come up during your discussion in your Personal Journal.

Extra Effort: How do you think the roles of women in the army or other military branches have changed? With classmates, organize a debate to explore the group's questions and ideas.

Open Court Classics ✦ Behind Rebel Lines   **19**

Responding to Literature p. 19

Teacher Tip Women had many different reasons for enlisting in the army. Patriotism was a major factor for many women, including Emma Edmonds. (Students might find it interesting that Edmonds was born in Canada and came to the United States at the age of 16.) Some women wanted to go to war to be with their husbands or brothers; others saw the war as an opportunity to travel. Women who were poor might have enlisted because they needed a soldier's regular paycheck as well as meals.

Objective

Students will learn to consider challenging issues raised by a selection.

Thinking Skills

✦ Extrapolating information
✦ Formulating questions
✦ Comparing perceptions

Activity

Have students infer why women, knowing the risks involved, made the choice to go to war. You might suggest that students investigate the roles of women in society during this time. Explain that this background information will enhance their discussions and help them generate new questions. Then have students meet with partners to talk about and to compare each other's ideas. Have students make a list of complex questions sparked by the selection and their discussion. Let students know the questions might not have single, concise answers.

The Next Step

Have students find out more about women who joined the army during the Civil War by reading additional historical works, such as biographies or autobiographies. Then have students write an expository essay about why women, knowing the risks involved, joined the army.

Wrap-Up

Knowledge-Building Project

Students have completed their preparatory work and should be ready to present their findings. Make available any audiovisual equipment that is needed for the presentations, which may be done in small groups or before the entire class. Encourage students to respond to presentations by offering constructive feedback and telling what they learned about the risks and consequences associated with particular professions. Use the Research Rubrics: Overall Assessment of Research on Appendix page 149 of the **Teacher's Edition** to assess students' knowledge-building projects as a whole.

> **Teacher Tip**
> Encourage students to read a variety of biographies to learn about other people's risks and consequences. You might suggest that students keep a journal in which they record risks and consequences that they contemplate, experience, or observe.

Reviewing the Concepts

In this unit students investigated many different types of risks and consequences. Students read about three main characters taking careless, selfless, and fearless risks that resulted in some surprising consequences. Students investigated some of the following key concepts in this unit:

✦ Choosing not to follow instructions can sometimes lead to negative consequences.

✦ Some people are willing to take a risk on someone else's behalf or for a cause.

✦ Many professions require people to face risks and consequences on a regular basis.

Evaluating the Unit

✦ Ask students to evaluate each selection on the basis of effectiveness of reading/vocabulary, literary value, interest of the subject matter, style of writing, application of theme, and the selection's personal value to the student.

✦ Ask students to evaluate the different activities in the unit, including the knowledge-building project. Have them consider these questions: Which activities made you think? Which ones did you find less challenging and why? Which ones seemed confusing? Which activities did you most enjoy and why? Which activities best contributed to your intellectual growth? Which activities changed your opinions and offered new ideas? What activities would you like to add to the unit?

✦ Ask students to evaluate this **Open Court Classics** unit. They can describe how the theme was explored in the unit. They can also compare and contrast each of the selections based on the characters' reasons for taking risks, the importance of the risks, and the appropriateness of the consequences.

Assessment

Vocabulary Assessment

To assess students' understanding of the vocabulary words, you might want to do one of the following:

✦ Have students create a game using the vocabulary words from the unit in the correct context.

✦ Have students design a test to exchange with a partner. This can be used to assess their knowledge of the vocabulary words in each selection.

✦ Administer an informal oral assessment. Have students supply the definition of the vocabulary word or use the word properly in a sentence.

Informal Comprehension Strategies Rubrics

Use the Informal Comprehension Strategies Rubrics: Visualizing, Predicting, and Monitoring and Clarifying on Appendix pages 144–145 of the *Teacher's Edition* to determine whether a student is using a particular strategy or strategies as he or she reads the selections. Note these and any other strategies a student is using instead of the degree to which a student might be using any particular strategy. In addition, encourage the student to tell of any strategies other than the ones being taught that he or she is using.

Research Rubrics

Use the Research Rubrics: Recognizing Information Needs, Finding Needed Information, Communicating Research Progress and Results, and Overall Assessment of Research on Appendix pages 148–149 of the *Teacher's Edition* to assess a student's performance throughout the investigation. The rubrics range from 1 to 4 in most categories, with 1 being the lowest score. In addition, you can use the rubrics to assess a group's collaborative work as well as an individual's participation in that group.

Writing Rubrics

Use the Getting Ideas Writing Rubric, the Poetry Writing Rubric, and the Persuasive Writing Rubric on Appendix page 146 of the *Teacher's Edition* to assess student writing. The rubrics range from 1 to 4 in most categories, with 1 being the lowest score.

UNIT 2 — Dollars and Sense

He does not possess Wealth, it possesses him.

He that is of Opinion Money will do every Thing, may well be suspected of doing every Thing for Money.

Beware of little Expences, a small Leak will sink a great Ship.

Pay what you owe, and you'll know what's your own.
—Ben Franklin—

Unit Goals

- To recognize the value of hard work and persistence
- To identify the elements of realistic fiction
- To understand that an autobiography is written by a person about his or her life
- To recognize the significance of sentimental value
- To investigate reasons people sacrifice things they value
- To identify ways a character is developed
- To investigate how the Great Depression affected people's concepts of value or worth

Introduction

Some of the things that mean the most to us are those that cannot be bought. The satisfaction of hard work, the pleasure and excitement of seeing a new place, and the gratification of helping a loved one are a few of the priceless experiences students will investigate in this unit. Selection 1 is "Where the Red Fern Grows" on page 52; Selection 2 is "The Endless Steppe: Growing Up in Siberia" on page 62; and Selection 3 is "A Telegram" on page 72. Reading and discussing these selections will encourage students to consider how people place different values on possessions and experiences.

Unit Discussion

Write the unit theme, *Dollars and Sense*, on the board, and ask students to identify the play on words in this title. Then have students discuss what they think this unit might be about. Continue the discussion by asking questions such as the following:

✦ What are some things you consider to be valuable, and why?

✦ What is the difference between monetary value and sentimental value?

✦ What kinds of sacrifices do people make to get things that they need and want?

✦ What do the adages in the unit opener mean to you?

Knowledge-Building Project

The first selection is set prior to the Great Depression, and students will be investigating this time in American history, when many people suffered great hardships. The sacrifices many people experienced during the Depression affected their outlook on life, including their ideas about what is valuable. Have students generate a list of questions about the Great Depression. If some students have difficulty formulating questions, suggest that they read and collect information about this topic from sources such as biographies, encyclopedias, or the Internet. In this unit students will discover how people value things differently and will be able to relate what they learn to their investigations. As a final product, students will write a diary from the perspective of someone who lived through the Great Depression. Explain that a diary is a daily record of personal experiences and observations. This type of writing is different from other forms, such as expository writing, because its purpose is to express personal thoughts and feelings instead of to inform readers. Students can use any point of view they wish—child or adult, fiction or nonfiction—from which they will write their diaries.

Teacher Tip Although the Great Depression started in the United States, its effects were felt worldwide. As a variation to the outlined project, students whose ancestors lived in another country at that time might wish to investigate how the Great Depression affected their family members.

Unit 2 Project Overview	
Unit Overview	Students begin by generating a list of questions about the Great Depression.
Selection 1	Students begin research and consider perspectives from which they will write their diaries.
Selection 2	Students select their writing perspectives.
Selection 3	Students continue with their investigations and writing.
Unit Wrap-Up	Students present their investigation findings in the form of diary entries.

Student Anthology pp. 52–61

Selection Goals

- To identify the elements of realistic fiction
- To recognize the value of hard work and persistence

Selection Summary

When 11-year-old Billy Colman finds an advertisement for redbone coon hound puppies, he can think of nothing else. Billy becomes determined to earn enough money to buy a pair of the pups. As two years pass by, Billy stays focused as he works odd jobs to turn his savings of 23 cents into the 50 dollars he needs to buy the puppies.

Genre: Realistic Fiction

Share with students some of the elements of realistic fiction, which include

- ✦ characters who behave like real people or animals.

- ✦ events that could happen in real life.

- ✦ settings that are real or could be real.

- ✦ conflicts similar to those in real life.

✦ Part 1 ✦
Building Background

Activate Prior Knowledge

✦ Ask students to share information or ideas they have about the book *Where the Red Fern Grows.* Invite students to tell what they know about the plot and various characters.

✦ Ask students whether they have ever saved their money to buy something special. Encourage them to discuss how it feels to work for something they want.

Background Information

✦ Wilson Rawls grew up on a farm like the one he describes in *Where the Red Fern Grows.* Because there were no schools in the area at that time, Rawls's mother taught him to read. After reading Jack London's *The Call of the Wild*, Rawls knew he wanted to be a writer. Although he had little formal education, he eventually achieved that goal. Like Billy Colman in this selection, Rawls had an unlikely dream that he made come true through hard work and persistence.

✦ The title of the novel refers to a Native American legend that tells of a boy and girl who froze to death in a blizzard. In the place where they were found, a red fern grew. According to the legend, the spot where a red fern grows is sacred. At the end of *Where the Red Fern Grows*, Billy discovers that a red fern has grown between the graves of his two dogs.

✦ Life on a farm in the Ozark Mountains during the 1920s was not easy. Most houses had no running water or electricity. Today the Ozark Mountains are a popular tourist area. The region's natural beauty and resources—including forests, streams, and mineral springs—attract many visitors. Encourage students to locate the Ozark Mountains on a map and to read more about this area.

Previewing the Literature

Browse the Selection

✦ Have students read the title aloud as well as the names of the author and the illustrator. Then have students browse the first page or two of the selection for clues that tell them something about the story. Ask students how they think this selection relates to the unit theme.

✦ Note on the board those things students mention as a result of their browsing and any questions they have about the selection.

> **Teacher Tip**
> The original title Rawls gave his novel was *The Secret of the Red Fern.* The selection first appeared in 1961 as a three-part serial in the *Saturday Evening Post* with the title "The Hounds of Youth." The book was published as *Where the Red Fern Grows* later that same year.

Set Purposes for Reading

Encourage students to set purposes for reading. As they read the selection, remind students to ask themselves questions such as the following: Why is having the dogs so important to Billy? What is it about the dogs that motivates Billy throughout the two years? Why does it take Billy a long time to save the money he needs?

Expanding Vocabulary

The words listed below can be found in the Glossary of the **Student Anthology.** Page numbers indicate where the words can be found in the selection.

festered, p. 52
To have caused increasing aggravation.

prowl, p. 53
To move quietly or secretly.

mulled, p. 54
To have considered or pondered extensively in one's mind.

heft, p. 57
To lift in order to estimate weight. [From 15th century *heave,* after pairs such as *weave, weft.*]

quavering, p. 61
Trembling [Middle-English *quaven,* "to tremble."]

> **Teacher Tip**
> Point out the inflectional endings *-ed* and *-ing* in three of the vocabulary words. Ask students to tell how the endings change the meaning of each base word.

✧ Part 2 ✧
Reading the Selection

Read

✦ Have students silently read **Student Anthology** pages 52–61, stopping at the end of each page if they have any questions or need clarification.

✦ Encourage students to use asking questions or any other comprehension strategies that might help them read the selection.

Discuss

The following discussion suggestions can be carried out on different days, depending upon how much time you allot to each selection.

✦ Have students discuss their general reactions to the selection.

✦ Ask students how this selection relates to the theme.

✦ Encourage students to review the questions they listed on the board before reading to see if the selection answered their questions.

✦ Have students discuss why this selection belongs in the genre of realistic fiction.

✦ Have students discuss the challenges Billy faces in earning the money he needs.

After students have discussed the selection, choose from **Responding to Literature** pages 20–25, and ask students to complete the assigned pages.

⁂ Part 3 ⁂
Knowledge-Building Project

Suggest that students review their lists of questions about the Great Depression and choose two or three to investigate. Encourage students to read some biographies and autobiographies for information about people who lived through the Great Depression. Students might also collect additional information by interviewing a person who experienced the Great Depression. Remind them to consider from what perspective they want to write their diaries. Explain that collecting information from a variety of sources will help them determine a perspective that interests them. Reiterate that the fictional or nonfictional perspective they choose to write from could include a child, an adult, a grandparent, a store owner, and so on.

Have students begin creating a profile of the perspective from which they will write their diaries. Students should use the information from their research to form their personas and should note such things in their profiles as the person's age, gender, family background, place of residence, and so on. Students should also make conjectures regarding the Great Depression's effects on the values of the person they chose. Remind students that they may make changes and revisions to this information.

By the end of the next selection, students should have selected a persona and identified their investigation needs, such as encyclopedias, films, and other resources they will examine.

> **Assessment**
> Use the Research Rubrics: Making Conjectures on Appendix page 148 of the *Teacher's Edition* to assess how well students make conjectures. Review with students the rubrics that will be used to evaluate them on their projects.

Objective

Students will use the information they gather from their interview questions and responses to write a news story.

Thinking Skills

✦ Formulating questions
✦ Drawing conclusions
✦ Summarizing information

Activity

Remind students that a news story should identify who, what, when, where, and why. The answers to these questions provide the most important details of a news story, which are presented in the lead paragraph.

The Next Step

Explain to students that news stories like the ones they wrote about Billy are often called *human interest* stories. Ask students what they think are the elements of a good human interest story. Then have them read their local newspaper to distinguish human interest stories from other news stories. Encourage students to focus on articles that could relate to the unit theme. Invite students to bring in the articles they discover to share with the rest of the class.

Name_____ Date_____

Getting Started

You are writing an article for the Colman family newsletter. The subject is how Billy Colman gets his dogs. One way to gather information is to interview the subject or the people who know him or her. Interview Grandpa to find out what he thinks of Billy's accomplishment. When formulating your interview questions, consider what interests and appeals to your audience.

1. Make a list of questions for your interview. What would your audience like to know about Grandpa's relationship with Billy? How does Grandpa feel about Billy's work?
Questions may vary.

_____

_____

2. Find another student who read "Where the Red Fern Grows." Take turns interviewing each other and playing the role of Grandpa. Use the lines below to take notes while you interview.
Notes may vary.

_____

_____

_____

_____

_____

3. Use the information you gathered from your interview to write your article for the newsletter in your Personal Journal. Remember that writing is a process and takes planning, drafting, revising, and editing.

See Appendix pages 118–119 to read more about a news story.

20   Where the Red Fern Grows ✦ **Open Court Classics**

Responding to Literature p. 20

Teacher Tip Encourage students to use various comprehension strategies while reading the selection. Meet with individual students to determine which strategies a student is using while he or she is reading.

Name_____ Date_____

Make It Happen

Billy, the main character in "Where the Red Fern Grows," stays focused on his goal of earning 50 dollars even though it takes a long time to achieve it. Think about if Billy ever thought of giving up. How would you achieve your goal of earning the money for something you really wanted?

On the line below, identify something you would like to buy. Then write a *process paper*, or step-by-step instructions, describing your plan and the steps you will take to earn the money. Organize your thoughts and ideas in your Personal Journal before you begin writing.

What I would like to buy:
Answers may vary.

How I plan to accomplish my goal of earning the money:
Responses may vary.

_____

_____

_____

_____

_____

_____

_____

See Appendix pages 116–117 for explaining a process.

Extra Effort: Make a list of books you have read in which the main character sets a goal and then works to achieve it. Share your list with classmates. Then choose a book from a classmate's list to read.

Open Court Classics ✦ Where the Red Fern Grows   **21**

Responding to Literature p. 21

Objective

Students will explain the process for achieving goals.

Thinking Skills

✦ Identifying a goal
✦ Describing a plan
✦ Sequencing steps in a process

Activity

Have students identify something they would like to buy and the various options they have for earning the money they will need. Then have students write a step-by-step explanation of how they plan to accomplish their goals. Before they begin to write, encourage students to create a graphic organizer to arrange their steps and to help plan their process. Remind students to describe each step in its sequence.

The Next Step

Ask students to consider how Billy's determination and hard work help him reach his goal of earning 50 dollars. Then have students evaluate their own work habits. In a personal narrative, students should describe their work habits as they write about a time they displayed determination and hard work. Encourage students to share their experiences with their peers.

Teacher Tip **Writing** Have students use signal words, such as *first, next, then,* and *finally,* to indicate the order in which the steps of a process occur. Remind students to prewrite, draft, revise, and proofread before sharing their work.

Assessment Use the Prewriting/Organizing Writing Rubric on Appendix page 146 of the *Teacher's Edition* to assess how well students develop a plan for writing.

Objective

Students will learn to analyze a character and support their ideas with examples.

Thinking Skills

- ✦ Evaluating a character
- ✦ Proving with examples

Activity

Ask students to think about how Rawls developed Billy's character through his actions and thoughts. Then encourage students to reread the selection to take notes on what they learned about Billy. Have students create a list of character traits that they think describe Billy and an example from the selection of Billy exhibiting each listed quality.

The Next Step

Ask students how Billy's character might have been affected if his parents or grandpa had simply given him the 50 dollars to buy the pups. Encourage students to record their responses in their Personal Journals and then discuss their thoughts with classmates.

Name_____ Date_____

Quite a Character

Think about the selection you just read and its narrator and main character, Billy. How do Billy's thoughts and actions tell about the kind of person he is?

In the space below, list some traits that you think describe Billy. Then find examples of Billy showing each trait in the story. You might want to create a graphic organizer to arrange your ideas.

Possible graphic organizer and answers below:

Traits	Examples
Determined	1. Billy works hard. 2. Billy picks blackberries while barefoot.
Responsible	1. Billy saves his money. 2. He makes a bank to keep his money safe.
Respectful	1. Billy takes whatever the fishermen offer. 2. Billy respects his grandfather.

Explain why Billy Colman is or is not someone you would like to have as a friend.
Answers may vary.

_____

Where the Red Fern Grows ✦ **Open Court Classics**

Responding to Literature p. 22

Teacher Tip Comprehension Strategies
Encourage students to discuss the strategies they used as they read the selection. Ask students to share some of the questions they asked as they read to better understand the selection.

Assessment Use the Informal Comprehension Strategies Rubrics: Asking Questions on Appendix page 144 of the *Teacher's Edition* to assess students' use of this strategy.

Name_____ Date_____

I Can Do It, Too

On page 56 of the anthology, Billy says that he "could almost feel the pups" in his hands. Imagine that you are Billy and you are holding the puppies. What words would you use to describe what you are feeling?

Write a descriptive paragraph describing how it feels to hold the puppies. Remember to write from the first-person point of view. When you have finished writing, exchange papers with a partner. Carefully read your partner's description, and draw an illustration in your Personal Journal to go with it. The drawing you create should illustrate how your partner's paragraph affects the feelings of its reader.

Descriptions may vary.

_____

_____

_____

_____

_____

_____

_____

_____

_____

_____

_____

_____

See Appendix pages 128–129 for writing a description and Appendix pages 133–134 for writing a paragraph.

Open Court Classics ✦ Where the Red Fern Grows   **23**

Responding to Literature p. 23

Teacher Tip **Writing** Before they begin writing, encourage students to review the selection and pay close attention to the language Billy uses.

Assessment Use the Descriptive Writing Rubric on Appendix page 146 of the *Teacher's Edition* to assess students' use of language and sensory details in their descriptive paragraphs.

Lesson 4

Objective

Students will write a descriptive paragraph using their thoughts and ideas.

Thinking Skills

✦ Making inferences
✦ Determining sensory details
✦ Visualizing

Activity

In addition to describing Billy's emotions, encourage students to include vivid descriptions that appeal to the senses. For example, how do the puppies move, feel, and smell? You might also encourage a discussion about the importance of word choice and how words such as *move* and *squirm* or *bark* and *yip* change what readers feel. Remind students that because they are writing from Billy's point of view, they should use words and phrases that he would use.

The Next Step

Have students conduct research to discover more about the various kinds of hound dogs and their distinctive characteristics. Then have students choose one particular kind to investigate further. Students might be especially interested in learning more about the redbone hound, which is the type of dog that Billy Colman bought.

Objectives

✦ Students will compare and contrast how people value things.

✦ Students will reflect on an adage and relate it to their ideas and experiences.

Thinking Skills

✦ Comparing and contrasting values

✦ Evaluating values

Activity

Have students read and respond to each of the questions on page 24 of *Responding to Literature.* In addition to objects they treasure, encourage students to name abstract qualities or ideas, such as honesty, family, and poetry, that are important to them. Ask students to explain how the intangibles are valued differently than the tangible items.

The Next Step

Tell students that Rawls once said that his first treasure was a book, *The Call of the Wild,* given to him by his mother. Ask students to consider this information about Rawls in relation to what they know about Billy. Then have students discuss how Rawls's treasure compares to what Billy treasures.

Name_____ Date_____

UNIT 2 Dollars and Sense • *Where the Red Fern Grows*

Hidden Treasures

In this excerpt from *Where the Red Fern Grows,* Billy describes how he enjoys searching campsites after the campers leave. Billy thinks of the sportsman's magazine that someone threw out as "a real treasure for a country boy." Later, when he sells fresh vegetables to the campers, he often finds the vegetables left on the ground. Think about these examples and what they show about how people value things differently as you answer the questions below.

Possible answers below:

1. List some things you treasure. Why do you consider them treasures?
   Answers may vary.

   _____

2. Consider the saying "One person's trash is another person's treasure." What does this mean to you?
   Something valued by one person might not be valued by another.

3. Think about the selection. What are some other things you think Billy would consider treasures?
   Billy treasures nature and "the beautiful silence that follows the setting sun . . ."

4. How are the things Billy treasures different from the things the campers treasure? How are they different from the things you treasure?
   The things that Billy treasures are taken for granted by the campers. Answers may vary.

Extra Effort: Meet with a partner and discuss the saying "One person's trash is another person's treasure." How do your treasures and your partner's treasures relate to this saying?

24   Where the Red Fern Grows ✦ Open Court Classics

Responding to Literature p. 24

Teacher Tip This activity could raise some sensitive issues for students from low-income families. For this reason, it is especially important to emphasize abstract things of value and the simplicity of the things Billy treasures, such as nature and his magazine.

Name_____ Date_____

Where the Red Fern Grows • Dollars and Sense **UNIT 2**

Life Lessons

Wilson Rawls based his novels on his own boyhood experiences in the Ozark Mountains of Oklahoma. The main character in Rawls's novel *Summer of the Monkeys* is a young boy named Jay Berry Lee. In *Summer of the Monkeys*, Jay Berry Lee's father says, "You know, if a fellow can learn something through experience when he's young, he doesn't ever forget it."

Consider how this might be true for Billy. What parts of his experience do you think he will never forget? Then on the lines below, list the names of three adults you know. Ask each adult to share something he or she learned as a child and never forgot. Write each adult's response on the lines below. **Responses may vary.**

1. **Adult's Name:** _____

   Experience: _____

   _____

   _____

2. **Adult's Name:** _____

   Experience: _____

   _____

   _____

3. **Adult's Name:** _____

   Experience: _____

   _____

   _____

Extra Effort: Compile your notes into a summary, and share the experiences with classmates. Then discuss an experience that you have had and do not think you will ever forget.

Open Court Classics ✦ Where the Red Fern Grows   **25**

Responding to Literature p. 25

 Assessment Use the *Responding to Literature* pages as an informal assessment of students' understanding of the selection and of comparing and contrasting.

Teacher Tip As students complete the assigned *Responding to Literature* pages, be sure they continue to make conjectures about potential research subjects for their knowledge-building projects.

Objective

Students will relate a quotation from another selection written by Rawls to the selection they read.

Thinking Skills

✦ Comparing ideas
✦ Making connections

Activity

Have students consider how the quotation from *Summer of the Monkeys* applies to Billy Colman. Then have students ask three adults to share a childhood experience that taught them a lesson they never forgot. Students should ask each adult's permission before sharing his or her story with the class.

The Next Step

Ask students to think about an experience they had and will never forget. Then have students write a personal narrative about their experiences. Remind them that narrative writing tells a story or gives an account of an event. Encourage students to describe what happened in detail and to write about the events in a logical order. Students should also be reminded that the experiences they describe should be ones that taught them a lesson about life.

The Endless Steppe

The
ENDLESS
STEPPE:
GROWING UP IN SIBERIA

an excerpt from *The Endless Steppe*
by Esther Hautzig
illustrated by Stacey Schuett

In June of 1941, Esther Rudomin was enjoying the simple comforts of life in Poland even though Europe was at war. However, the peacefulness of her world was suddenly shattered when two Russian soldiers arrested her family for political reasons. The family was forced into a cattle car and sent on a long journey across Russia. The Rudomins soon arrived at their destination—the endless steppe of Siberia. They would spend the next five years living in exile.

In this excerpt, Esther and her grandmother have been given permission to travel into Rubtsovsk, a nearby village, and trade their belongings at an outdoor market. This story is an autobiography, the author's true story.

We received permission to go in two weeks. When we heard that Rubtsovsk had a market, a *baracholka*, where one could exchange goods for *rubles* and which was open on Sunday, it was agreed that Grandmother and I should do some trading. *Rubles* meant food—potatoes perhaps; anything but bread and *brinza*. We spent every night deciding which of our few belongings we were ready to sell. One of Mother's lace-trimmed French silk slips went in and out of a bag a dozen times. "I really don't need this for dynamiting gypsum," she said.

"Nor do I need this," Father said, holding up a custom-made silk shirt, "for driving a wagon."

Grandmother wasn't so sure they wouldn't need them, and she herself was most reluctant to part with a black silk umbrella with a slender silver handle.

I thought that Sunday would never come. When it did, Grandmother and I set off down the dusty road before anyone else. Along with our wares—the slip, the shirt, and the umbrella, after all—we had wrapped some bread in one of my father's handkerchiefs; the bread was to be our lunch.

Student Anthology pp. 62–71

Selection Goals

- To understand that an autobiography provides information about the author's life and includes events that really happened
- To recognize the significance of sentimental value

Selection Summary

In this excerpt from *The Endless Steppe: Growing Up in Siberia*, Esther Rudomin Hautzig details a rare bright spot in her life at a forced-labor camp. Hautzig tells about this true event with descriptive language that re-creates the scene at the *baracholka*, or market, she attends with her grandmother. Hautzig also describes the decisions her family makes as they are forced to consider what they value.

Genre: Autobiography

Share with students some of the elements of an autobiography, which include

✦ an account by a person about his or her life.

✦ details about how the person talks, feels, or thinks.

✦ the entirety of the person's life or only an important part of the person's life.

✦ the most important events in the person's life, including his or her achievements or talents.

⬦ Part 1 ⬦
Building Background

Activate Prior Knowledge

✦ Tell students that this selection is an autobiography. Ask students to share information about other autobiographical selections they have read.

✦ Point to Siberia on a map or a globe, and ask students to share what they know about this region. With students, make a list of adjectives to describe Siberia. Encourage students to research more about Siberia and record additional characteristics of this region in their Personal Journals.

Background Information

✦ Students might have heard about Jewish people being sent to Nazi concentration camps during World War II. In this selection however, the author and her family are sent to a different kind of camp—a labor camp. In 1941 an agreement between Germany and the Soviet Union split Poland in two. In the part of Poland that was claimed by the Soviet Union, many Jews were forced to go to labor camps where they were not paid for their work and received barely enough food to stay alive.

✦ Students might wonder why the Rudomins had silk clothing with them in the cold and brutal environment of Siberia. Explain that the family had no idea where they were going when Russian soldiers took them from their home. As a result, the Rudomins could not have known what kind of supplies to take.

✦ Esther Hautzig lived in Siberia from the age of 10 to the age of 15.

Previewing the Literature

Browse the Selection

✦ Tell students that because this is a nonfiction piece, they may browse the entire selection, if they wish. Have students identify anything that catches their attention, such as challenging or unfamiliar words or clues that tell them something about the selection.

✦ Note on the board those things students mention as a result of their browsing and any questions they have about the selection.

Set Purposes for Reading

Have students set purposes for reading, such as for personal enjoyment or comprehension of a subject. As they read, encourage students to focus on descriptive words that create vivid images in their minds and evidence about the kind of relationship Esther had with her grandmother.

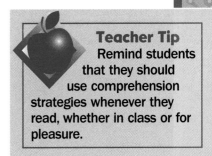

Teacher Tip
Remind students that they should use comprehension strategies whenever they read, whether in class or for pleasure.

Expanding Vocabulary

In "The Endless Steppe: Growing Up in Siberia," several foreign words are introduced. All the words listed below can be found in the Glossary of the **Student Anthology.** Page numbers indicate where the words can be found in the selection.

Foreign Vocabulary

baracholka, p. 63 — Type of market.

rubles, p. 63 — The basic unit of money in Russia. [Possibly from Old Russian *rubli*, "cut piece" (a piece cut from wood).]

brinza, p. 63 — A type of goat cheese similar to feta.

grande dame, p. 64 — A woman of great authority or stature. [French, "great lady."]

babushkas, p. 66 — Scarves folded triangularly and worn on women's heads.

Kazakhs, p. 66 — Members of a Turkic people inhabiting Kazakhstan and parts of China.

Diaspora, p. 70 — A community of people separated from their original homeland. [Greek, from *diaspeirein*, "to scatter."]

General Vocabulary

steppe, p. 62 — A vast grass-covered plain, as found in southeast Europe and Asia.

mean, p. 66 — Shabby; in poor condition.

ravishing, p. 66 — Very appealing or captivating.

Teacher Tip
Tell students that derivations are words that come from other languages. Even the General Vocabulary words from this selection are derived from other languages (*steppe* is derived from Russian; *mean* is derived from Old English; and *ravishing* is derived from Latin).

⟡ Part 2 ⟡

Reading the Selection

Read

✦ Have students silently read **Student Anthology** pages 62–71, stopping at the end of each page if they have any questions or need clarification.
✦ Encourage students to use visualizing or any other comprehension strategies that might help them read the selection.

Discuss

The following discussion suggestions can be carried out on different days, depending upon how much time you allot to each selection.

✦ Have students discuss their general reactions to the selection.

✦ Ask students what this selection adds to the theme that the other selection did not.

✦ Encourage students to review the questions they listed on the board before reading to see if the selection answered their questions.

✦ Have students discuss the elements of an autobiography.

✦ Have students draw conclusions about Esther's relationship with her grandmother. Ask them to support their conclusions with examples from the selection.

✦ Have students compare the sentimental value with the monetary value of items that Esther's family brought with them from Poland.

After students have discussed the selection, choose from *Responding to Literature* pages 26–31, and ask students to complete the assigned pages.

✧Part 3✧
Knowledge-Building Project

Students should be making final decisions about the perspective from which they will write their diaries. Remind students that they may choose any identity they wish, but that their diaries should reflect realistic ideas, emotions, and experiences for that person. Encourage students to include anecdotes that make the diary more personal and interesting. For example, if a student is writing from the perspective of Herbert Hoover, who was president of the United States when the Great Depression began, that student might write about the challenge of remaining positive in public while having private concerns about the country's future. Suggest that students also provide an artifact, such as a ticket stub, a coin, a news clipping, and so on, that supports their writing.

Once students choose an identity, they should determine the resources they will need in order to learn more about the Great Depression. Remind students to keep recording questions they have about their subjects in their Personal Journals. This will help students discover the types of information they need, and it will add depth to their investigations. The number of entries students write for their diaries may vary; however, suggest that students write at least three entries to present to the class.

By the end of the next selection, students will have completed their diaries.

> **Assessment**
> Use the Research Rubrics: Recognizing Information Needs on Appendix page 148 of the *Teacher's Edition* to assess how well students identify the information needed for their investigations. Discuss with students the rubrics that will be used to evaluate their projects.

UNIT 2

The Endless Steppe
Lesson 1

Objective

Students will learn to ask comprehension questions related to the selection and draw conclusions as they respond to questions.

Thinking Skills

✦ Comprehending main ideas
✦ Drawing conclusions
✦ Distinguishing points of views

Activity

Have students write three open-ended questions to ask Esther's grandmother. The questions should be answered from Esther's grandmother's point of view. Partners should be able to answer each other's questions by citing examples or drawing conclusions from the selection. Encourage students to record any new questions that were generated during the discussion with their partners.

The Next Step

Have a class discussion about how children view situations differently than adults. Tie the discussion to the selection by asking students what they think Esther will remember about the *baracholka* and what they think her grandmother will remember. For example, Esther does not appear to have any misgivings about parting with her family's belongings, but her grandmother is reluctant to give up her umbrella.

Name_____ Date_____

UNIT 2 Dollars and Sense • *The Endless Steppe*

Getting Started

In this selection, the author describes a day at the *baracholka*, or market, as "the happiest time I had had in a long, long time." Hautzig writes that her grandmother also is "having a marvelous time." While Esther and her grandmother share some of the same feelings, we see the events of the day through Esther's eyes only. Her grandmother might have a different view of some of the things they experience at the *baracholka*.

Write three *open-ended questions* that you would like to ask Esther's grandmother about going to the *baracholka*. An open-ended question cannot be answered with a simple "yes" or "no," but it can be answered by reading the selection. Then exchange papers with a classmate and answer each other's questions as if you were Esther's grandmother.

Questions and answers may vary.

1. **My Question:** _____

   _____

   My Partner's Answer: _____

   _____

2. **My Question:** _____

   _____

   My Partner's Answer: _____

   _____

3. **My Question:** _____

   _____

   My Partner's Answer: _____

   _____

26   The Endless Steppe ✦ **Open Court Classics**

Responding to Literature p. 26

Teacher Tip **Comprehension Strategies** Ask students what they visualized as they read this selection. Have them explain how visualizing helped them better understand what they read.

Assessment Use the Informal Comprehension Strategies Rubrics: Visualizing on Appendix page 145 of the **Teacher's Edition** to assess how well students are visualizing what they read.

Name_____ Date_____

A Closer Look

Going to the *baracholka* is a very exciting adventure for Esther. She enjoys it so much that she wishes for her family to "be allowed to live in the village within sight and sound of the Sunday *baracholka*."

Think about some of the sights and sounds Esther describes. Now think about some of the sights and sounds at a place where your family shops. Compare the *baracholka* to the store you visit. Write your ideas on the lines below, and then answer the question. **Possible answers below:**

Where I shop: **a grocery store**_____

How it is like the *baracholka:*
A grocery store, like the *baracholka,* sells food

such as potatoes, meat, and bread.

_____

How it is different from the *baracholka:*
The grocery store where I shop is inside a physical

structure, unlike the *baracholka* that is outside.

_____

Explain why you would or would not like to go to a *baracholka*.
Answers may vary._____

_____

_____

_____

_____

Responding to Literature p. 27

Teacher Tip The concept of trading might be unfamiliar to some students. Discuss with students how trading is similar to and different from the use of currency.

Objective

Students will learn to draw comparisons between similar situations.

Thinking Skills

◆ Comparing and contrasting environments
◆ Recalling details
◆ Making connections

Activity

Encourage students to include sensory details as they describe the sights, sounds, activities, people, and so on. Suggest that students return to the selection and identify sensory details used by the author. Students might wish to use these examples as a model for their own sensory details. If students have difficulty identifying a place where they shop, ask if they have been to a garage sale, flea market, farmers' market, or auction.

The Next Step

Have students read more about markets in different countries throughout the world. They can use their Personal Journals to take notes about the information they uncover. Then have each student use his or her notes to write an expository essay on one of the markets. Encourage students to note details, such as the most common and most prized items sold or traded.

Objective

Students will make decisions based on information provided in the selection and justify their choices.

Thinking Skills

✦ Recalling details
✦ Determining importance based on need and availability
✦ Proving importance with reason

Activity

Discuss with students the importance of good decision-making skills. Have students describe how making the right decision was a matter of survival for Esther and her family. Then have students put themselves in Esther's place and select three items to purchase. Remind students to provide detailed reasons to support their choices.

The Next Step

Engage students in a discussion about the distinctions between need and want. For example, ask students to explain when clothing, such as boots or food, is a need and when it is a want.

Name_____ Date_____

What Would You Do?

Imagine that you are Esther. You have just sold some of your personal belongings at the *baracholka*, and it is now your turn to be the buyer. At the market you are surrounded by different kinds of goods; however, you have enough *rubles* to buy only three things. What will you choose to buy? How will you determine what is a necessity and what is not?

On the lines below, specify three items that you will buy at the *baracholka*. Then explain why each item you have selected is important to you and is worth the *rubles* you must spend to buy it. **Possible answers below:**

Item: At the market I would buy a coat.

Reason: I would buy a coat because of the cold weather in Siberia.

_____

Item: I would buy some meat at the *baracholka*.

Reason: Meat is important because my family has been eating only bread and cheese.

_____

Item: I would buy a new pair of boots.

Reason: It is important to have a good pair of boots while working in the mines.

_____

28   The Endless Steppe ✦ Open Court Classics

Responding to Literature p. 28

Teacher Tip As students complete the assigned *Responding to Literature* pages, be sure they are moving forward with recognizing information needs as they conduct research for their knowledge-building projects.

Think like a Historian

A *historian* is a person who studies the past, including the history of countries, cultures, and specific people or events. Historians examine diaries, reports, newspapers, and other sources for information about the past. Often they make inferences from the information they collect and compare historical events to current events.

Imagine that you are a historian studying the Russian *baracholka* of the 1940s. Using "The Endless Steppe" as your source of information, thoroughly answer two of the three questions below.

1. What inference can you make about the economic level of the people who traded at the *baracholka?* Support your answer with evidence from the selection.
   Possible answer: They were poor. Hautzig writes about the girls showing off their dolls made from rags.

2. What role did the *baracholka* play in people's lives other than being a place to buy and exchange goods?
   Possible answer: The *baracholka* provided an opportunity for socializing and gave the people a chance to forget about their hardships.

3. How might modern citizens in developed countries view the *baracholka* of the 1940s? Explain your answer.
   Answers may vary.

Responding to Literature p. 29

Teacher Tip **Writing** Explain that historians must be good writers because they often present their findings in magazine articles and books. Part of being a good writer is supporting one's ideas with facts, examples, and reasons.

Assessment Use the Expository Structure Writing Rubric on Appendix page 146 of the *Teacher's Edition* to assess the organization of students' writing and use of supporting details.

Objective

Students will learn to make inferences and support their ideas with examples from the text.

Thinking Skills

✦ Making inferences
✦ Extrapolating importance
✦ Proving with examples

Activity

Students should use examples and evidence from the selection to support their answers to the first two questions. For the third question, have students give reasons to support their opinions.

The Next Step

Ask students what they know about prisoners of war throughout history, and have them share their ideas. Then have students further examine this concept by using resources to collect information about prisoners of war. Because this research might raise some sensitive issues for students, you might want to provide materials in the classroom that you have reviewed for students to explore. Then have students use the information they gather to write an expository essay in their Personal Journals. Encourage students to discuss how their research affected their ideas about the Rudomin family.

Objectives

- Students will make decisions based on their values and ideas and provide support for their choices.
- Students will apply concepts from the selection in a role-playing situation.

Thinking Skills

- Distinguishing necessities from luxuries
- Prioritizing items of importance
- Evaluating value of possessions

Activity

As students make their lists of items to pack, remind them not to spend too much time thinking about what to take. Encourage students to make their lists quickly to help them relate to the urgency of the Rudomins' situation. While the role-playing activity should be fun for students, explain that they should take the situation and the decision-making process seriously, as Esther's family would have.

The Next Step

Allow each "family" group to share its role-playing experience with the class. Then have a class discussion about the insights into the Rudomin family's circumstances this activity provided. Ask students how this activity helped them gain a better understanding of the unit theme.

Name_____ Date_____

UNIT 2 Dollars and Sense • *The Endless Steppe*

Make It Happen

Suppose that you are in the same situation as the Rudomins. You are spending an ordinary day at home when there is a knock on your door. You are told that you must leave your home, and you have only a few minutes to pack a suitcase. You do not know where you are going or how long you will be gone.

In the short time that you have, what will you pack? List the most important items that you will take, and give a reason for choosing each one. **Answers may vary.**

Item 1: _____ Reason: _____

Item 2: _____ Reason: _____

Item 3: _____ Reason: _____

Item 4: _____ Reason: _____

Item 5: _____ Reason: _____

Form a "family" with several classmates. Assign a role to each family member (mother, uncle, daughter, grandfather, and so on). Imagine that your family needs money and must sell some belongings. Role-play this situation with your classmates using the lists you made. Discuss what will be sold, what each person feels he or she can or cannot part with, and who will make the final decision about what is to be sold.

How did this role-playing activity affect your view of the Rudomins' situation? Write your ideas below.
Answers may vary.

_____

_____

_____

_____

30   The Endless Steppe ✦ Open Court Classics

Responding to Literature p. 30

Assessment Use the *Responding to Literature* pages as an informal assessment of students' understanding of the selection, making inferences, and the importance of decision making.

Name_____ Date_____

Life Lessons

Before the Rudomin family is taken from their home and sent to the labor camp, they live a comfortable life. They are a wealthy family with a good home, nice clothes, and plenty to eat. As prisoners at the labor camp, the Rudomins are often cold, hungry, and exhausted from hard work. Imagine what it must be like for Esther to go through such a big change in her life. Keep in mind that she is only ten years old when she leaves Poland to go to Siberia.

Possible answers below:

In what ways do Esther's experiences change when she arrives in Siberia? Write your ideas below.

In Poland, Esther might have experienced feelings

of security; however, in Siberia, Esther might

experience feelings of fear and uncertainty.

_____

_____

_____

Esther is fifteen years old when Russian soldiers come to free her from the labor camp. In the five years she spends in Siberia, how do you think Esther's ideas about what is important to her might change? Write your thoughts below.

Esther might value family, health, and happiness

more than material things.

_____

_____

_____

_____

Open Court Classics ✦ The Endless Steppe   **31**

Responding to Literature p. 31

Teacher Tip If students have trouble with the second portion of this activity, initiate a discussion about priorities. Explain that many different kinds of experiences can cause a person's priorities to change. Priorities also change as a person gets older. Point out that at first Esther might have missed physical objects or possessions. However, as she matured and experienced the hardships of life at the labor camp, she might have come to place a higher value on security, family, and health.

Objective

Students will learn to make conjectures in order to answer questions about a character.

Thinking Skills

✦ Extrapolating information
✦ Evaluating a character's situation and experiences

Activity

Have students write about how Esther's values might have changed from the time she arrived in Siberia to the time she was released. Encourage students to put themselves in Esther's place as they consider these challenging questions and to reference events that might have influenced her thinking.

The Next Step

Hautzig has written other autobiographies about this time in her life. Some of her stories are collected in a book called *Remember Who You Are: Stories about Being Jewish.* Have students think about this title as they identify sentences from the selection that they think best illustrate who Esther is. Encourage students to explain their reasons for choosing each sentence. Then ask them to write their own short "Who I Am" stories.

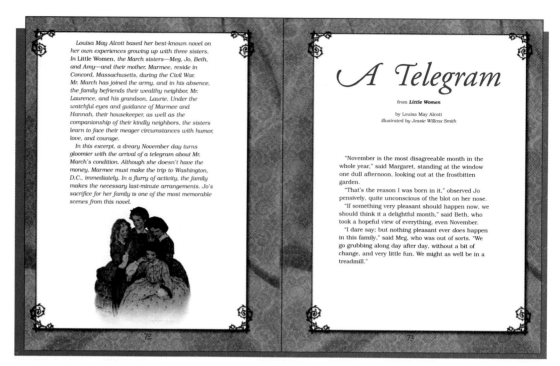

The following appears within the illustrated book pages:

Louisa May Alcott based her best-known novel on her own experiences growing up with three sisters. In Little Women, the March sisters—Meg, Jo, Beth, and Amy—and their mother, Marmee, reside in Concord, Massachusetts, during the Civil War. Mr. March has joined the army, and in his absence, the family befriends their wealthy neighbor, Mr. Laurence, and his grandson, Laurie. Under the watchful eyes and guidance of Marmee and Hannah, their housekeeper, as well as the companionship of their kindly neighbors, the sisters learn to face their meager circumstances with humor, love, and courage.

In this excerpt, a dreary November day turns gloomier with the arrival of a telegram about Mr. March's condition. Although she doesn't have the money, Marmee must make the trip to Washington, D.C., immediately. In a flurry of activity, the family makes the necessary last-minute arrangements. Jo's sacrifice for her family is one of the most memorable scenes from this novel.

$\mathscr{A}$ Telegram

from *Little Women*

by Louisa May Alcott
illustrated by Jessie Willcox Smith

"November is the most disagreeable month in the whole year," said Margaret, standing at the window one dull afternoon, looking out at the frostbitten garden.

"That's the reason I was born in it," observed Jo pensively, quite unconscious of the blot on her nose.

"If something very pleasant should happen now, we should think it a delightful month," said Beth, who took a hopeful view of everything, even November.

"I dare say; but nothing pleasant ever *does* happen in this family," said Meg, who was out of sorts. "We go grubbing along day after day, without a bit of change, and very little fun. We might as well be in a treadmill."

Student Anthology pp. 72–89

Selection Goals

- To identify ways the author develops characters
- To recognize the significance of personal sacrifice

Selection Summary

When a telegram arrives announcing that Mr. March, a soldier in the Civil War, has been hospitalized, his family rushes to make arrangements for Mrs. March to join him in Washington, D.C. Jo, one of the four March daughters, finds a creative and selfless way to make a contribution to her mother's trip and to her father's well-being.

Genre: Realistic Fiction

Share with students some of the elements of realistic fiction, which include

- ✦ characters who behave like real people or animals.
- ✦ events that could happen in real life.
- ✦ settings that are real or could be real.
- ✦ conflicts similar to those in real life.

❖ Part 1 ❖
Building Background

Activate Prior Knowledge

✦ Ask students if they are familiar with the novel *Little Women*. Encourage them to tell something about the plot and/or characters.

✦ Explain to students that one of the characters mentioned in this selection, Mr. March, is a soldier in the Civil War. Ask students to share what they know about this war and this period in American history. Encourage students to recall what they learned from the selection "Behind Rebel Lines: The Incredible Story of Emma Edmonds, Civil War Spy" in Unit 1.

Background Information

✦ Louisa May Alcott based each of the March sisters in *Little Women* on herself and her three sisters. The character that Alcott patterned after herself was Jo March. Following the success of *Little Women*, Alcott wrote two sequels: *Little Men* (1871) and *Jo's Boys* (1886).

✦ Alcott's book *Hospital Sketches* was based on letters she wrote to her family while working as a nurse in Washington, D.C. during the Civil War—a time and place that turns up in this selection as well.

✦ Like the March family in this selection, Alcott's family was often in debt. As a teenager Alcott began working at various jobs to contribute to her family's income. When she became an established writer, Alcott provided the primary financial support for her family.

Previewing the Literature

Browse the Selection

✦ Have students read aloud the title of the selection and the names of the author and illustrator. Then have students browse the first couple of pages for any challenging or unfamiliar words in the selection.

✦ Note on the board those things students mention as a result of their browsing and any questions they have about the selection.

Set Purposes for Reading

Encourage students to set purposes for reading this selection. Ask students to think about how the selection connects to their personal interests or experiences as well as to the unit theme.

> **Teacher Tip**
> Louisa May Alcott's father, Bronson, was an educator and philosopher. He encouraged Alcott to keep a diary as a child which probably helped her discover and develop her talent as a writer. Friends of Bronson, noted writers Henry David Thoreau and Ralph Waldo Emerson were also influential in developing Alcott's talent.

A Telegram

Expanding Vocabulary

The words listed below can be found in the Glossary of the **Student Anthology.**
Page numbers indicate where the words can be found in the selection.

despondent, p. 74
Showing or feeling discouragement.

obliged, p. 75
To be made thankful for a service or favor.

assurances, p. 78
Statements supposed to make one certain; without doubt.

perturbed, p. 81
To have upset or made anxious. [Middle English, from Latin *perturbare,* "to throw into confusion," from *per-* + *turbare,* "to disturb."]

commissions, p. 81
Tasks given to a person to do.

vanity, p. 83
Too much pride in one's appearance.

ninepence, p. 83
An old English coin; "nine pennies."

amiably, p. 88
In a friendly and kindly manner.

> **Teacher Tip**
> As students read, remind them to use various word attack skills, such as word structure, apposition, and context clues, to help figure out the meanings of unfamiliar words.

⊹*Part 2*⊹

Reading the Selection

Read

✦ Have students silently read **Student Anthology** pages 72–89, stopping at the end of each page if they have any questions or need clarification.

✦ Encourage students to use summarizing or any other comprehension strategies that might help them read the selection.

Discuss

The following discussion suggestions can be carried out on different days, depending upon how much time you allot to each selection.

✦ Have students discuss their general reactions to the selection.

✦ Ask students what this selection adds to the theme that the other selections do not.

✦ Encourage students to review the questions they listed on the board before reading to see if the selection answered their questions.

✦ Have students discuss their impressions of the characters in this selection. Ask them to give examples of how Alcott developed distinct personalities for each character.

✦ Have students make inferences from the selection and discuss things they think Alcott considered to be of value.

After students have discussed the selection, choose from *Responding to Literature* pages 32–37, and ask students to complete the assigned pages.

→ Part 3 ←
Knowledge-Building Project

Students should continue to collect information and begin working on the final drafts of their diaries. Encourage them to use a variety of resources, such as encyclopedias, videos, nonfiction books, and the Internet. Suggest that students format their diaries to represent the fictional or nonfictional perspective from which they are writing. For example, if a student is writing from the perspective of the president of the United States, he or she might present a diary that is covered and protected by a fine, expensive-looking material. If a student is writing from the perspective of a worker in a factory, he or she might present a diary with tattered and yellowed pages that are bound with twine.

> **Assessment** Use the Research Rubrics: Communicating Research Progress and Results on Appendix page 149 of the *Teacher's Edition* to assess students' progress on their projects. Share with students the rubrics that will be used to evaluate them.

As students prepare final drafts of their Great Depression diaries, they should be thinking about entries they would like to present to the class. Encourage students to practice reading their diaries aloud. Suggest that they ask for feedback from friends or family members. Explain to students that they should focus on their tone, clarity, and volume of voice and should judge whether they are reading with expression.

By the end of this selection, students should be ready to present their completed diaries.

Objective

Students will formulate interview questions and apply their questions in an interview situation.

Thinking Skills

✦ Formulating questions
✦ Drawing conclusions

Activity

As students formulate questions for their interview with Alcott, encourage them to think about what they would most like to know about the author and *Little Women*. Remind them that good questions often lead to additional questions. After their interviews, have students think about how their new questions were formulated from their interview questions.

The Next Step

Have students research Alcott's life to find or confirm answers to their questions about the author. Students can then write a biography about Alcott in their Personal Journals. Remind them that a biography is the story of a real person's life written by someone else. Encourage students to share their biographies with classmates.

Name_____ Date_____

Getting Started

Imagine you have a radio program called *Writer's Corner*. Your next guest on the program is Louisa May Alcott, author of *Little Women*. What would you like to ask Alcott?

1. What would you and your listeners be interested in knowing about Alcott and *Little Women*? Make a list of questions for your interview on the lines below.

Questions may vary.

_____
_____
_____

2. Find a classmate who has read the story. Interview your classmate using the questions you wrote. Your classmate should play the role of Alcott. Use the lines below to take notes while conducting your interview. Then trade places and let your partner interview you as you play the role of Alcott.

Notes may vary.

_____
_____
_____
_____
_____

3. With your partner, discuss the questions each of you asked the author. After the discussion, what new questions were formed from your interview questions? Record any new questions that you have in your Personal Journal.

Extra Effort: Read another selection written by Alcott. Record any new information you learn about the author and her writing in your Personal Journal.

32

A Telegram ✦ Open Court Classics

Responding to Literature p. 32

Teacher Tip Encourage students to listen to a radio program in which guests are interviewed. Hearing the kinds of questions someone else asks can help students learn how to phrase their own questions. Have students consider what other kinds of questions might elicit interesting information in this situation. Ask students also to consider how interesting questions vary in different contexts.

Name_____Date_____

A Telegram • Dollars and Sense **UNIT 2**

I Wonder

To *sacrifice* means "to give up something for the sake of someone or something else." In "A Telegram" Jo makes a sacrifice by selling her hair for money to bring her ill father home. How does Jo's sacrifice relate to the unit theme?

Possible answer: Jo believes that her father's

comfort is of more value than her hair.

Think about the other selections you read in this unit and the unit theme. Then read each question, and express your ideas and thoughts on the lines below.

1. Why do you think some people are willing to sacrifice what is valuable to them?

   Possible answer: They want to make others

   happy.

   _____

   _____

2. What is the greatest sacrifice you would make, and for whom would you make it?

   Answers may vary.

   _____

   _____

   _____

   _____

Extra Effort: What other books or poems have you read that relate to the unit theme? Choose one to bring to class and share with classmates. Discuss how the book or poem relates to the unit theme.

Open Court Classics ✦ A Telegram

33

Responding to Literature p. 33

Teacher Tip Comprehension Strategies Have students explain what strategies they used to understand the selection. Because of the length of this selection, summarizing might have been especially useful. Ask students how often they summarized as they read.

Assessment Use the Informal Comprehension Strategies Rubrics: Summarizing on Appendix page 145 of the *Teacher's Edition* to assess students' use of summarizing to better understand the text.

Objective

Students will relate the selection, their personal experiences, and their inferences regarding the experiences of others to the unit theme.

Thinking Skills

✦ Making connections
✦ Making inferences
✦ Evaluating ideas

Activity

Have students think about what it means to make a sacrifice. As they answer the questions, ask them to consider how the personal sacrifices and the different levels of sacrifice demonstrated in each selection of this unit relate to the unit theme and themselves. Encourage students to develop their answers by providing examples and reasons.

The Next Step

This selection gives some clues about the role of women in the mid-1800s when the story is set. You might draw students' attention to Meg's comment on page 74 of the *Student Anthology.* Have students read more about this topic and take notes about the information they find. Then have them write a persuasive paragraph in which they express their ideas about how women's roles in modern society are the same and/or different than they were 150 years ago.

Objective

Students will learn to make connections among characters from two selections.

Thinking Skills

- ✦ Making connections
- ✦ Proving with examples

Activity

Have students consider the similarities between Jo and Billy, as well as their family members, and then answer the questions. Remind students to support their answers with evidence from the selections. In addition, you might suggest that students recall the sacrifices made by Esther and her family in *The Endless Steppe.* Ask students to discuss how the Rudomins' sacrifices compare and contrast with Jo's and Billy's sacrifices.

The Next Step

Have students search for other literary works that deal with personal sacrifice. Ask each student to present a summary of one of the selections he or she found. Then encourage a class discussion about the various ways personal sacrifice is dealt with as a theme. Ask students how the selections they found also relate to the unit theme.

Name_____ Date_____

UNIT 2 Dollars and Sense • *A Telegram*

Making Connections

Jo from "A Telegram" and Billy from "Where the Red Fern Grows" make sacrifices for things they believe to be important. Think about the events in each story. Consider the sacrifices each character makes as you answer the questions below. **Possible answers below:**

1. How are Jo's and Billy's situations similar?

   The families in both stories have little money; therefore, Jo and Billy find their own ways to earn money.

2. How do the other characters in each story respond to Jo's and Billy's sacrifices? How are their responses similar?

   The families are shocked at Jo's and Billy's actions, but they are proud of both characters.

3. What do the sacrifices Jo and Billy make tell about their characters?

   Jo's and Billy's sacrifices show that they are strong-willed and determined characters.

4. How do Jo's and Billy's actions demonstrate fairness?

   Jo and Billy earn the money honestly by giving up things they value.

34

A Telegram ✦ Open Court Classics

Responding to Literature p. 34

Teacher Tip Use the last question on page 34 of *Responding to Literature* as an opportunity for a class discussion about character. Ask volunteers to share their ideas about how Jo and Billy demonstrate fairness. Then have students discuss what fairness means to them and how they can promote fairness through their actions.

Quite a Character

Alcott provides her readers with insight into the character of Meg, Jo's older sister. Review the story for information about Meg, and then answer the questions below. Use the text to support your views.

Possible answers below:

1. What do you know about Meg . . .

   from her behavior?
   Meg is kind: Meg comforts Jo as she cries about her hair.

   from what she expresses?
   Meg takes charge: Meg "begged her [mother] to sit quietly in her room for a little while, and let them work."

   from what other people say about her?
   Meg is generous: Jo says, "Meg gave all her quarterly salary toward the rent . . ."

2. How do you think Meg perceives her role in the family?
   Meg sees herself as a caregiver to her family.

Responding to Literature p. 35

Teacher Tip As students complete the assigned *Responding to Literature* pages, be sure they are making progress with their research and writing for their projects.

Assessment Use the *Responding to Literature* pages as an informal assessment of students' understanding of the selection and of their ability to make connections and conjectures.

Objective

Students will learn to analyze a character from the selection and support their character analyses with examples from the text.

Thinking Skills

✦ Evaluating a character's traits
✦ Drawing conclusions

Activity

Explain to students that authors sometimes reveal characters' traits through their thoughts and actions, instead of describing them directly. Encourage students to make a list of adjectives that they think describe Meg *before* they reread the selection. This will emphasize to them the general impression they had of Meg after the first reading of the selection. Students should then reread the selection and complete the activity. When they have finished, have students revisit the list of adjectives to see whether their first impression changed or was reinforced.

The Next Step

Have students select another character from the selection and write a character analysis. Encourage students to create a character web detailing the character's traits before writing their analyses.

Objective

Students will learn to make conjectures about a character, investigate causes and issues of the Civil War, and write a friendly letter.

Thinking Skills

✦ Evaluating a character's motives
✦ Identifying causes and issues
✦ Substituting personal perspective with a character's

Activity

Have students research some of the causes and issues of the Civil War and, based on the information they collect, identify the reasons Mr. March joins the Union army. Students will then write a letter from Mr. March to his family explaining his reasons for fighting in the war. Remind students that because they will be writing from Mr. March's perspective, they should use a first-person point of view in their letters.

The Next Step

Have students find letters that were written by real Civil War soldiers. Suggest that students use resources, such as the Internet, to locate authentic letters. Encourage them to share interesting letters with the rest of the class. Students can record their reactions to the letters in their Personal Journals.

Name_____ Date_____

Think like a Soldier

In *Little Women*, Mr. March joins the army and leaves to fight in the Civil War. How do you think Mr. March's absence affects the family's financial situation? Why do you think Mr. March feels that fighting in the war is important? What struggles do you think he faces when choosing between the war and his family?

Research some of the causes and issues of the Civil War, and take notes in your Personal Journal. Then on the lines below, write a letter from Mr. March to his family. In the letter explain your reasons for joining the army and your feelings about the causes for which you are fighting. Remember to follow the steps of the writing process as you write your letter.

Letters may vary.

_____

_____

_____

_____

_____

_____

_____

_____

See Appendix page 130 for writing a friendly letter.

Extra Effort: Read more about the Civil War, and then choose a cause or issue to investigate. Record what you learned in your Personal Journal, and share your discoveries with classmates.

36   A Telegram ✦ Open Court Classics

Responding to Literature p. 36

Teacher Tip **Writing** Remind students that the body of a letter contains the message but can also include questions. Writing questions adds variety and encourages a response from the recipient.

Assessment Use the Personal Writing Rubric on Appendix page 146 of the *Teacher's Edition* to assess the development and expression of thoughts in students' writing.

Name_____Date_____

Lesson 6

A Closer Look

Jo's selling her hair causes a great deal of excitement among the characters in *Little Women*. Since ancient times, hair has been an important part of the way people present themselves. In addition to adornment, hairstyles in some cultures can indicate a person's social status, beliefs, age, or occupation.

1. Write some questions you have about these ideas on the lines below.

_____

_____

_____

2. Then conduct research to find more information related to one of your questions. Use your Personal Journal to take notes as you collect information. You can also record new ideas and questions you have as you discover additional information.

3. Decide how you will organize and present your ideas and information. For example, you might create a time line with pictures of different hairstyles or write and present a report.

4. After presenting your ideas and information, write what you learned from your research on the lines below. Include your ideas about using hair as an accessory and any new questions that you have.

_____

_____

_____

_____

_____

_____

_____

Responding to Literature p. 37

Teacher Tip Resource materials, such as the book *Hair There and Everywhere* by Karin Luisa Badt or the Web site www.springfield.k12.il.us/schools/springfield/eliz/hairstyles.html might be helpful to students as they collect information for this activity. However, you should always review materials for appropriateness before suggesting them to students.

Objective

Students will research a question and present their findings.

Thinking Skills

✦ Formulating research questions
✦ Identifying information
✦ Proving with evidence

Activity

If students find it challenging to formulate questions, have them consider what their own hairstyles could indicate about them. Encourage students to generate original ideas for their presentations. Also remind students to use their Personal Journals for recording information and new questions that arise as they investigate their research topics.

The Next Step

Have students discuss the value placed on hairstyles in their culture. Encourage students to consider the amount of time and money people spend on their hair. You might also suggest that students predict hairstyles of the future. Students can record and share their predictions through drawings and/or descriptions.

*W*rap-Up

Knowledge-Building Project

Students have completed their preliminary work and should be ready to present their findings. Suggest that each student read aloud two or three entries from his or her diary. Encourage students to respond to each presentation, offering constructive feedback. Also have students tell what new facts they learned and new questions they have about people's concepts of value. Make the diaries available for students to examine after the presentations. Use the Research Rubrics: Overall Assessment of Research on Appendix page 149 of the *Teacher's Edition* to assess students' knowledge-building projects as a whole.

Teacher Tip
• Suggest that students investigate how the advertising business influences society's ideas about what is valuable.

• Encourage students to keep a journal for recording short- and long-term goals and plans for achieving them. Remind students to consider what they value.

Reviewing the Concepts

In this unit students explored different ideas about what people judge as valuable. The hard work and sacrifice of characters in these selections demonstrated the value of immaterial as well as material possessions. Students investigated some of the following key concepts in this unit:

✦ Working hard to accomplish a goal has its own rewards.

✦ Sentimental value can have more importance than monetary value.

✦ The Great Depression deeply affected many people's ideas about what is valuable.

Evaluating the Unit

✦ Ask students to evaluate each selection on the basis of effectiveness of reading/vocabulary, literary value, interest of the subject matter, style of writing, application of theme, and the selection's personal value to the student.

✦ Ask students to evaluate the different activities in the unit, including the knowledge-building project. Have them consider these questions: Which activities made you think? Which ones did you find less challenging and why? Which ones seemed confusing or challenging? Which activities did you most enjoy and why? Which activities changed your opinions and offered new ideas? Which activities stimulated novelty and original thinking? What activities would you like to add to the unit?

✦ Ask students to evaluate this *Open Court Classics* unit. They can describe how the theme was explored in the unit. They can also compare and contrast the selections based on what the characters valued, sacrifices that were made, and the importance of family.

Assessment

Vocabulary Assessment

To assess students' understanding of the vocabulary words, you might want to do one of the following:

✦ Have students provide synonyms and/or antonyms for the vocabulary words from the unit.

✦ Have students design a test to exchange with a partner. This can be used to assess their knowledge of the vocabulary words in each selection.

✦ Administer an informal oral assessment. Have students supply the definition of the vocabulary word or use the word properly in a sentence.

Informal Comprehension Strategies Rubrics

Use the Informal Comprehension Strategies Rubrics: Asking Questions, Visualizing, and Summarizing on Appendix pages 144–145 of the ***Teacher's Edition*** to determine whether a student is using a particular strategy or strategies as he or she reads the selections. Note these and any other strategies a student is using, instead of the degree to which a student might be using any particular strategy. In addition, encourage the student to tell of any strategies other than the ones being taught that he or she is using.

Research Rubrics

Use the Research Rubrics: Making Conjectures, Recognizing Information Needs, Communicating Research Progress and Results, and Overall Assessment of Research on Appendix pages 148–149 of the ***Teacher's Edition*** to assess a student's performance throughout the investigation. The rubrics range from 1 to 4 in most categories, with 1 being the lowest score. In addition, you can use the rubrics to assess a group's collaborative work as well as an individual's participation in that group.

Writing Rubrics

Use the Prewriting/Organizing Writing Rubric, the Descriptive Writing Rubric, the Expository Structure Writing Rubric, and the Personal Writing Rubric on Appendix page 146 of the ***Teacher's Edition*** to assess student writing. The rubrics range from 1 to 4 in most categories, with 1 being the lowest score.

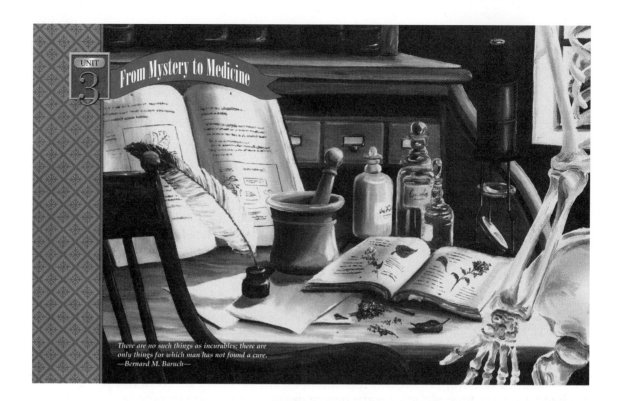

UNIT 3 From Mystery to Medicine

There are no such things as incurables; there are only things for which man has not found a cure.
—Bernard M. Baruch—

Unit Goals

- To recognize the elements of expository text
- To understand that folk medicine has a place in modern medicine
- To write and deliver a speech regarding medical treatments
- To identify the elements of narrative nonfiction
- To recognize that medicine can produce unexpected results
- To recognize Edward Jenner's contribution to world health
- To identify major developments in medicine
- To investigate a scientist's discovery and the ways in which his or her discovery affected society

Introduction

Throughout history, medical mysteries have puzzled humans; however, they have also inspired people to examine the unknown and make discoveries. In this unit students will explore some medical mysteries that have been solved and some that remain. Selection 1 is "Lingering Leeches" on page 92; Selection 2 is "A Spot or Two of Bother" on page 98; and Selection 3 is "Dr. Jenner's Marvelous Vaccine" on page 108. These selections will encourage students to consider how medicine has advanced and continues to progress.

Unit Discussion

Invite students to make predictions about the theme of this unit. Then have students discuss what they know about medicine. Continue the discussion by asking questions such as the following:

✦ What are some different kinds of doctors, and what do they do?

✦ What is the importance of understanding the cause of diseases?

✦ What are some medical mysteries of the past and of the present?

✦ How do these mysteries relate to the quotation in the unit opener?

Knowledge-Building Project

Advances in medicine would not be possible without the efforts of scientists and their medical research. While improved medicines, techniques, and equipment are generally welcomed by doctors and patients, some aspects of medical research are controversial. Have students develop a list of questions they have about scientists. Students might consider questions about a scientist's branch of medical research, how key discoveries were made, and how his or her work affected the field of medicine. If students have difficulty formulating questions, encourage them to read about some well-known scientists, such as Robert Koch, Jonas Edward Salk, John Franklin Enders, and Gertrude Elion, who have impacted society with their medical research. Students should record the information they gather in their Personal Journals. Remind students that throughout the unit they should return to this list to record new questions and ideas. As students move through the selections in this unit, they will discover some evolutions in medicine that they can relate to their projects. As a final product, students will write and deliver an informative speech about a scientist and his or her significant discovery that evolved from medical research.

Teacher Tip
As an alternative to the outlined project, encourage interested students to investigate a medical tool or instrument. Students might compare and contrast early models of a particular implement with modern versions. Students might also create a model or a diagram to accompany their final presentations.

	Unit 3 Project Overview
Unit Overview	Students begin their investigations by developing questions about scientists and their branch of medical research.
Selection 1	Students begin research and select a subject to investigate.
Selection 2	Students continue with their investigations and begin working on their speeches.
Selection 3	Students prepare final drafts of their speeches.
Unit Wrap-Up	Students deliver their speeches.

Student Anthology pp. 92–97

Selection Goals

- To recognize the elements of expository text
- To understand that folk remedies play a role in modern medicine
- To write and deliver a speech regarding medical treatments

Selection Summary

Like author Edel Wignell, most people would probably be distressed to find a leech on their skin. However, sometimes leeches are purposely applied to the skin. In this expository selection, Wignell explains the past and present medical uses of leeches.

Genre: Expository Text

Share with students some of the elements of an expository text, which include

- ✦ factual and verifiable information about a specific subject.
- ✦ events presented in the order in which they occurred.
- ✦ writing organized by topics.
- ✦ diagrams, photographs, maps, or illustrations.

⋄ Part 1 ⋄
Building Background

Activate Prior Knowledge

✦ Ask students to share what they know about leeches. Have students use their prior knowledge about leeches and medicine to predict the outcome of this selection.

✦ Have students share information about any alternative medical treatments that are familiar to them. For example, ask if anyone is familiar with herbal medicines or acupuncture. Encourage students to discuss the validity of these practices.

Background Information

✦ Australian Edel Wignell taught for 15 years before becoming a full-time writer. Wignell writes in a variety of genres, but her best-known works are children's books. Her award-winning books include *Raining Cats and Dogs*, *Escape by Deluge*, and *I Wonder Who Lives Upstairs*.

✦ There are 650 known species of leeches. The type that is most commonly used by plastic surgeons and reconstructive surgeons is *Hirudo medicinalis*, which is now an endangered species.

✦ Using maggots to treat wounds is an old folk remedy that is making a comeback. Maggot therapy, used in hospitals throughout the United States and Europe, is prescribed to treat seriously injured tissue. The maggots eat infected and dead flesh from a wound and remove harmful bacteria. This restores blood flow to the area and promotes the growth of new tissue.

> **Teacher Tip**
> Remind students that good readers browse nonfiction differently from the way they browse fiction. When readers browse nonfiction, they look through the entire selection. However, when readers browse fiction, they skim only the first couple of pages. This is because nonfiction is usually read to gather information rather than for entertainment.

Previewing the Literature

Browse the Selection

✦ Have students note the title and the name of the author, and then have them browse the entire selection. Ask students to look for clues about how this selection relates to the unit theme.

✦ Note on the board those things students mention as a result of their browsing and any questions they have about the selection.

Set Purposes for Reading

Encourage students to set purposes for reading, such as comprehension of a subject. Remind students that good readers ask themselves questions as they read, such as the following: Why was bloodletting thought to be an effective treatment for disease? Why and when do modern doctors use leeches instead of more sophisticated treatments?

Expanding Vocabulary

The words listed below can be found in the Glossary of the **Student Anthology.**
Page numbers indicate where the words can be found in the selection.

larvae,
p. 93 — Newly hatched, wormlike forms of insects before transformation through other stages of growth.

sustain,
p. 93 — To maintain. [From Latin *sustinēre*, "to hold up."]

ingested,
p. 94 — To have taken into the body through the mouth. [Latin *ingestus*, past participle of *ingerere*, "to carry in."]

legitimate,
p. 95 — Based on accepted standards; reasonable.

surplus,
p. 95 — An amount greater than needed. [Medieval Latin *superplus*, "more."]

secrete,
p. 96 — To release a chemical substance into the body.

saliva,
p. 96 — A clear liquid found in the mouth; produced by glands in the mouth to keep the mouth moist and to help in chewing and digestion.

> **Teacher Tip**
> Point out the irregular plural word *larvae,* and ask students if anyone knows the singular form *(larva).* Take this opportunity to review other irregular plurals with students.

⟡ *Part 2* ⟡

Reading the Selection

Read

◆ Have students silently read **Student Anthology** pages 92–97, stopping at the end of each page if they have any questions or need clarification.

◆ Encourage students to use making connections or any other comprehension strategies that might help them read the selection.

Discuss

The following discussion suggestions can be carried out on different days, depending upon how much time you allot to each selection.

✦ Have students discuss their general reactions to the selection.

✦ Ask students how this selection relates to the theme.

✦ Encourage students to review the questions they listed on the board before reading to see if the selection answered their questions.

✦ Have students discuss the relationship between folk medicine and modern medicine.

✦ Ask students what this selection added to their knowledge of medicine.

After students have discussed the selection, choose from *Responding to Literature* pages 38–43, and ask students to complete the assigned pages.

⊹ *Part 3* ⊹
Knowledge-Building Project

Have students review their list of questions about scientists and medical research. Encourage students to select several scientists and branches of medical research to investigate. This preliminary investigation should help students narrow their focus and select a subject that interests them. Encourage students also to use a variety of print references, such as books and journals, and nonprint references, such as films and recordings, when gathering their information. Students might need help finding appropriate resources. Encourage students to share with classmates any reference materials or other resources they find particularly helpful in their investigations. Consider inviting a speaker with experience in medical research or a related field, such as a parent, grandparent, or school nurse, to talk with students.

By the end of this selection, students should have selected a subject for their investigations. Remind students that they will be writing a speech with the purpose to inform, which means they will need to use a variety of credible resources.

By the end of the next selection, students should have begun working on their speeches.

> **Assessment**
> Use the Research Rubrics: Recognizing Information Needs on Appendix page 148 of the *Teacher's Edition* to assess how well students identify relevant information. As a group or with individual students, discuss the rubrics that will be used to evaluate students on their projects.

UNIT 3

Lingering Leeches

Lesson 1

Objective

Students will create a survey to collect information for the purpose of analyzing reactions.

Thinking Skills

✦ Formulating survey questions
✦ Evaluating reactions of peers

Activity

Have students create a survey to collect information about their classmates' responses to the selection. Encourage them to include open-ended questions that require some thought instead of questions that require simple yes or no answers. Remind students that open-ended questions allow for more personal responses and usually generate additional discussion and questions. Encourage students to discuss their responses after they have completed the surveys.

The Next Step

Tell students that surveys are conducted for several different purposes. Then have them research some famous surveys, such as the Gallup poll and the Nielsen ratings. Ask students to determine the purpose of each survey they research by examining the kind of information collected. Then have students compare the techniques used by each survey to gather information. Have students record their findings in their Personal Journals.

Name_____ Date_____

Getting Started

You want to find out what your classmates think about the selection "Lingering Leeches." One way to *analyze*, or examine, their thoughts is by making a *survey*. A survey is used to collect information from a group of people. Information can be gathered through interviews, research, or questionnaires. Create a survey that allows your classmates to share their ideas about the selection.

1. Make a list of questions for your survey. The questions you write should make classmates evaluate their feelings about and reactions to the selection.

Questions may vary.

_____

_____

_____

_____

2. Make copies of your survey and give them to classmates who have read "Lingering Leeches." Ask your classmates to write their answers to your questions. You can take your own survey, too.

3. After your classmates have completed your survey, have a group discussion. Ask classmates to share their answers to the questions you created. Record any new questions that were generated from the discussions on the lines below.

Questions may vary.

_____

_____

_____

See Appendix page 137 for writing a survey.

38   Lingering Leeches ✦ **Open Court Classics**

Responding to Literature p. 38

Teacher Tip Point out to students that thought-provoking questions begin with words and phrases such as *why, what if,* and *what do you think.*

Name_____ Date_____

Lingering Leeches • From Mystery to Medicine **UNIT 3**

Lesson 2

I Wonder

Writer Edel Wignell says that she "got the horrors" when she found a leech on her. Refer to the selection and review the information about leeches provided by the author. Use this information and your reactions to respond to the questions below. When you have finished, take turns sharing your responses with classmates.

1. What do you think you would do if you found a leech on your skin?
I would ask an adult I know for help.

_____
_____
_____
_____
_____

2. How would you react if a doctor told you it was necessary to treat your illness with leeches?
I probably would be surprised.

_____
_____
_____
_____
_____

Extra Effort: Read more about leeches and their purposes in today's medicine. Record your discoveries in your Personal Journal, and then share your new information with classmates.

Open Court Classics ✦ Lingering Leeches

39

Responding to Literature p. 39

Teacher Tip As students complete the assigned *Responding to Literature* pages, be sure they progress with recognizing information needs about a potential research subject for their knowledge-building projects.

Objective

Students will make connections between information in the selection and their ideas and experiences.

Thinking Skills

✦ Making connections
✦ Describing personal reactions
✦ Making inferences

Activity

Have students use the information presented in the selection and their feelings to respond to the questions. Encourage students to describe both their physical and emotional reactions. Explain that word choice is an integral part of writing to convey personal thoughts and feelings. Encourage students to use vivid words to help capture the essence of the experiences they describe in the activity.

The Next Step

In this selection Wignell writes about her terror of leeches. Ask students to think about the fears people have at different stages of their lives. Have students create a chart to shown how fears that people have vary from young children to adults to the elderly and so on. Then ask students to write about the things they do to overcome their fears and how their strategies have changed through the years.

Lingering Leeches

Lesson 3

Objective

Students will assess challenges presented by a product and then identify needed information to create an appealing advertisement.

Thinking Skills

✦ Determining challenges
✦ Judging informational needs

Activity

Encourage students to research the products and services provided by an actual leech farm to generate ideas before creating their advertisements. Then have students develop, design, and create a brochure or poster that advertises a leech farm's products and services. As students create their advertisements, remind them to judge whether their choice of words and illustrations will convince consumers to buy the products and services.

The Next Step

Have students compare and contrast advertisements for different types of products, such as movies, beauty supplies, car dealerships, and so on. Encourage students to discuss how the advertising techniques are different even though they all have the same purpose—to sell the products they feature.

Name_____ Date_____

Think like an Advertiser

In "Lingering Leeches" the author mentions that there are farms that provide leeches for medical use. Imagine that you work for an advertising company and a leech farmer has asked you to create an advertisement for a product. What challenges will this job present to you as an advertiser?

Possible answer: Appealing to customers will be one challenge of this job.

What kind of information should be included in the advertisement? Think about the issues that are important to doctors and scientists.

Possible answer: The positive aspects of using leeches to treat patients should be included.

Use the space below to generate and organize ideas for the advertisement. Then create a brochure or poster advertising your client's product.

Advertisements may vary.

See Appendix page 124 for tips for writing an advertisement.

40

Lingering Leeches ✦ **Open Court Classics**

Responding to Literature p. 40

Teacher Tip Comprehension Strategies Ask students what connections they made between the text and their prior knowledge as they read. Encourage them to explain how using this strategy helped them better understand the selection.

Assessment Use the Informal Comprehension Strategies Rubrics: Making Connections on Appendix page 144 of the *Teacher's Edition* to assess students' use of this strategy.

Name_____ Date_____

Lesson 4

I Can Do It, Too

In the selection "Lingering Leeches," you read about the practice of leech rental more than 200 years ago. How do you think doctors discovered that this was causing diseases to spread?

Possible answer: A connection was made between

patients on whom leeches were used and patients

who contracted the disease.

Make a list of questions you have about the use of leeches in the eighteenth and nineteenth centuries. Then use encyclopedias, magazines, books, the Internet, and other appropriate resources to research the medical use of leeches hundreds of years ago. Take notes in your Personal Journal.

Questions may vary.

In your Personal Journal, write an expository paragraph to add to the selection "Lingering Leeches." Consider the author's style, and *emulate*, or match, the style in your writing. Also think about the best place to insert your paragraph in the text and how to write a smooth transition. When you have finished, answer the question below.

How did you decide where to insert your paragraph in "Lingering Leeches"? Give your reasons below.

Answers may vary.

See Appendix pages 133–134 for writing a paragraph and Appendix page 138 for writing an expository essay.

Open Court Classics ♦ Lingering Leeches   **41**

Responding to Literature p. 41

Teacher Tip You might want to first review other works written by the author, and then provide students with a list of appropriate articles and books from which they can choose.

Objectives

♦ Students will formulate questions and gather needed information.

♦ Students will learn to emulate the author's style in their own expository paragraphs.

Thinking Skills

♦ Formulating questions
♦ Identifying relevant information
♦ Adding to expository text

Activity

Have students conduct research to find information about the medical use of leeches in the 1700s and 1800s. Then have them write an expository paragraph to add to the selection. Remind students to pay particular attention to matching Wignell's style and creating a smooth transition. Encourage students to meet with partners to discuss characteristics of Wignell's writing style and to review the elements of expository text.

The Next Step

Have students read other articles and books by Edel Wignell and compare the writing style of those works with that of this selection.

Objectives

✦ Students will formulate
questions and draw
conclusions about folk
medicine.

✦ Students will learn to debate
the effectiveness of folk
medicine versus modern
medicine.

Thinking Skills

✦ Formulating questions
✦ Proving with evidence
✦ Drawing conclusions

Activity

Tell students that participants in
a debate should show respect for
their opponents. Explain that
during a debate students should
stay focused on the issue and
avoid personal insults or attacks.
Then have students use the
information they collected from
print and nonprint sources to
debate the practice of folk
medicine versus modern
medicine. Students should
record what they learned and
additional questions in their
Personal Journals.

The Next Step

Have students find out about the
formal rules for debating.
Encourage them to follow these
guidelines and stage a debate
about an issue related to the
unit theme.

Name_____ Date_____

A Closer Look

Using leeches to treat disease began as a kind of *folk
medicine.* Folk medicine is a term for the practice of medicine
that often involves the use of organic, herbal, or other natural
remedies, such as those produced from plants.

1. Write some questions you have about folk medicine on the
   lines below.
   ## Questions may vary.
   _____
   _____
   _____

2. Next search for information related to one of your
   questions. Take notes in your Personal Journal. Keep a
   list of new questions and ideas you have as you research
   folk medicine.

3. Using various resources, work with a classmate to
   prepare a debate between a folk medicine practitioner and
   a doctor who went to medical school. Then on the lines
   below, write any conclusions you have drawn or
   statements you have formulated about folk medicine.
   ## Responses may vary.
   _____
   _____
   _____

4. Record what you learned from your debate in your
   Personal Journal. Include your ideas about why people
   might choose folk medicine instead of modern medical
   treatments.

See Appendix pages 120–121 for persuasive writing.

42   Lingering Leeches ✦ Open Court Classics

Responding to Literature p. 42

Teacher Tip Writing Remind students that the
main purpose of persuasive writing is to change the
way their audience thinks or feels about a topic. Tell
students that providing evidence to support their ideas
is one effective way to persuade their audience. As students
prepare to present their arguments to the class, encourage
them to provide facts and reasons that support their opinions.
Suggest that students also practice presenting their facts in a
calm and clear manner to help persuade their audience.

Name_____ Date_____

Dr. Jenner's Marvelous Vaccine • From Mystery to Medicine **UNIT 3**

Think like a Guardian

The first person on whom Edward Jenner tested his vaccine was eight-year-old James Phipps. "Although he could not guarantee the boy's safety, Jenner obtained the permission of James's parents to conduct an experiment on their son."

How do you think James's parents reached this decision? Put yourself in their place as you answer the questions below.
Possible answers below:

1. What difficulties did you confront when deciding whether to let James be part of this experiment?

   One difficulty confronted was the risk of James

   contracting smallpox.

   _____

   _____

2. Why were you willing to take this risk?

   If Dr. Jenner's theories were correct, his new

   vaccine would save the lives of many people.

   _____

   _____

3. How did you feel while the experiment was being conducted on James?

   We were nervous, because we did not know how

   James would respond to the vaccine.

   _____

   _____

Extra Effort: Write a letter to James from the point of view of his parents. Express your concerns for James and your reasons for letting Dr. Jenner conduct an experiment on him. See Appendix page 130 for writing a friendly letter.

Open Court Classics ✦ Dr. Jenner's Marvelous Vaccine   **51**

Responding to Literature p. 51

Teacher Tip Having students "think like a guardian" might give them an appreciation of the challenging decisions their own parents or guardians make on their behalf.

Lesson 2

Objective

Students will assume a different perspective and analyze the rationale behind a difficult decision.

Thinking Skills

✦ Evaluating a situation
✦ Drawing conclusions

Activity

Before students begin the activity, discuss the risk smallpox posed to the population. Then have students put themselves in the place of James Phipps's parents as they answer questions about the decision to let Jenner test his vaccine on James. Remind students that Jenner was the town's only doctor and was probably very well respected. Encourage students to consider what influence Jenner's position might have had on the Phipps's decision.

The Next Step

In their Personal Journals have students write about this issue from their own perspective. Ask whether they would want their parents or guardians to allow them to be involved in such an experiment. Encourage students to share their reasons with classmates.

Objective

Students will write a relevant headline and introductory paragraph for a news story.

Thinking Skills

+ Formulating headlines
+ Determining relevant information
+ Summarizing information

Activity

Explain that a good newspaper headline grabs readers' attention and makes them want to find out more. Use current newspapers to investigate how headlines are used and formulate a set of guidelines for writing a good headline. You also might want to have books about Jenner available for students to use as reference. Encourage them to look for quotations by Jenner to use in their news stories.

The Next Step

Have students use the library, the Internet, or other resources to find a headline that was printed to announce an actual medical advancement. Then ask students to compare the real headlines they chose with the headlines they wrote to introduce their news stories. Students can note the comparisions in their Personal Journals.

Name_____ Date_____

In the News

When Edward Jenner's work was finally accepted, "[t]he good news about vaccination traveled far beyond the borders of England." Imagine the excitement over Jenner's discovery. How do you think it would have been announced to the public?

Imagine that you are a newspaper editor. The main story on the front page is about Edward Jenner's new vaccine. What headline would you write for this story? Write several ideas below.

Ideas for newspaper headline: **Headlines may vary.**

_____

_____

_____

_____

_____

Choose one of the headlines from your list. In your Personal Journal, begin planning and organizing the information you want to include in your article. Then write the first paragraph of the story for this article. Remember that the first paragraph of a news story answers the questions *What? Who? Where? When?* and *Why?*

See Appendix pages 118–119 to read more about a news story.

Extra Effort: Consider the *format*, or layout, of a newspaper. Why are columns important in a newspaper's format? Complete your news story, then format your news story in columns to look like a page in a newspaper.

52

Dr. Jenner's Marvelous Vaccine ✦ **Open Court Classics**

Responding to Literature p. 52

Teacher Tip Writing Explain that the first paragraph of a news story is called a *lead*. It captures a reader's interest by telling what, when, where, who, and why.

Assessment Use the Drafting Writing Rubric on Appendix page 146 of the *Teacher's Edition* to assess how well students arrange their ideas and follow their plans.

Name_____ Date_____

Dr. Jenner's Marvelous Vaccine • From Mystery to Medicine **UNIT 3**

A Closer Look

Edward Jenner worked for many years learning about smallpox, testing his theories, and spreading the news about vaccination. Jenner deserves a lot of credit for his discovery, but other people also played a part in his accomplishments.

Evaluate how the *collaborations*, or joint efforts, and the cooperation of each person listed below contributed to Jenner's discovery. Write your ideas next to each person's name. **Possible answers below:**

1. Stephen Jenner: **Stephen arranged for Edward to be an apprentice to a physician.**

Effect on Jenner: **Jenner began learning about medicine at a young age.**

2. Farm workers: **The farm workers refused to be inoculated.**

Effect on Jenner: **Jenner began looking more closely at cowpox and smallpox.**

3. Sarah Nelmes: **Sarah came to Jenner after she contracted cowpox.**

Effect on Jenner: **Jenner was able to take pus from the sore.**

4. James Phipps: **Jenner could test his theories on a patient.**

Effect on Jenner: **Jenner discovered a vaccine for smallpox.**

Open Court Classics ✦ Dr. Jenner's Marvelous Vaccine   **53**

Responding to Literature p. 53

Objective

Students will learn to analyze relationships and assess their significance.

Thinking Skills

✦ Making connections
✦ Analyzing correlations
✦ Determining significance

Activity

Have students write an evaluation of the role each person played in Jenner's work with the smallpox vaccine. Encourage students to return to the selection to look for information about each person listed and to take notes in their Personal Journals before they complete the activity.

The Next Step

Have students write a mock interview with a physician. Students might include questions and answers about his or her branch of medicine and how the collaboration of others helped in his or her success.

Teacher Tip Ask students how the Royal Society contributed to Jenner's work. If necessary, explain that rejection can have a positive effect by forcing people to try different ways of achieving their goals.

Teacher Tip As students complete the assigned *Responding to Literature* pages, be sure they progress with their speeches for their projects.

UNIT 3

Dr. Jenner's Marvelous Vaccine
Lesson 5

Objective

Students will express their ideas about the characteristics that led to Jenner's success.

Thinking Skills

- ✦ Making inferences
- ✦ Analyzing characteristics

Activity

List the following creative problem-solving steps for students to consider: identifying challenges, identifying potential problems, generating solution ideas, evaluating solution ideas, applying solution ideas, and developing a plan of action. Ask students whether they use these steps when solving a problem. Then ask students how Jenner might have used these creative problem-solving steps. Encourage students to create a graphic organizer to illustrate the creative problem-solving steps and how Jenner's actions follow each step.

The Next Step

Have students find out more about the Royal Society that rejected Jenner's findings. Students might research how one became a member of the Society, the Society's role in public health affairs, and whether the Society still exists.

I Wonder

Members of the Royal Society rejected Jenner's findings and "thought it most unlikely that anyone would believe cowpox could be used to prevent smallpox." Although it seemed like an unusual idea, Jenner did prove it to be true.

How do you think Jenner's willingness to make conjectures and consider unlikely solutions to problems helped him succeed? Write a paragraph expressing your ideas.
Paragraphs may vary.

_____

_____

_____

_____

_____

_____

_____

_____

_____

_____

_____

_____

See Appendix pages 133–134 for writing a paragraph.

Extra Effort: Think about other discoveries that might have resulted from unlikely conjectures that were proven to be true. Choose a discovery you would like to read more about, and then record your findings in your Personal Journal.

54   Dr. Jenner's Marvelous Vaccine ✦ Open Court Classics

Responding to Literature p. 54

Teacher Tip Meet with individual students to determine which comprehension strategies a student is using while he or she is reading.

Teacher Tip Point out that many great ideas are initially met with ridicule. Ask students how the problem-solving process is affected by skeptics or disbelievers.

Name_____ Date_____

Dr. Jenner's Marvelous Vaccine • From Mystery to Medicine **UNIT 3**

Reality Check

Although smallpox was a terrible disease, it led to a very important discovery. Jenner's success in creating a smallpox vaccine led to great *medical advances* in the knowledge and treatment of diseases. A medical advancement is an improvement or higher phase of progress in the study or practice of medicine.

1. What questions do you have about other medical advances?
   Questions may vary.
   _____

   _____

2. List some sources where you could find information about major developments in medicine.
   Sources may vary.
   _____

   _____

3. Examine your sources. Then list some important medical advances and the year each one happened.

   Year   Important Medical Advance
   Answers may vary._____

   _____ _____

   _____ _____

   _____ _____

   _____ _____

   _____ _____

   _____ _____

4. In your Personal Journal, create a time line to display the information you collected. Think about the relationship between the medical advancement and the year in which it occurred as you construct your time line. Include drawings or pictures from magazines to illustrate your time line.

Open Court Classics ✦ Dr. Jenner's Marvelous Vaccine   **55**

Responding to Literature p. 55

Objective

Students will recognize major developments in medicine and sequence them on a time line.

Thinking Skills

✦ Identifying medical advances
✦ Making connections
✦ Sequencing events

Activity

Students will research important medical advances and then create an illustrated time line to present their information. Remind students that the events listed on a time line should appear in chronological order. In their Personal Journals encourage students to record any significant connections between a medical advancement and the year in which it occurred.

The Next Step

Have students work together to create a comprehensive time line of medical advances. As they compile their information, have students note those items that appeared most frequently on their individual time lines. Encourage students also to consider cause-and-effect relationships that appear on their time lines.

Teacher Tip Time lines present a good opportunity for cross-curricular investigation. Encourage students to consider the social history surrounding the medical advancements they choose to include in their time lines.

Assessment Use the *Responding to Literature* pages as an informal assessment of students' understanding of the selection and of analyzing relationships and making inferences.

Wrap-Up

Knowledge-Building Project

Students have completed their research and should now be ready to present their speeches to an audience. Presentations may be done in small groups or before the entire class. Encourage students to respond to each speech and offer constructive feedback. Also have students tell what new facts they learned and new questions they have about a scientist or a key medical discovery. Use the Research Rubrics: Overall Assessment of Research on Appendix page 149 of the *Teacher's Edition* to assess students' knowledge-building projects as a whole.

Reviewing the Concepts

Teacher Tip
Suggest that students investigate medical services and facilities in less-developed countries. Have students consider how the availability and level of medical care relate to a population's quality of life.

In this unit students explored a variety of medical wonders, including the renewed practice of a centuries-old treatment, the unexpected complication of a simple procedure, and a discovery that resulted in the eradication of a deadly disease. Students investigated some of the following key concepts in this unit:

✦ Folk remedies have a place in modern medicine.
✦ Even experienced doctors can be surprised by a patient's mysterious response to medicine.
✦ Edward Jenner's success in developing a smallpox vaccine changed the course of medical history.
✦ Medical research is necessary for advancing medical treatments.

Evaluating the Unit

✦ Ask students to evaluate each selection on the basis of effectiveness of reading/vocabulary, literary value, interest of the subject matter, style of writing, application of theme, and the selection's personal value to the student.
✦ Ask students to evaluate the different activities in the unit, including the knowledge-building project. Have them consider these questions: Which activities made you think? Which ones seemed confusing or challenging? Which activities did you most enjoy and why? Which activities best contributed to your intellectual growth? Which activities changed your opinions and offered new ideas? Which activities stimulated novelty and original thinking? What activities would you like to add to the unit?
✦ Ask students to evaluate this *Open Court Classics* unit. They can describe how the theme was explored in the unit. Students can also compare and contrast the selections based on what they added to students' knowledge of medicine.

Assessment

Vocabulary Assessment

To assess students' understanding of the vocabulary words, you might want to do one of the following:

✦ Have students create pictures that represent vocabulary words from the selections.

✦ Have students write meaningful sentences using two or more of the vocabulary words from the selections in each sentence.

✦ Administer an informal oral assessment. Have students supply the definition of the vocabulary word.

Informal Comprehension Strategies Rubrics

Use the Informal Comprehension Strategies Rubrics: Making Connections, Predicting, and Monitoring and Adjusting Reading Speed on Appendix pages 144–145 of the *Teacher's Edition* to determine whether a student is using a particular strategy or strategies as he or she reads the selections. Note these and any other strategies a student is using, instead of the degree to which a student might be using any particular strategy. In addition, encourage the student to tell of any strategies other than the ones being taught that he or she is using.

Research Rubrics

Use the Research Rubrics: Recognizing Information Needs, Finding Needed Information, Communicating Research Progress and Results, and Overall Assessment of Research on Appendix pages 148–149 of the *Teacher's Edition* to assess a student's performance throughout the investigation. The rubrics range from 1 to 4 in most categories, with 1 being the lowest score. In addition, you can use the rubrics to assess a group's collaborative work as well as an individual's participation in that group.

Writing Rubrics

Use the Persuasive Writing Rubric, the Expository Structure Writing Rubric, and the Drafting Writing Rubric on Appendix page 146 of the *Teacher's Edition* to assess student writing. The rubrics range from 1 to 4 in most categories, with 1 being the lowest score.

$\mathcal{O}$verview

Do what you can, with what you have, where you are.
—Theodore Roosevelt—

Unit Goals

- To identify personal qualities of a survivor
- To explore the human need for community versus the need for solitude
- To recognize the characteristic elements of an adventure tale
- To explore the relationship between writing and survival
- To identify descriptive writing
- To effectively communicate opinions in a book review
- To create original survival stories

Introduction

The range of human experience leads people to have different ideas of what it means to survive. To some people, survival is equivalent to sustaining life; to others, survival is associated with quality of life. Students will investigate concepts of survival as they read about three intriguing survivors. Selection 1 is "Robinson Crusoe" on page 120; Selection 2 is "Letters from Rifka" on page 130; and Selection 3 is "In Which I Have a Good Look at Winter and Find Spring in the Snow" on page 146. These selections will encourage students to examine the attributes of a survivor and develop their ideas about survival.

Unit Discussion

Before students begin reading the selections, invite them to discuss their ideas about survival. Continue the discussion by asking questions such as the following:

✦ What books, stories, movies, and current or historical events have you read about or seen that relate to survival?

✦ What human behaviors support the theory that survival is an instinct? How might these behaviors relate to the quotation in the unit opener?

✦ What are different ways that people survive?

These selections are about people surviving in extraordinary circumstances. It is not likely that students will have had such experiences, but this should not prevent them from connecting with the characters or the unit theme. Encourage students to predict how they would react to similar challenges and to explain the basis on which they made their predictions.

> **Teacher Tip**
> As an alternative to the outlined project, you might suggest that students work in groups to prepare a panel discussion with audience participation. The discussion should focus on a question or problem related to survival.

Knowledge–Building Project

Stories of survival have a universal appeal. Readers enjoy learning about how someone has overcome obstacles or persisted in the face of danger in order to survive. Ask students to consider elements that are essential for a good survival story. Then encourage them to develop a list of ideas for stories about survival. The list might include perilous situations or the names of people who have overcome adversity. As a final product, students will use these ideas to write a story about survival to share with the class. In this unit students will discover some of the strengths and abilities that people use to survive. Students should view each selection as a source for learning and should relate what they learn to their knowledge-building projects. Point out that even authors of fictional stories must conduct research for information about the subject and the details needed to support the story.

Unit 4 Project Overview	
Unit Overview	Students begin their investigations by evaluating elements of survival stories and generating story ideas.
Selection 1	Students begin taking notes for their chosen story topics.
Selection 2	Students write and revise the first draft of their stories.
Selection 3	Students prepare their final drafts.
Unit Wrap-Up	Students present their completed survival stories.

Robinson Crusoe

Student Anthology pp. 120–129

Selection Goals

- To recognize the elements of an adventure tale
- To value the strength of character required to survive challenging situations

Selection Summary

After battling a hurricane for 12 days with his shipmates, Robinson Crusoe is the only sailor to survive the terrible storm. Washed onto a foreign, deserted island, Crusoe must use all his resourcefulness to form a plan for staying alive. This selection is from Daniel Defoe's classic novel *Robinson Crusoe.*

Genre: Adventure Tale

Share with students some of the elements of an adventure tale, which include

- ✦ characters who behave like real people and animals.

- ✦ settings that are real or could be real.

- ✦ events that could happen in real life.

- ✦ action or suspense, or both.

⟡ *Part 1* ⟡
Building Background

Activate Prior Knowledge

✦ Ask students whether they are familiar with the story of *Robinson Crusoe*. If so, ask them to tell a little about the plot and how it relates to the unit theme. Tell students who are familiar with the story not to give away the ending of the selection.

✦ Have students share what they know about the challenges associated with surviving in an unfamiliar place with few supplies.

Background Information

✦ Daniel Defoe was a prolific writer. In addition to novels, Defoe produced hundreds of essays and articles. *Robinson Crusoe* was Defoe's first novel and remains his most famous. It was published in 1719, when the author was nearly 60 years old.

✦ Some literary scholars credit Defoe with being among the first writers to create realistic stories with believable characters. The first-person point of view and diary format Defoe used in *Robinson Crusoe* contribute to the sense of reality in the novel.

✦ Defoe's inspiration for writing *Robinson Crusoe* was the true story of Scottish sailor Alexander Selkirk. In 1704 Selkirk was sailing as a privateer, a sailor on a privately owned ship commissioned by the English government to attack enemy ships. When he had a dispute with the ship's captain, William Dampier, Selkirk asked to be left on one of the Juan Fernández Islands, where he believed he would wait only a short time for another ship to come. It was four years and four months before Selkirk was rescued from the island. Ironically, the pilot of the ship that came to Selkirk's aid was William Dampier.

Previewing the Literature
Browse the Selection

✦ Have students note the title and the names of the author and illustrator. Then have them browse the first page or two of the selection to search for clues that tell them something about the selection.

✦ Note on the board those things students mention as a result of their browsing and any questions they have about the selection.

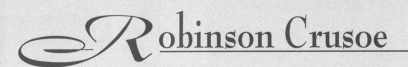
Set Purposes for Reading

Encourage students to set purposes for reading, such as to investigate how the selection relates to their personal interests or experiences. As they read, have students focus on the tools and equipment Crusoe salvaged and created to help him survive, the effectiveness of the first-person narrator in this selection, and passages or phrases that created suspense.

Expanding Vocabulary

The words listed below can be found in the Glossary of the **Student Anthology.** Page numbers indicate where the words can be found in the selection.

hurricanes, p. 120 — Storms with heavy rains and strong winds. [Spanish *huracán*, after *Huracán*, the wind god of the Carib people.]

sandbar, p. 125 — A mound of sand that has been built up by waves in a river or in coastal waters.

tide, p. 127 — The rise and fall of the sea's surface.

> **Teacher Tip**
> Ask students to identify the compound word in the vocabulary list (*sandbar*). Remind students that a compound word is made of two or more smaller words and that some compound words are hyphenated. Point out that most hyphenated compound words are adjectives, such as *thirty-seven* and *state-of-the-art*.

✧ Part 2 ✧
Reading the Selection

Read

✦ Have students silently read **Student Anthology** pages 120–129, stopping at the end of each page if they have any questions or need clarification.

✦ Encourage students to use predicting or any other comprehension strategies that might help them read the selection.

Discuss

The following discussion suggestions can be carried out on different days, depending upon how much time you allot to each selection.

+ Have students discuss their general reactions to the selection.

+ Ask students how this selection relates to the theme.

+ Encourage students to review any questions they listed on the board before reading to see if the selection answered their questions.

+ Have students discuss the author's tone and its appropriateness for an adventure tale.

+ Ask students to discuss Crusoe's emotional responses to his situation. Have them support their ideas with evidence from the text.

+ Have students discuss examples of Crusoe's resourcefulness.

After students have discussed the selection, choose from **Responding to Literature** pages 56–61, and ask students to complete the assigned pages.

⇢ Part 3 ⇠
Knowledge-Building Project

Have students review their list of ideas for survival stories and begin narrowing their focus. Have them find out more about several of the people, events, or circumstances on their list to determine which subject interests them most. Remind students that fictional stories involve research. Information gathered from research will allow them to learn more about the subject and to collect details that will support the main ideas and events of the story. Tell students that their survival stories should include elements of an adventure tale. As they select a topic and begin their research, encourage students to think about how they will include elements of this genre in their writing. It would be worthwhile to meet with students to discuss their chosen topic, how the topic relates to the unit theme, and what elements of the adventure tale genre they might include.

Once students have chosen a topic, they should begin making notes and planning their stories. Encourage students to organize their ideas in lists, outlines, character webs, T charts, Venn diagrams, or other graphic organizers in their Personal Journals.

By the end of the next selection, students should have written and edited the first draft of their survival stories.

Assessment
Use the Research Rubrics: Recognizing Information Needs on Appendix page 148 of the *Teacher's Edition* to assess how well students identify their topics and their information needs. Discuss with students the rubrics that will be used to evaluate them on their projects.

Objective

Students will learn to make distinctions between types of questions.

Thinking Skills

✦ Formulating questions
✦ Distinguishing types of questions

Activity

Have students write three different types of questions, and then exchange papers with a partner and respond to one another's questions. Encourage partners to meet and discuss the various types of questions they explored in this activity. Ask them which kind of question is most challenging to answer and which kind of question helps them learn the most about a selection. Encourage students also to discuss which kind of question will lead them to additional research and learning.

The Next Step

Ask students the following evaluative question: What basic needs and wants would you have to satisfy if you were stranded on a deserted island? Then in their Personal Journals, have students write about these basic needs and wants. Tell students to include explanations of how they would make the products they need, including what materials they would use.

Name_____ Date_____

Getting Started

The way you ask a question can influence the kind of answer you get. *Knowledge, factual analysis,* and *evaluation* are three kinds of questions, and each involves a different level of thinking. For example, a knowledge question requires a reader to recall specific information and often begins with words such as *Who, What, When,* and *Where.* An analysis question asks a reader to identify relationships and comparisons. This type of question begins with words and phrases such as *How, Why,* and *In what ways.* An evaluation question asks a reader to make judgements or choices based on his or her values and usually begins with phrases such as *How can you defend, What justifies,* and *What do you think.*

On the lines below, write a knowledge, an analysis, and an evaluation question that can be answered by reading the story. Then exchange papers with a partner and answer each other's questions. **Possible answers below:**

1. **Knowledge Question:** Where was the ship sailing before the hurricane struck?

   Partner's Answer: The ship was sailing "near the coast of South America."

2. **Analysis Question:** Why does Crusoe think of the tools as having more worth than gold?

   Partner's Answer: He can use the tools to build shelter.

3. **Evaluation Question:** When two men fell overboard, no attempts were made to save them. What do you think about this?

   Partner's Answer: Answers may vary.

56   Robinson Crusoe ◆ Open Court Classics

Responding to Literature p. 56

Teacher Tip Comprehension Strategies Ask students whether they made, confirmed, and revised predictions as they read this selection. Have volunteers share with the rest of the class examples of how they used this strategy.

Assessment Use the Informal Comprehension Strategies Rubrics: Predicting on Appendix page 145 of the *Teacher's Edition* to assess students' use of this strategy.

Robinson Crusoe • Survival **UNIT 4**

Picture This

This selection includes information that helps the reader *visualize*, or create a mental picture of, the island on which Robinson Crusoe is stranded. For example, you know that there is at least one big rock, which Crusoe is thrown against by a wave. What other clues does the author provide about this location?

Review the selection for other details about the physical characteristics of the island. On the lines below, make a list of features that you will include in a map. Then on a large sheet of paper or poster board, create a map of the island. Remember to include a title, compass rose, and legend with your map.

Students might list the following features:

a grassy area next to the sand, a small stream, tall

trees, a hill near the shore.

_____

_____

_____

_____

_____

_____

_____

_____

Extra Effort: Investigate other types of maps, such as a topographic map, a relief map, or a physical map. Choose one of the maps you explored, and re-create the map of your island accordingly.

Open Court Classics ✦ Robinson Crusoe   **57**

Responding to Literature p. 57

Objective

Students will use context clues to create a map of Robinson Crusoe's island.

Thinking Skills

✦ Recalling details
✦ Visualizing
✦ Extrapolating information

Activity

Explain that visualizing is a strategy used by readers to form mental images of what the text describes. Then have students use details from the text to help them visualize the island on which Crusoe was stranded and to create a map. Encourage students to look at actual maps to note any general characteristics they would like to include in their maps.

The Next Step

Have students compare their maps to a map of the real Robinson Crusoe Island. Explain that this is where the sailor who inspired Defoe's novel was stranded for more than four years. Encourage students to find out what the island is like today and to record their findings in their Personal Journals.

Teacher Tip Alexander Selkirk was stranded on one of the Juan Fernández Islands formerly known as Más a Tierra. In 1966 the Chilean government renamed the island Robinson Crusoe Island. A nearby island, once called Más Afuera, was renamed Alejandro Selkirk Island.

Robinson Crusoe
Lesson 3

Objective

Students will think critically about items necessary for their survival.

Thinking Skills

✦ Prioritizing personal needs
✦ Judging basic necessities
✦ Distinguishing essentials from nonessentials

Activity

Ask students what basic necessities they need to survive for one day. Then have students imagine that they are in a situation similar to Crusoe's and must prioritize the supplies necessary for survival. Encourage students to think about the importance of companionship. Point out that in addition to the supplies Crusoe took from the ship, he retrieved two cats and a dog to keep him company.

The Next Step

Have students conduct research to identify different kinds of survival kits, such as wilderness or natural disaster survival kits. Then have students investigate the contents of each survival kit, such as a flashlight, compass, and water bottle, and the emergency situation for which each kit is intended. You might also suggest that students create a survival kit for their home or classroom based on the needs of the area in which they live.

Name_____ Date_____

What Would You Do?

The morning after Robinson Crusoe washes ashore, he returns to his ship looking for supplies. Because the small raft he built cannot carry much weight, he must carefully choose what to take. The items he selects are food, clothing, and tools.

Imagine that, like Crusoe, you have only three boxes to fill with supplies. You do not know how long you will be stranded or what you will find on the island. If you could take whatever you want from your home, what would you choose to help you survive? Choose a category label for each box, such as *Food* or *Clothing*. Then choose the items that will go in it. Explain why you chose each item. **Possible answers below:**

Box 1 Category: __Clothing__

Items: __Shoes to protect my feet; long pants to protect my legs from sharp rocks; a coat to wear if it is cold.__

Box 2 Category: __Gear__

Items: __A flashlight to see in the dark; a net to catch fish.__

Box 3 Category: __First-aid Kit__

Items: __Bandages to cover scratches or cuts; sunscreen to protect my skin.__

When your list is complete, meet with a classmate to discuss and compare items.

58   Robinson Crusoe ✦ **Open Court Classics**

Responding to Literature p. 58

> **Teacher Tip** As students complete the assigned *Responding to Literature* pages, be sure they progress with recognizing information needs related to the topics of their knowledge-building projects.

A Closer Look

Out of the 17 sailors on board Robinson Crusoe's ship, he is the only one to survive the storm at sea. What do you think sets Crusoe apart from the other men?

Think about the challenges that Crusoe faces in this selection and how he handles each one in order to survive. Then on the lines below, list some character traits that suggest Robinson Crusoe is a survivor. Support each trait with examples from the selection. **Possible answers below:**

1. **Trait:** Determined

   Example(s): "But I knew I could not rest until I was out of reach of the waves."

2. **Trait:** Resourceful

   Example(s): Crusoe "tied the poles together to make a raft."

3. **Trait:** Hard-working

   Example(s): "I then came back to my raft and unloaded my goods. This took me the rest of the day."

Recall other stories you have read in which the main character is a survivor. How do the traits of this character compare to those of Robinson Crusoe?
Answers may vary.

Responding to Literature p. 59

Teacher Tip Encourage students to begin making a list of personality traits that they think are common to survivors. Explain that they should add to and revise the list as they progress through the unit.

Objectives

✦ Students will analyze a character and identify the traits that make him a survivor.
✦ Students will compare and contrast survivor characteristics of other characters.

Thinking Skills

✦ Analyzing a character
✦ Proving with examples
✦ Comparing and contrasting characteristics

Activity

Explain to students that character webs are one way to organize and examine a character's traits. In their Personal Journals encourage students to construct a character web to analyze Robinson Crusoe and identify the personality traits that contributed to his survival. Tell students that Venn diagrams or character webs might be helpful tools when comparing Crusoe's traits to the traits of other survivors. Have students use the information in their graphic organizers to complete the activity page.

The Next Step

Have students find other literary selections, including nonfiction selections (such as newspaper articles), that reinforce the concept of survival. Encourage students to bring the selections they discover to class and share them with classmates.

Objective

Students will practice writing dialogue.

Thinking Skills

✦ Adding to the selection
✦ Formulating dialogue
✦ Drawing conclusions

Activity

Remind students that because the selection is written from Crusoe's point of view, they have some idea of how he thinks and what kind of language he uses. Have students incorporate these ideas in their dialogues. Ask students who are familiar with the story and its later events to write a paragraph expressing their ideas about the need for community versus the need for solitude and instances when each is necessary for survival. Remind students that this adventure tale is a realistic story and that these qualities should be reflected in their writing.

The Next Step

Have students research information about the effects isolation can have on a person's speaking ability and other communication skills. Ask students to record the information they uncover in their Personal Journals, and if possible, provide examples for support. Encourage students to incorporate these ideas in their knowledge-building projects.

Name_____ Date_____

I Can Do It, Too

Robinson Crusoe knows little about the island on which he is stranded. He tells the reader, "I still did not know whether or not there were other people on this land. If there were other people, I did not know whether they would be friendly or whether they would try to kill me."

Imagine that Crusoe does find another person living on the island. What might this person tell Crusoe about the island? What questions might Crusoe ask the stranger? On the lines below, write dialogue for the conversation between Crusoe and the stranger. When you have finished, work with a partner to perform your dialogue for the rest of the class.

Dialogue may vary.

_____

_____

_____

_____

_____

_____

_____

_____

_____

_____

_____

_____

See Appendix page 127 for using dialogue.

60　　　　　　　　　　Robinson Crusoe ✦ **Open Court Classics**

Responding to Literature p. 60

Teacher Tip **Writing** In narrative writing the characters should sound and act like real people. Encourage students to read their dialogues aloud to help them identify phrases that sound unnatural and need to be revised.

Assessment Use the Narrative Writing Rubric on Appendix page 146 of the *Teacher's Edition* to assess students' elaboration on the plot and character as well as students' development of a new character.

Name_____Date_____

Lesson 6

Reality Check

Daniel Defoe's *Robinson Crusoe* was based on the story of a real sailor named Alexander Selkirk. Selkirk lived alone on an island off the coast of Chile for almost four and a half years. However, he landed on the island by choice rather than as the result of a shipwreck. Because of a serious disagreement Selkirk had with the captain of his ship, he asked to be left on one of the islands in the area where they were sailing. On this rugged, deserted island, Selkirk found a way to survive.

1. Write some questions that you have about Alexander Selkirk.
   Questions may vary.

   _____

   _____

   _____

   _____

2. Use the Internet and other reference sources to find answers to your questions and more information about Selkirk. Take notes in your Personal Journal as you research.

3. In your Personal Journal, write a short biography of Alexander Selkirk. Draw some conclusions about Selkirk, and support them with details and examples from his life. Remember to follow the steps of the writing process as you write your biography.

See Appendix page 115 to read more about a biography.

Extra Effort: Write a monologue from Alexander Selkirk's point of view. Then perform your work for the class. See Appendix page 132 for writing a monologue.

Open Court Classics ✦ Robinson Crusoe   **61**

Responding to Literature p. 61

Objective

Students will formulate research questions, identify credible reference sources, and write a biography.

Thinking Skills

✦ Formulating questions
✦ Determining information needs
✦ Drawing conclusions

Activity

Encourage students to think about what evidence they will need to include in their biographies in order to support their conclusions about Selkirk. Remind students to utilize reference sources, such as books, journals, encyclopedias, and so on. Encourage students to include pictures of Selkirk to add interest to their biographies.

The Next Step

Tell students that Alexander Selkirk was a sailing master on a ship when a dispute with the ship's captain led to his stay on the uninhabited island. Ask students what they know about the ranks given to sailors. Then have students research those ranks. Encourage them to explore the origins and importance of the ranking system and its relationship to surviving at sea.

Assessment Use the *Responding to Literature* pages as an informal assessment of students' ability to understand the selection, formulate questions, and analyze characters.

UNIT 4

Letters from Rifka

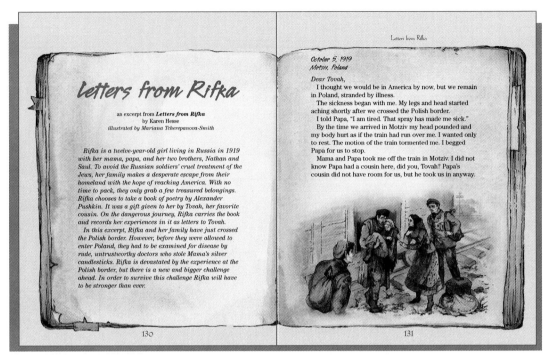

Student Anthology pp. 130–145

Selection Goals

- To recognize the importance of family to Rifka
- To appreciate the significance of personal writing and its connection to survival

Selection Summary

Rifka and her family leave their home in Russia to protect Rifka's brothers from serving in the Russian army. In letters to her cousin, 12-year-old Rifka describes the hardships that her family endures while fleeing to America. Battling typhus, loneliness, and hunger, Rifka struggles to continue the journey. This selection is an excerpt from Karen Hesse's award-winning novel *Letters from Rifka*.

Genre: Historical Fiction

Share with students some of the elements of historical fiction, which include

- ✦ a story that is set in a particular time and place in the past.
- ✦ realistic characters that act appropriately for the time in which the story is set.
- ✦ details that make the story more realistic.
- ✦ real people and actual events.

⭈ *Part 1* ⭇
Building Background

Activate Prior Knowledge
✦ Ask students whether they write letters to friends and relatives. Have them discuss reasons people communicate in writing and how writing is different from other forms of communication. Encourage students to consider a variety of forms of personal writing, such as friendly letters, e-mail messages, cards, and so on.

✦ Have students share what they know about refugees, including some reasons people leave their homelands.

Background Information
✦ This selection is set in 1919, a time of great poverty and political instability in Russia. Many Russian peasants had no work, no money, and no food and were disgruntled with their government. Political leaders attempted to distract the peasants and shift the focus from the government by promoting violence against Jews. These organized campaigns, called *pogroms*, encouraged Russian peasants to rob and burn homes and businesses of Jewish citizens.

✦ The main character writes "letters" in the margins of a book of poetry by Alexander Pushkin. Pushkin, a poet and author, has been called the most important writer of Russian literature. His commitment to social reform and support of literary radicals caused him to continually be in conflict with the Russian government.

✦ Karen Hesse was awarded the prestigious John Newbery Medal for her book *Out of the Dust*. Her novel *Letters from Rifka* has won the Christopher Award, the *School Library Journal* Best Book of the Year, the ALA Best Book for Young Adults, and the National Jewish Book Award. Hesse's other books for children include *Come on, Rain!*, *The Music of Dolphins*, *Witness*, and *A Time of Angels*.

Previewing the Literature
Browse the Selection
✦ Have students note the title as well as the names of the author and illustrator. Then have students browse the first page or two of the selection and discuss how they think it might relate to survival.

✦ Note on the board those things students mention as a result of their browsing and any questions they have about the selection.

UNIT 4

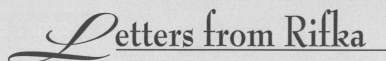

Letters from Rifka

Set Purposes for Reading

Before they read, have students set purposes for reading the selection. Encourage students to ask themselves questions such as the following: Why did Rifka write letters? What effect did illness have on Rifka and her family? How does this selection relate to the unit theme?

Expanding Vocabulary

The words listed below can be found in the Glossary of the **Student Anthology.** Page numbers indicate where the words can be found in the selection.

cossacks, p. 132
Members of a group in southern Russia classified as cavalry in the czarist army.

shalom, p. 137
A traditional Jewish greeting or good-bye.

Bubbe, p. 142
Yiddish, "Grandmother."

> **Teacher Tip**
> Students should use a variety of skills to determine the meaning of a word. Context clues, word structure, and apposition can help students clarify unfamiliar words. Encourage students to explain which skills they are using and how they figured out the meanings of words.

⋄ Part 2 ⋄

Reading the Selection

Read

✦ Have students silently read **Student Anthology** pages 130–145, stopping at the end of each page if they have any questions or need clarification.

✦ Encourage students to use asking questions or any other comprehension strategies that might help them read the selection.

Discuss

The following discussion suggestions can be carried out on different days, depending upon how much time you allot to each selection.

✦ Have students discuss their general reactions to the selection.

✦ Encourage students to review any questions they listed on the board before reading to see if the selection answered their questions.

✦ Have students discuss Rifka's relationship with her brother Saul and how it changes over the course of the selection.

✦ Have students discuss the role Rifka's family plays in her survival. Remind them to consider relatives Rifka left behind in Russia.

✦ Have students discuss different ways in which Rifka is a survivor, such as physically and emotionally.

After students have discussed the selection, choose from *Responding to Literature* pages 62–67, and ask students to complete the assigned pages.

⊹ Part 3 ⊹
Knowledge-Building Project

Students should continue collecting information to include in their survival stories. Additional information that is not used in students' stories will still enrich the project by contributing to students' knowledge. Students should also review the characteristic elements of an adventure tale to include in their writing.

When writing their first drafts, students should refer to their lists, outlines, character webs, T charts, Venn diagrams, or other graphic organizers they created in their Personal Journals. This will help them sequence the main and supporting ideas of their stories. Tell students to include all of their ideas in the first draft and then begin the revising phase. Remind them to look for places where they can improve their word choice and sentence fluency. Encourage students to exchange their stories with a partner for peer review. Classmates can give each other feedback that will help them identify weak or confusing parts of their stories.

By the end of the next selection, students should have prepared the final draft of their stories.

Teacher Tip
Writing Explain that peer reviews are beneficial during the writing process. Encourage students to be specific when commenting on another person's writing. Explain that specific comments will better enable the writer to revise his or her work.

Assessment
Use the Research Rubrics: Finding Needed Information on Appendix pages 148–149 of the *Teacher's Edition* to assess students' collection of information. Discuss the rubrics that will be used to evaluate students on their projects.

Use the Revising Writing Process Rubric on Appendix page 146 of the *Teacher's Edition* to assess students' pursuit and use of constructive feedback.

UNIT 4

Letters from Rifka

Lesson 1

Objective

Students will analyze a character's circumstances and draw conclusions about her personality.

Thinking Skills

✦ Recalling details
✦ Evaluating circumstances
✦ Drawing conclusions

Activity

Explain to students that throughout history people around the world have become refugees for various reasons. The stories of their journeys, like Rifka's, are often extraordinary tales of survival. Have students recall and list challenges that Rifka encountered on her journey. Then have them draw conclusions about Rifka's abilities to survive based on how she responded to the tribulations.

The Next Step

Ask students to consider what it means to be a refugee. Then have them conduct research for more information about refugees today. Encourage students to identify some of the reasons people are forced to leave their homelands and the challenges of surviving encountered by refugees in a new environment.

Name_____ Date_____

UNIT **4** Survival • *Letters from Rifka*

Getting Started

This selection tells about some of the difficult situations Rifka experiences during her journey to the United States. On your own or with a partner, make a list of challenges Rifka faces. Examine how Rifka handles each challenge. Then respond to the questions below.

Possible answers below:

Rifka's Challenges:

Rifka is challenged with illness and loneliness. The thought of America gives Rifka the strength to overcome typhus. When she is lonely, she writes to her cousin Tovah.

1. What do you think is the most difficult challenge Rifka faces? Justify your choice.

   The most difficult challenge Rifka faces is the separation from her family. She misses them a lot.

   _____

2. What do you learn about Rifka from the way she handles hardship?

   Rifka has a positive attitude and is determined to survive.

   _____

   _____

   _____

62   Letters from Rifka ✦ **Open Court Classics**

Responding to Literature p. 62

Teacher Tip Comprehension Strategies Have students share the questions they asked themselves as they read "Letters from Rifka." Have them explain how asking questions helped them better understand the selection.

Assessment Use the Informal Comprehension Strategies Rubrics: Asking Questions on Appendix page 144 of the *Teacher's Edition* to assess students' use of this strategy.

Name_____ Date_____

Letters from Rifka • Survival **UNIT 4**

What Would You Do?

The letters from Rifka are actually written in the margins and other white spaces of a book given to her by her cousin Tovah. The book, which Tovah gave Rifka as a gift, is a book of poems by Alexander Pushkin. Pushkin was a famous and important Russian author. Having a book by Pushkin may have been a comforting reminder of her homeland for Rifka as she endured many difficult events on her journey.

Imagine that you are in Rifka's situation and are forced to leave your home to go live in another country. Which book or author symbolizes *home* for you? Answer the questions below.

Answers may vary.

1. If you could take only one book with you, which book would you select?

_____

2. Why is this book or its author important to you?

_____

_____

_____

_____

3. Meet with a partner to discuss books or authors you think symbolize your homeland. Make a list of your ideas.

_____

_____

_____

_____

Extra Effort: Ask your teacher for a list of poems by Alexander Pushkin. Choose one or more poems that you would like to read. Write your reactions to Pushkin's writing in your Personal Journal.

Open Court Classics ✦ Letters from Rifka   **63**

Responding to Literature p. 63

Teacher Tip As students complete the assigned *Responding to Literature* pages, be sure they continue to find information about a selected topic for their knowledge-building projects.

Objective

Students will make a personal choice about a book that represents their homeland.

Thinking Skills

✦ Making connections
✦ Judging importance

Activity

Have students imagine themselves in a situation similar to Rifka's. As they complete the activity on **Responding to Literature** page 63, have students think about how they would feel if they were forced to leave their homes and travel to another country. Remind them that the book or author they select should not necessarily be their favorite, but should be one that best symbolizes the meaning of home for them.

The Next Step

Have students conduct research for information about the life and poetry of Alexander Pushkin. Then have them discuss the connection between Pushkin's poetry and "Letters from Rifka." Encourage students to consider how Pushkin's writing was a comfort for Rifka.

UNIT 4
Letters from Rifka
Lesson 3

Objective

Students will write a journal entry from a character's point of view and make connections between writing and survival.

Thinking Skills

✦ Determining relevance
✦ Making connections
✦ Substituting personal perspective with a character's

Activity

Prompt students to think about the relationship between writing and survival by asking them to recall a stressful time when they wrote a letter or kept a journal or diary. What were their reasons for writing? Did writing help ease their tension? Then have students consider why it was important for Rifka to write about her experiences and how this activity might have contributed to her survival.

The Next Step

Have students do a literature search to find other published diaries or stories written as diaries. Ask them to read one of these works and then compare it to this selection. Students can record their comparisons in their Personal Journals. Encourage students to discuss why people enjoy writing in a diary or journal and its importance.

Name_____ Date_____

In My Opinion

In this selection, Rifka uses her book like a *journal* to write letters to her cousin Tovah. A journal is a place to write about personal experiences and feelings. Although she cannot send the letters, Rifka continues to write about her experiences. Why do you think Rifka writes about her experiences? How do you think writing helps Rifka survive?

Write a journal entry from Rifka's point of view to express your thoughts. Then meet with a partner to share journal entries and other ideas you have about writing and survival.

Journal entries may vary.

_____
_____
_____
_____
_____
_____
_____
_____
_____
_____
_____
_____

Extra Effort: What important roles have letters played throughout history? Research historical letters, and then choose a letter to investigate further. Identify the importance and purpose of the letter; then write your findings in your Personal Journal.

64   Letters from Rifka ✦ Open Court Classics

Responding to Literature p. 64

Teacher Tip Writing Explain to students that journal writing is more worthwhile if they include details about what their ideas, thoughts, observations, and experiences mean to them.

Assessment Use the Personal Writing Rubric on Appendix page 146 of the *Teacher's Edition* to assess the development and expression of thoughts in students' journal entries.

Name_____ Date_____

A Closer Look

One of the main ideas of this selection is the importance of family. In fact, Rifka's family members have become refugees in order to protect Saul from serving in the Russian army. In their efforts to save each other and stay together, this family endures great struggles.

At the end of the selection, Rifka writes, "I am trying to be clever, Tovah, but how much more clever I could be surrounded by my family." What do you think Rifka means by this? Write your thoughts and ideas in the form of a paragraph on the lines below. Then answer the question that follows.

Paragraphs may vary.

_____

_____

_____

_____

_____

_____

_____

_____

_____

How does the author Karen Hesse show the importance of family relationships?

Possible answer: Hesse writes about the members

of a family making sacrifices for each other.

See Appendix pages 133–134 for writing a paragraph.

Open Court Classics ✦ Letters from Rifka   **65**

Responding to Literature p. 65

Teacher Tip Encourage students to use various comprehension strategies while reading the selection. Meet with individual students to determine which strategies a student is using while he or she is reading.

Objective

Students will learn to interpret a character's words and write a paragraph in response.

Thinking Skills

✦ Evaluating text
✦ Making inferences
✦ Understanding author's purpose

Activity

Before students write a paragraph in response to the quotation, ask them to consider how Rifka's family members help each other survive. What evidence from the text supports their ideas? Then discuss with students how the author uses the word *clever* in this passage. Encourage students to share their ideas of how Hesse conveys the importance of family in this selection.

The Next Step

Have students discuss ways that people throughout history have helped each other survive. Encourage students to consider groups of people who have provided relief in the past, such as the people who worked on the Underground Railroad, as well as current humanitarian organizations, such as the Red Cross.

Objective

Students will learn to collect information for constructing a family tree.

Thinking Skills

- ✦ Determining and identifying facts
- ✦ Classifying and categorizing relationships

Activity

Have students assume the role of a genealogist as they collect information to construct their family trees. Encourage students to interview family members and study family keepsakes, such as diaries and pictures, to find information for their family trees. If students have difficulty identifying information needed for their family trees, suggest that they include data, such as dates and places of birth, names of relatives, dates and places of marriage, names of children, and dates and places of death. Encourage students to find out who were the first members of their families to come to the United States.

The Next Step

Have students write a biography about a family member whom they consider to be a survivor. Encourage students to share their biographies with the rest of the class.

Name_____ Date_____

UNIT 4 Survival • *Letters from Rifka*

Think like a Genealogist

The word *genealogy* means "the study of ancestry and family history." A genealogist is someone who conducts research to identify ancestors and their family relationships.

Genealogists use several methods to collect information about a family's history. Researching public records available at libraries and courthouses is one way information is gathered. A genealogist then organizes the collected information in a *family tree*. A family tree is a chart that shows how the members of a family are related through generations.

Karen Hesse based her book *Letters from Rifka* on the experiences of her great-aunt Lucy. Think about how Hesse might have learned about Lucy's journey to the United States. How would you discover information about your family history? List your resources.
Resources may vary.

_____

_____

_____

On the lines below, identify the data you will need to gather before constructing your family tree. Then research your family history to find this data. Take notes in your Personal Journal.
Data may vary.

_____

_____

_____

Organize the information you have collected, and create your family tree. You might want to make your family tree on a sheet of poster board and, if possible, include copies of photographs.

66   Letters from Rifka ✦ **Open Court Classics**

Responding to Literature p. 66

Teacher Tip This activity might raise sensitive issues for students who are not living with or in contact with their biological relatives. Encourage these students to complete their family trees with people who play an important role in their lives.

Name_____Date_____

Lesson 6

I Wonder

At the end of "Letters from Rifka," readers are left to make a *conjecture*, or conclusion based on little evidence, about what will happen next on Rifka's journey to America. What do you think will happen to Rifka and her family?

Use what you have learned about Rifka and her family from the selection to make a conjecture about their futures. Use your Personal Journal to organize your ideas. Then on the lines below, write a persuasive paragraph expressing your thoughts. Support your reasons with information from the text. When you have finished, share your conjecture with classmates.

Persuasive paragraphs may vary.

_____

_____

_____

_____

_____

_____

_____

_____

_____

_____

_____

_____

_____

See Appendix pages 120–121 for persuasive writing.

Open Court Classics ✦ Letters from Rifka   **67**

Responding to Literature p. 67

Assessment Use the *Responding to Literature* pages as an informal assessment of students' understanding of the selection and of ways to express personal opinions and ideas.

Objective

Students will learn to make conjectures based on evidence from the selection.

Thinking Skills

✦ Predicting
✦ Extrapolating information
✦ Proving with evidence

Activity

Explain to students that a conjecture is a conclusion based on speculation. Then have students make conjectures about Rifka's and her family's future. Some students might have read the complete work *Letters from Rifka* and already be familiar with the selection's ending. Have these students make conjectures about what happened to Rifka and her family after the book's conclusion.

The Next Step

Have students use the ideas expressed in their persuasive paragraphs to write an ending for "Letters from Rifka." Remind students that the selection's ending should be supported with evidence from their reading and should be cohesive with the rest of the selection. Students should pay particular attention to matching their writing style to the author's writing style.

Student Anthology pp. 146–165

Selection Goals

- To appreciate the author's descriptive language and vivid imagery
- To recognize the challenges and rewards of living in the wilderness
- To effectively communicate opinions in a book review

Selection Summary

Having left his family and home in New York City, Sam Gribley endures a brutal winter in his outdoor home in the Catskill Mountains. Through Sam's journal entries, readers learn about his survival techniques and his attachment to the mountain. This selection is an excerpt from Jean Craighead George's Newbery Honor Book *My Side of the Mountain.*

Genre: Realistic Fiction

Share with students some of the elements of realistic fiction, which include

- ✦ characters who behave like real people or animals.

- ✦ events that could happen in real life.

- ✦ settings that are real or could be real.

- ✦ conflicts similar to those in real life.

⁂ *Part 1* ⁂

Building Background

Activate Prior Knowledge

✦ Ask students what they know about camping. Have them share information and personal stories about the challenges and benefits of living outdoors.

✦ Discuss with students their ideas about what it would be like to live alone in the wilderness and depend only on the environment for food and shelter.

Background Information

✦ George enjoys sharing her love of nature through writing. She has said that she prefers children as an audience because they have enthusiasm and excitement for nature. George's efforts have been appreciated and acknowledged by critics as well as readers. Her novel *Julie of the Wolves* won the Newbery Medal in 1973, and her book *My Side of the Mountain* was selected as a 1960 Newbery Honor Book.

✦ *My Side of the Mountain* is the first book in a trilogy. Thirty years after writing the first story, George wrote the sequel *On the Far Side of the Mountain*. Ten years later, she wrote the third installment, *Frightful's Mountain*, which is told from the falcon's point of view.

✦ This selection is set in the Catskill Mountains of upstate New York. Much of the Catskills is a forest preserve; however, more than 60 percent of the land is privately owned. Remind students of this fact if they are confused by the reference in the selection to the Gribley farm.

> **Teacher Tip**
> Tell students that one of George's techniques for creating vivid images is the use of similes. She writes, "The sky was as thick as Indiana bean soup," and "The deer-hide door grew stiff with ice as darkness came, and it rattled like a piece of tin when the wind hit it." Encourage students to identify other examples of similes from the selection as they read.

Previewing the Literature

Browse the Selection

✦ Have students note the title of the selection and the name of the author/illustrator. Then have students browse the first couple of pages to look for clues that tell them what the selection has to do with survival. Remind students that good readers make connections between what they already know and what they are reading.

✦ Note on the board those things students mention as a result of their browsing and any questions they have about the selection.

In Which I Have a Good Look . . .

Set Purposes for Reading

Have students set purposes for reading this selection. As they read, encourage students to ask themselves questions such as the following: Why would Sam choose to put himself in a difficult situation? What survival techniques does Sam exhibit? What character traits enable him to survive? What elements of realistic fiction appear in this selection?

Expanding Vocabulary

The words listed below can be found in the Glossary of the **Student Anthology.** Page numbers indicate where the words can be found in the selection.

barometer, p. 148 An instrument used to measure atmospheric pressure and to predict changes in the weather.

whittling, p. 148 Cutting small pieces from a portion of wood using a knife.

concoction, p. 153 Something made up of a combination of things.

resilient, p. 156 Ability to recover easily or return to original shape or position.

cavity, p. 158 A hole or hollow place.

> **Teacher Tip**
> Tell students that the base word of *resilient* is the less commonly used verb *resile.* Have students look up the word *resile* and the suffix *-ent* to figure out the meaning of the vocabulary word. Explain that the meaning of an unfamiliar word can often be determined by looking at the word's parts, such as prefixes and suffixes.

⇒Part 2⇐

Reading the Selection

Read

✦ Have students silently read **Student Anthology** pages 146–165, stopping at the end of each page if they have any questions or need clarification.

✦ Encourage students to use making connections or any other comprehension strategies that might help them read the selection.

Discuss

The following discussion suggestions can be carried out on different days, depending upon how much time you allot to each selection.

✦ Have students discuss their general reactions to the selection.

✦ Ask students what this selection adds to the theme that the other selections do not.

✦ Encourage students to review any questions they listed on the board before reading to see if the selection answered their questions.

✦ Ask students to discuss Sam Gribley's relationship with nature and the responsibility he feels toward his environment.

✦ Have students consider and discuss Sam's motivation for living alone in the mountains.

✦ Ask students to discuss the author's use of descriptive language and its effect on the reader.

After students have discussed the selection, choose from *Responding to Literature* pages 68–73, and ask students to complete the assigned pages.

✧ Part 3 ✦
Knowledge-Building Project

At this point in their projects, students should have received feedback from their peers regarding their first drafts. Have students review the suggestions made by their peers to determine which comments will add to the quality of their survival stories. Remind students that the revising stage of the writing process is the time for them to make sure their ideas are clear, well-supported, and well-organized. Students should then begin writing their final drafts.

As students prepare their final drafts, remind them to proofread for errors in spelling, grammar, capitalization, and punctuation. Suggest that students incorporate illustrations or charts to add visual appeal to their stories.

By the end of this selection, students should be ready to present their survival stories to the class.

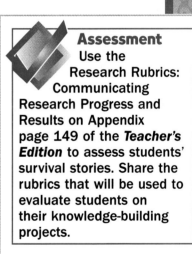

Assessment
Use the Research Rubrics: Communicating Research Progress and Results on Appendix page 149 of the *Teacher's Edition* to assess students' survival stories. Share the rubrics that will be used to evaluate students on their knowledge-building projects.

UNIT 4

In Which I Have a Good Look . . .

Lesson 1

Objective

Students will learn to examine an author's message and writing techniques.

Thinking Skills

- ✦ Understanding author's purpose
- ✦ Analyzing text
- ✦ Proving with examples

Activity

Students might find it interesting that many of the characters in Jean Craighead George's stories evolved from the animals that lived around her home. Explain that George learned about these animals by observing and making notes about their behavior. Have students consider ways George portrayed the importance of the animals in this selection. Encourage students to discuss and compare ideas.

The Next Step

Have students research the different ways animals communicate and how this contributes to their survival. Then have students use George's writing style to write a realistic short story that reveals an animal's personality and survival techniques without giving the animal the ability to talk. Encourage students to include the elements of realistic fiction in their writing.

Name_____ Date_____

Getting Started

The author of this selection, Jean Craighead George, grew up close to animals. From the way George writes about animals, readers can tell she knows and cares about them. Focus on the important role animals play in this selection as you answer the questions below. Support your answers with examples from the selection. **Possible answers below:**

1. Why does George choose to give names to three of the animals, Frightful, The Baron Weasel, and Barometer?
   George names the animals to make them more
   distinct characters.
   _____

2. How does George show that people and animals need each other?
   Sam predicts changes in the weather by watching
   the animals. The deer depend on Sam for food.
   _____

3. How does George develop the animals' personalities without giving them the ability to speak?
   She describes the way they act in their
   environment and interact with Sam.
   _____

Extra Effort: Go to the library, and select another book written by Jean Craighead George. Compare how George portrays the relationship between animals and humans in the book and in this selection. Record your ideas in your Personal Journal.

68 In Which I Have a Good Look at Winter and Find Spring in the Snow ✦ **Open Court Classics**

Responding to Literature p. 68

Teacher Tip **Comprehension Strategies**
After students read the selection, ask them what connections they made between the selection and what they already knew. Have volunteers tell how making connections helped them better understand what they read.

Assessment Use the Informal Comprehension Strategies Rubrics: Making Connections on Appendix page 144 of the *Teacher's Edition* to assess students' use of this strategy.

Name_____ Date_____

In Which I Have a Good Look at Winter • Survival **UNIT 4**
and Find Spring in the Snow

Making Connections

This selection and the selection from *Robinson Crusoe* are both about a person trying to survive on his own in the wilderness. Compare the two main characters, assessing each one's situation. Fill in the Venn diagram with examples of how Sam Gribley and Robinson Crusoe are alike and how they are different. **Answers may vary.**

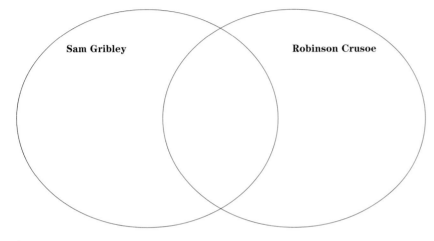

Based on what Sam Gribley and Robinson Crusoe have in common, what do you think are important qualities of a survivor? How do Sam Gribley and Robinson Crusoe compare to other survivors you have read about?

Possible answer: Important qualities of a survivor

are courage, determination, respect, and

responsibility. Answers may vary.

Open Court Classics ✦ In Which I Have a Good Look at Winter and Find Spring in the Snow **69**

Responding to Literature p. 69

Teacher Tip Comparing and contrasting is one comprehension skill that students can apply to achieve a more complete understanding of what they read. Encourage students to apply comprehension skills, such as cause and effect, drawing conclusions, and sequence, as they read. Ask students to share the skills they used to better understand the selection.

Objectives

✦ Students will compare and contrast characters from two selections.

✦ Students will recognize characteristics of a survivor.

Thinking Skills

✦ Comparing and contrasting characters

✦ Identifying characteristics

Activity

Have students use the Venn diagram to show how Sam Gribley and Robinson Crusoe are alike and different. Remind them that words such as *like, just as, both,* and *also* signal comparisons, and words such as *different, instead of, rather,* and *than* signal contrasts. Encourage students to practice using these words as they respond to the questions.

The Next Step

Have students research Henry David Thoreau to find out more about the man and his ideas. Then have students identify ways in which Sam exhibits some of Thoreau's personal characteristics and philosophies. Suggest that students record their thoughts and ideas in the form of dialogue between Sam and Thoreau.

UNIT 4

In Which I Have a Good Look . . .

Lesson 3

Objective

Students will learn to identify devices that humans use to mimic a particular animal trait that helps them survive in a certain environment.

Thinking Skills

✦ Identifying survival gear
✦ Making connections
✦ Determining relevance

Activity

Have students identify connections between human inventions and the animal traits that each imitates. Encourage students to consider a variety of environments, such as a swamp, a desert, or a jungle. Then have students explain the use of each human invention as a survival aid.

The Next Step

Ask students to think about the fundamental needs humans must satisfy in order to survive in a given situation. For example, students might consider the different way humans can collect fresh water for survival. Then have students design their own inventions that could help humans survive in a particular environment. Encourage students to create diagrams or models of the inventions they design.

Name_____ Date_____

Reality Check

Sam Gribley is so impressed with the deer he observes that he writes this in his journal: "They manage the deep snows so effortlessly on those slender hooves."

Think about other physical traits of animals that help them survive in their environment. How might humans benefit from traits like wings, tails, fins, or fur? Research different types of *gear*, or equipment, that have been invented for humans to imitate a specific animal trait. For example, flippers people wear while swimming imitate fins. Then on the lines below, identify the invention and animal trait it imitates. Explain the purpose of each invention and how it helps humans survive. **Possible answers below:**

1. **Invention:** Snorkel

   Animal Trait: Fish gills

   Purpose for Survival: Allows humans to breathe underwater.

2. **Invention:** Coat

   Animal Trait: Fur

   Purpose for Survival: Allows humans to survive in cold temperatures.

3. **Invention:** Parasail

   Animal Trait: Wings

   Purpose for Survival: Allows humans to glide in the sky.

70 In Which I Have a Good Look at Winter and Find Spring in the Snow ✦ **Open Court Classics**

Responding to Literature p. 70

Teacher Tip As students complete the assigned *Responding to Literature* pages, be sure they progress with their knowledge-building projects and make necessary preparations for their presentations.

Name_____ Date_____

Lesson 4

Making Sound Decisions

This selection includes a lot of descriptive writing that appeals to readers' sense of hearing. Jean Craighead George describes how "the trees cry out and limbs snap and fall, and the wind gets caught in a ravine and screams until it dies." George uses words to create the sounds of the forest on a cold, windy night.

Think of how you would put sounds to George's words. How could you make the sounds of trees crying out? Work with one or more classmates to create an audiocassette with sound effects. Choose one page from the selection to use for your recording. Make a list of sound effects you will create to go with the text. Then decide how you will make each sound, and gather the props you need. Make your audiocassette with one person reading the text and one or more partners making sound effects in the background.

Sound effects and props may vary.

Sound Effects	Props
_____	_____
_____	_____
_____	_____
_____	_____
_____	_____
_____	_____
_____	_____
_____	_____

Extra Effort: Think about a song you enjoy listening to. What makes the song appealing to your sense of hearing? Discuss with classmates how the techniques described above are used in the music industry.

Open Court Classics ✦ In Which I Have a Good Look at Winter and Find Spring in the Snow **71**

Responding to Literature p. 71

Teacher Tip Encourage students to review the selection and identify other examples of descriptive writing, such as adjectives, adverbs, verbs, or nouns, that George uses to appeal to the readers' senses.

Objective

Students will identify descriptive writing in a selection and create appropriate sound effects.

Thinking Skills

✦ Identifying descriptive text
✦ Adding to text

Activity

Tell students that the sound effects they create should help listeners hear what George describes in the text. Explain that the sound effects should also make the phrases or passages seem more realistic. If students have difficulty locating props, suggest they use objects in the classroom, such as spiral notebooks, books, folders, and so on.

The Next Step

Have students investigate sound effects. For example, you might encourage them to research the history of early radio shows to identify techniques used to create sound effects, such as sheets of tin used for thunder. You might also suggest students research Foley artists to discover how they add realistic sound effects to match the actions in films.

UNIT 4

In Which I Have a Good Look . . .

Lesson 5

Objective

Students will formulate and defend their opinions in a book review.

Thinking Skills

✦ Evaluating text
✦ Formulating opinions
✦ Proving with evidence

Activity

Have students write a book review in which they express their opinions about whether the events portrayed in this selection are realistic. Explain that their opinions should be clearly stated in their book reviews. Tell students that they should also provide examples from the selection to defend their opinions.

The Next Step

Have students research reference materials for information about the lifestyles of early Native Americans and their symbolic relationship with nature. Then in their Personal Journals, have students compare their findings to modern Americans' relationship with nature. Encourage students to investigate environmental organizations, such as the Sierra Club, Greenpeace, and the National Park Conservation Association.

Name_____ Date_____

In My Opinion

Works of realistic fiction are stories that could actually happen. In realistic fiction, the characters behave as they would in real life, the setting is or could be a real place, and the events could really happen. *My Side of the Mountain* is a work of realistic fiction. How realistic do you think the story is? How could a boy from the city survive on his own in the wilderness? What would he have had to do to prepare himself?

Write a book review to express your opinion of whether this story is or is not realistic. Support your ideas with examples from the selection.

Book reviews may vary.

_____

_____

_____

_____

_____

_____

_____

_____

_____

_____

See Appendix pages 122–123 for reviewing a fiction book.

Extra Effort: Choose another work of realistic fiction that you would like to read. Look for elements in the piece that characterize this genre.

72 In Which I Have a Good Look at Winter and Find Spring in the Snow ✦ **Open Court Classics**

Responding to Literature p. 72

Teacher Tip Writing A book review includes a summary of the selection and the writer's opinion of it. Before summarizing suggest that students create a story map to organize main events. Students should then state their opinions and provide support for their evaluations.

Assessment Use the Expository Structure Writing Rubric on Appendix page 146 of the *Teacher's Edition* to assess students' book reviews.

Name_____Date_____

Lesson 6

Life Lessons

The introduction to this selection explains that Sam Gribley leaves his home and family to live in the wilderness. As a result, we might think Sam does not care about or need the comforts that he leaves behind. However, on page 147 of the anthology, Sam describes his attachment to his new home in this way: "Not that I was afraid of being caught far from home in a storm, for I could find food and shelter and make a fire anywhere, but I had become as attached to my hemlock house as a brooding bird to her nest." Choose two of the three questions below to answer thoroughly.

Possible answers below:

1. Based on this quotation and the rest of the selection, what do you think is Sam Gribley's idea of home?

   Sam's idea of home is a place where he has the

   necessities to survive.

2. Describe how this selection has affected your ideas about what *home* means.

   Answers may vary.

3. Compare the ideas of *home* and *survival*. How do you think the two ideas are related? If possible, use examples from the selection to support your answer.

   Answers may vary.

Open Court Classics ✦ In Which I Have a Good Look at Winter and Find Spring in the Snow **73**

Responding to Literature p. 73

Teacher Tip The activity on *Responding to Literature* page 73 might raise sensitive issues for students from troubled homes. Assure all students that you will not share their responses with the rest of the class.

Assessment Use the *Responding to Literature* pages as an informal assessment of students' ability to understand the selection, analyze characters, and express opinions.

Objective

Students will respond to philosophical questions about concepts from the selection.

Thinking Skills

✦ Making inferences
✦ Describing ideas
✦ Analyzing text

Activity

Explain to students that the word *home* might have different meanings for different people. Point out that to one person *home* might signify a physical structure but to another person *home* might symbolize security and happiness. Have students consider their definitions of *home*. Then have them write detailed answers to two of the three questions.

The Next Step

Have students write a letter to Sam Gribley in which they attempt to persuade him to return to his home in New York City. Encourage them to consider a variety of perspectives, such as a guardian or friend, from which they could write. Then have students write a response from Sam's perspective in which he explains why he wants to continue living in the wilderness. Suggest that students work in pairs, with each partner writing one of the letters from a different perspective.

$\mathcal{W}$rap-Up

Knowledge-Building Project

Students have completed the investigation of their topics and should now be ready to present their survival stories. Presentations may be done in small groups or before the entire class. Encourage students to respond to each presentation, telling what they found most interesting. Also have students tell what new facts they learned and new questions they have about survival. Use the Research Rubrics: Overall Assessment of Research on Appendix page 149 of the ***Teacher's Edition*** to assess students' knowledge-building projects as a whole.

Teacher Tip Encourage students to discuss how the following quotation by philosopher and psychologist William James (1842–1910) relates to the selections, as well as to their ideas about survival: "Great emergencies and crises show us how much greater our vital resources are than we had supposed."

Reviewing the Concepts

In this unit students encountered three characters with a strong will to survive. Although the characters found themselves in challenging circumstances for very different reasons, the marooned sailor, the young refugee, and the determined adolescent were all survivors. Students investigated some of the following key concepts in this unit:

✦ Resourcefulness is one of several personal characteristics that survivors have in common.

✦ The strength and support of family members can help one overcome challenging situations.

✦ Writing is a way to reflect on and cope with challenging experiences.

Evaluating the Unit

✦ Ask students to evaluate each selection on the basis of effectiveness of reading/vocabulary, literary value, interest of the subject matter, style of writing, application of theme, and the selection's personal value to the student.

✦ Ask students to evaluate the different activities in the unit, including the knowledge-building project. Have them consider these questions: Which activities made you think? Which ones did you find less challenging and why? Which ones seemed confusing or challenging? Which activities did you most enjoy and why? Which activities best contributed to your growth intellectually? Which activities stimulated novelty and original thinking? What activities would you like to add to the unit?

✦ Ask students to evaluate this ***Open Court Classics*** unit. They can describe how the theme was explored in the unit. They can also compare and contrast the selections based on the personal characteristics of the main characters and the journal- and letter-writing formats for a first-person narrator.

Assessment

Vocabulary Assessment

To assess students' understanding of the vocabulary words, you might want to do one of the following:

✦ Have students work alone or with a partner to role-play the meanings of the vocabulary words in this unit.

✦ Have students write a sentence for each vocabulary word in this unit and incorporate apposition or context clues.

✦ Administer an informal oral assessment. Have students supply the definition of the vocabulary word or use the word properly in a sentence.

Informal Comprehension Strategies Rubrics

Use the Informal Comprehension Strategies Rubrics: Predicting, Asking Questions, and Making Connections on Appendix pages 144–145 of the *Teacher's Edition* to determine whether a student is using a particular strategy or strategies as he or she reads the selections. Note these and any other strategies a student is using, instead of the degree to which a student might be using any particular strategy. In addition, encourage the student to tell of any strategies other than the ones being taught that he or she is using.

Research Rubrics

Use the Research Rubrics: Recognizing Information Needs, Finding Needed Information, Communicating Research Progress and Results, and Overall Assessment of Research on Appendix pages 148–149 of the *Teacher's Edition* to assess a student's performance throughout the investigation. The rubrics range from 1 to 4 in most categories, with 1 being the lowest score. In addition, you can use the rubrics to assess a group's collaborative work as well as an individual's participation in that group.

Writing Rubrics

Use the Narrative Writing Rubric, the Revising Writing Process Rubric, the Personal Writing Rubric, and the Expository Structure Writing Rubric on Appendix page 146 of the *Teacher's Edition* to assess student writing. The rubrics range from 1 to 4 in most categories, with 1 being the lowest score.

The difference between the right word and the almost right word is the difference between lightning and lightning bug.
—Mark Twain—

Unit Goals

- To recognize the need to communicate
- To investigate communication between humans and nature
- To write a poem or dialogue about communicating with nature
- To recognize elements of an author's style
- To understand the importance of written language as a means of communication
- To identify elements of science fiction
- To write and present a play about an aspect of communication

Introduction

Communication occurs all around us in various ways. Communication tools, from telephones to computers, help meet the same human need that has existed for ages—to give and receive information. In this unit students will investigate the past and the future of communication in a variety of fictional genres. Selection 1 is "Animal Language" on page 168, which is accompanied by the poem "Forgotten Language" on page 180; Selection 2 is "How the Alphabet Was Made" on page 182; and Selection 3 is "Someday" on page 202. These selections will encourage students to examine questions about how and why we communicate.

Unit Discussion

Invite students to discuss their ideas about communication. Questions such as the following can help continue the discussion:

✦ How have forms of communication changed throughout time?

✦ Why do people need to communicate? What message does the quotation found in the unit opener convey?

✦ What are the similarities and differences between verbal and nonverbal communication?

Knowledge-Building Project

Have students discuss their definitions of *communication* with classmates and list new ideas or questions that are generated. Reiterate that humans and animals communicate in many different ways. During their discussion, encourage students to consider not only verbal communication but also nonverbal communication, such as sign language, photographs, and art. Prompt students' thinking by pointing out different types of communication that they might incorporate in their discussions, such as sounds insects use to communicate or ways in which humans communicate with each other. As a final product, students will write a play about an aspect of communication they choose to investigate. Explain that the purpose of their plays will be to inform, as well as to entertain. The information they collect and include in their plays should provide the audience with a better understanding of the unit theme. Students will also examine the different ways characters in plays communicate with each other and the audience. Encourage students to continually think about ways they will have their characters convey the play's messages through verbal communication, such as dialogue, and nonverbal communication, such as stage directions. Encourage students to consider what they learn from the selections as they research topics for their projects.

> **Teacher Tip**
> As an alternative to the outlined project, suggest that students write and produce a television or radio commercial. Students can investigate various ways that advertisers communicate with audiences and incorporate these techniques in their commercials.

Unit 5 Project Overview	
Unit Overview	Students define communication and generate a list of ideas and questions.
Selection 1	Students select an idea or question for investigation and begin making a preliminary list of characters and scenes for their plays.
Selection 2	Students begin drafting their plays.
Selection 3	Students edit their scripts and prepare a final draft.
Unit Wrap-Up	Students present their plays for an audience.

𝒜nimal Language

Student Anthology pp. 168–181

Selection Goals

- To recognize elements of the author's style
- To investigate communication between humans and animals
- To write a poem or dialogue on the subject of communicating with nature

Selection Summary

When Doctor Dolittle's career as a physician reaches its lowest point, one of his patients suggests that he treat animals instead of humans. Polynesia, the pet parrot, likes the idea and begins teaching Doctor Dolittle the language of animals and the many ways in which they communicate. In addition to "Animal Language," students will read the poem "Forgotten Language."

Genre: Fantasy

Share with students some of the elements of a fantasy, which include

✦ people, animals, or objects that do things they cannot do in the real world.

✦ creatures and settings that do not exist in the real world.

✦ events that could not happen in the real world.

✦ *Part 1* ✦
Building Background

Activate Prior Knowledge

✦ Ask students whether they are familiar with the Doctor Dolittle stories and movies. Discuss with them the discrepancies between print and visual forms of communication.

✦ Have students share personal stories about ways in which they have communicated with pets or animals at a zoo or at an aquarium.

Background Information

✦ Tell students that this selection is the second chapter of Hugh Lofting's novel *The Story of Doctor Dolittle.* The first chapter of the book explains how Doctor Dolittle's love of animals leads to the failure of his medical practice. Dolittle's small home, where he treats patients, eventually becomes so overrun with pets that people no longer want to come there.

✦ Hugh Lofting was born in England. Although he became a resident of the United States, Lofting served in the British army during World War I (1914–1918). The Doctor Dolittle stories that made Lofting famous began as letters written to his children while he was away at war. *The Story of Doctor Dolittle* was originally published in 1920, and nine more stories followed. In 1923 Lofting received the Newbery Medal for *The Voyages of Doctor Dolittle.*

✦ The musical movie *Doctor Dolittle*, released in 1967, was based on the Doctor Dolittle books. In 1998 another movie titled *Doctor Dolittle* was released. However, other than featuring a doctor who can talk to animals, the recent version of the story has very little in common with Lofting's stories.

Previewing the Literature

Browse the Selection

✦ Have students note the title and the names of the author and illustrator. Then have them browse the first couple of pages of the selection and discuss how this selection relates to communication.

✦ Note on the board those things students mention as a result of their browsing and any questions they have about the selection.

$\mathcal{A}$nimal Language

Set Purposes for Reading
Encourage students to set purposes for reading. As they read, suggest that students focus on the author's use of dialogue, how the author incorporates humor, and elements of a fantasy that occur in the selection.

Expanding Vocabulary
The words listed below can be found in the Glossary of the **Student Anthology.** Page numbers indicate where the words can be found in the selection.

spavins, p. 175 — Bony enlargements of joints on horses' hind legs; often associated with strain.

mustard-plaster, p. 176 — A paste-like mixture (containing mustard) that hardens when dry; applied to the body to help healing.

booby, p. 176 — A person considered foolish or unthinking.

Teacher Tip
This selection contains a number of hyphenated compounds, such as the vocabulary term *mustard-plaster.* Explain that the accepted style for using hyphens is continually changing. Have students identify some hyphenated terms from the selection and tell how these words should be written according to current style guidelines. You might suggest that students consult various sources, such as *Writers INC: A Student Handbook for Writing and Learning,* to identify the current guidelines.

⇥ Part 2 ⇤
Reading the Selection

Read
✦ Have students silently read **Student Anthology** pages 168–181, stopping at the end of each page if they have any questions or need clarification.

✦ Encourage students to use asking questions or any other comprehension strategies that might help them read the selection.

Discuss

The following discussion suggestions can be carried out on different days, depending upon how much time you allot to each selection.

✦ Have students discuss their general reactions to the selection.

✦ Ask students how this selection relates to the theme.

✦ Encourage students to review any questions they listed on the board before reading to see if the selection answered their questions.

✦ Have students discuss how animals and humans communicate.

✦ Have students discuss the author's use of dialogue in this selection.

✦ Have students discuss how the author created humor.

After students have discussed the selection, choose from **Responding to Literature** pages 74–81, and ask students to complete the assigned pages.

⋆Part 3⋆
Knowledge-Building Project

Have students review their lists of ideas and questions about communication. Suggest that students collect information about several of the items on their lists to find a topic that interests them. Encourage students also to consider a topic's translation into a dramatization. Students should then begin researching their chosen topics to collect details that will add new ideas and interest to their plays. Students should also begin making preliminary lists of characters and scenes for their plays.

As students begin investigating and making notes about their topics, encourage them to watch a production of a play. Suggest that students who cannot view a live production watch a filmed production. Stress the importance of evaluating the elements of a play, such as the characters, dialogue, setting, and stage directions. Encourage students to focus on the verbal and nonverbal communication that characters use on stage. For example, suggest that students examine facial expressions and movements or gestures of the characters to determine the message they are conveying rather than focusing only on what the characters say. Have students also consider how the play's purpose is revealed to the audience. Have some published plays available for students to read as well. This will help them become more familiar with the elements of a play and learn how to format their writing.

By the end of the next selection, students should have completed the first drafts of their plays.

> **Assessment**
> Use the Research Rubrics: Recognizing Information Needs on Appendix page 148 of the *Teacher's Edition* to assess the depth and relevance of students' research questions. Discuss with students the rubrics that will be used to evaluate them on their knowledge-building projects.

Animal Language
Lesson 1

Objectives

✦ Students will conduct a survey for information about appealing qualities in a veterinarian.

✦ Students will write a job description based on their survey results.

Thinking Skills

✦ Formulating questions
✦ Summarizing survey responses

Activity

Explain that a job description details specific duties and responsibilities necessary for a job and it usually includes information such as job duties, skills, knowledge, employee attributes, experience, and so on. Encourage students to read some job listings in the classified section of a local newspaper for examples. Then have students create and conduct a survey in which they investigate the most important qualities in a veterinarian. Students should use their survey results to create a job description.

The Next Step

Have students locate a job description for a veterinarian. In their Personal Journals ask students to create a Venn diagram or a web to compare the real job description they located to the one they created.

Name_____ Date_____

Getting Started

Recall what you know about a survey. Think about when and how a survey is conducted and the kind of information it provides. Now imagine that you have the same talent as Doctor Dolittle, and you can talk with animals. Conduct a survey in which you interview animals about what they think are important qualities in a veterinarian.

1. Make a list of questions for your survey.
   Questions may vary.
   _____
   _____
   _____

2. Ask some classmates who have read "Animal Language" to complete your survey. Each student should imagine to be an animal from the story.

3. Write a job description or a "Help Wanted" ad for the position of veterinarian using the results of your survey.
   Job descriptions may vary.
   _____
   _____
   _____
   _____
   _____
   _____

See Appendix page 137 for writing a survey.

74   Animal Language ✦ Open Court Classics

Responding to Literature p. 74

Teacher Tip Comprehension Strategies
Encourage students to share the questions they asked as they read. Have students explain how asking questions helped them better understand the selection.

COMMUNICATION

Lesson 2

Quite a Character

Sometimes when authors create a character they *show* rather than *tell* the readers how that character thinks or feels. Readers then draw conclusions about a character based on the character's actions.

In the space below, create a web to analyze Doctor Dolittle. List the elements of Doctor Dolittle's character that are shown through his actions. Then write examples from the selection to support your ideas. When you have finished, meet with a partner to compare character webs.

Possible character web:

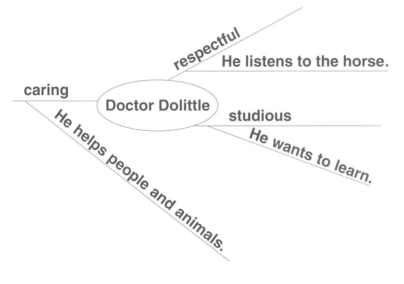

Extra Effort: In your Personal Journal, analyze another character from "Animal Language."

Open Court Classics ✦ Animal Language

75

Responding to Literature p. 75

Assessment Use the Informal Comprehension Strategies Rubrics: Asking Questions on Appendix page 144 of the *Teacher's Edition* to assess students' use of this strategy as they read.

Objective

Students will learn to create a character web to analyze a character's traits.

Thinking Skills

✦ Identifying traits
✦ Proving with evidence

Activity

Suggest that students return to the selection to look for clues about Doctor Dolittle's character traits in what he says, what he does, and what other characters say about him. Then have students create a character web to record what they learned about Doctor Dolittle's personality. Ask students to consider how Doctor Dolittle's personality traits might help him communicate with his animal patients.

The Next Step

Have students recall what they learned about real-life veterinarian James Herriot in Unit 3. Then in their Personal Journals, have students compare Doctor Dolittle with James Herriot. Encourage students to discuss the similarities and differences between the two veterinarians and the ways both characters communicated with their patients.

Objectives

✦ Students will translate the meanings of animals' gestures.

✦ Students will write a paragraph appropriate to the selection's style and theme.

Thinking Skills

✦ Identifying and interpreting animals' gestures

✦ Adding to the selection

Activity

Ask students what it usually means when a person nods his or her head up and down or when a person smiles. Explain that people and animals communicate nonverbally in a variety of ways, such as through body language. Then discuss with students different verbal and nonverbal ways people communicate with each other. Suggest that students create a chart to arrange and organize their "translations" in this activity.

The Next Step

Have students conduct research about hand signals and other gestures humans use to communicate with and train animals, such as horses, dogs, and dolphins. Encourage students to utilize sources, such as the Internet, to discover useful information. Ask students to demonstrate some examples for the class and to share the purpose of each gesture.

Name_____ Date_____

UNIT 5 Communication • *Animal Language*

I Can Do It, Too

In "Animal Language," Polynesia, the parrot, helps Doctor Dolittle learn the languages of different animals. For example, she explains that when Jip the dog twitches up one side of his nose, it means he is asking, "Can't you see that it's stopped raining?"

Think about other animal gestures and their possible *translations*, or meanings. For example, what does it mean when a dog flaps its ears or when a goldfish swims in a circle? Then create a graphic organizer to arrange your ideas in the space below. In your Personal Journal, use the information in the graphic organizer to write a paragraph to add to "Animal Language."

Ideas and graphic organizers may vary.

See Appendix pages 133–134 for writing a paragraph.

Extra Effort: Read an expository selection about animal communication. How does the information in the selection compare with your "translations"? What new information did you discover?

76 Animal Language ✦ Open Court Classics

Responding to Literature p. 76

> **Teacher Tip** **Writing** Have students review the characteristic elements of a fantasy and incorporate those elements in their paragraphs.

> **Assessment** Use the Genre Writing Rubric on Appendix page 146 of the *Teacher's Edition* to assess students' use of the elements of a fantasy in their writing.

Name_____ Date_____

Animal Language • Communication **UNIT 5**

In My Opinion

There are many reports of animals' ability to communicate. Dolphins, elephants, chimpanzees, and bees are just a few species that scientists have observed communicating through sound and/or movement. However, there are different opinions about the reasons or circumstances in which animals communicate. Some people believe that animals can think and make decisions, while others believe that animals only act according to their instincts.

Reflect on what you have read and your experiences with animals. Then in the form of a persuasive paragraph, explain why you believe animals communicate based on thinking and decision-making skills, or why you believe animals communicate only by instinct.

Persuasive paragraphs may vary.

_____
_____
_____
_____
_____
_____
_____
_____
_____
_____
_____

See Appendix pages 120–121 for persuasive writing and Appendix pages 133–134 for writing a paragraph.

Open Court Classics ✦ Animal Language

77

Responding to Literature p. 77

Teacher Tip Remind students to be respectful of one another's opinions as they exchange paragraphs. Students should consider what they might learn from a different point of view. Even partners who share the same opinion can learn from the different reasons and evidence they each use to support their arguments.

Objective

Students will formulate and defend their opinions about how and why animals communicate.

Thinking Skills

✦ Judging concepts
✦ Determining affect of a peer's opinion

Activity

Suggest that students read more about animal communication before completing the activity. Providing materials about this topic in the classroom might be helpful for students who wish to gather more information. Based on the appropriateness for your classroom, you might suggest the book *Bees Dance and Whales Sing: The Mysteries of Animal Communication* by Margery Facklam or the Web site www.oaklandzoo.org/atoz/atoz.html. After students complete the activity, encourage them to trade paragraphs with a classmate and write how their classmate's ideas affected their opinions.

The Next Step

Have students conduct research for information about various kinds of service animals, such as guide dogs. In their Personal Journals have students write an expository essay about how the animals are trained to do specific tasks and how they communicate with their owners.

Objective

Students will conduct research to discover how a particular culture interacts with nature.

Thinking Skills

✦ Formulating questions
✦ Identifying facts

Activity

Explain that many cultures, such as the Native American culture, have lived or do live close to nature and, as a result, have developed a strong appreciation for their environment. Point out that natural environment can also play a role in a culture's beliefs and ideas. As students proceed with their investigations, encourage them to explore the songs, dances, and art of a particular culture and how these artistic expressions relate to communication.

The Next Step

Have students investigate a conservation organization, such as The Nature Conservancy, Endangered Wildlife Trust, or National Wildlife Federation. Then in their Personal Journals, have students write a paragraph about one of the organizations they investigated and its goals and accomplishments.

Name_____ Date_____

A Closer Look

Respect for nature is an important part of many cultures. For example, many Native American myths and rituals deal with communication between people and elements of nature.

Look in some books and on the Internet for information about a particular culture. On the lines below, write questions you have about how and why the people of that culture have communicated with the natural world.
Questions may vary.

_____

_____

_____

_____

_____

_____

_____

_____

_____

Next search for more information related to one of your research questions. Take notes in your Personal Journal, and record any new ideas and questions you have as you discover additional information.

In your Personal Journal, write what you learned from your research and explain how this investigation relates to the unit theme of communication.

78   Animal Language ✦ Open Court Classics

Responding to Literature p. 78

> **Teacher Tip** Allow students to share their research results with the class and compare their findings about a particular culture with one another. Encourage a discussion about general attitudes toward nature in the students' community.

Animal Language • Communication **UNIT 5**

Reality Check

Some of the characters in "Animal Language" express their thoughts and ideas about *veterinarians*, or animal doctors, that they believe to be true. What do you think about their thoughts and ideas?

Answers may vary.

_____

_____

_____

Write some ideas that you think are true about veterinarians. They might be ideas from the selection or from your own experiences.

Ideas may vary.

_____

_____

_____

Where might you look for information to answer your questions? List some possible sources, including people whom you could interview.

Sources may vary.

_____

_____

_____

Check the sources you listed above to find out whether your ideas about veterinarians were accurate. Then in your Personal Journal, write about what you learned as a result of your investigation.

Open Court Classics ✦ Animal Language   **79**

Responding to Literature p. 79

Teacher Tip As students complete the assigned *Responding to Literature* pages, be sure they progress with recognizing information needs about a potential topic for their knowledge-building projects.

Objectives

✦ Students will learn to make conjectures about veterinarians.

✦ Students will learn to judge the accuracy of their ideas.

Thinking Skills

✦ Distinguishing fact from fiction

✦ Making inferences

Activity

If students interview someone for this activity, remind them to prepare a list of questions in advance. Also remind students that they should write a thank-you note to the person they interviewed. You might consider inviting a veterinarian to speak to the class about how he or she communicates with animals. Encourage students to prepare by formulating questions about animal communication.

The Next Step

Have students investigate the work of animal psychologists. Encourage students to find out how these doctors communicate with their patients to identify and resolve problems. Have students share their findings with classmates.

Poetry

Vocabulary

Have students look up the definitions of any challenging words they encounter while reading the poem. Encourage them to write the words and the definitions in their Personal Journals.

Activity

Encourage students to reread the poem several times to help them think about the effects of the language Silverstein uses and about the emotions associated with the poem. To help students with this activity, you might conduct a brief lesson on the elements of poetry. Be sure to discuss repetition, figurative language, and mood, as these elements are specifically addressed in the activity.

The Next Step

In their Personal Journals have students write about their reactions to the poem. In addition to communication, ask students to consider other themes this poem represents.

Name_____ Date_____

Think like a Poet

"Animal Language" and the poem "Forgotten Language" include similar ideas about communication. How do the main ideas of the two selections compare? **Possible answer: Both selections express ideas about humans communicating with nature.**

Read the poem aloud. Then answer the questions listed below. **Possible answers below:**

1. Why do you think Shel Silverstein called this poem "Forgotten Language"?
   He does not remember the language he once shared with nature.

2. Why do you think Silverstein used repetition and figurative language in this poem?
   The sound of language in a poem appeals to readers and listeners.

3. What mood do you think Silverstein was trying to create for his readers?
   I think he was trying to create a serious and thoughtful mood.

4. What emotions do you think Silverstein felt when he was writing this poem?
   Silverstein felt regret that he could no longer speak to nature.

80   Animal Language/Forgotten Language ✦ **Open Court Classics**

Responding to Literature p. 80

Teacher Tip Suggest that students close their eyes as you read the poem aloud. Then ask them to describe the images the poem creates in their minds. Discuss with students specific words that formed the images.

Assessment Use the *Responding to Literature* pages as an informal assessment of students' understanding of the selection and of their ability to formulate questions and write a paragraph.

Name_____ Date_____

Animal Language/Forgotten Language • Communication **UNIT 5**

I Wonder

Nature is the subject of many poems. In "Forgotten Language," the poet tells readers how he used to communicate with flowers, birds, and insects. Consider what it would be like to have that kind of conversation. What would you talk about with a tree, a hurricane, a robin's egg, or some other part of nature? Choose an object of nature with which you would like to have a conversation. Then write your ideas in a poem or a dialogue.

Responses may vary.

_____

_____

_____

_____

_____

_____

_____

_____

_____

_____

_____

_____

_____

_____

See Appendix page 125 for tips for writing poetry and Appendix page 127 for using dialogue.

Open Court Classics ✦ Animal Language/Forgotten Language   **81**

Responding to Literature p. 81

Activity

Encourage students to think about what they would discuss with an object of nature. Then have students write their imagined conversations in the form of a poem or a dialogue. Encourage students who are writing a dialogue to check their work carefully for correct punctuation and capitalization. Ask students to share their poems or dialogues with the rest of the class.

The Next Step

Have students read *The Giving Tree* by Shel Silverstein. As they read, encourage them to make comparisons between the theme in "Forgotten Language" and the theme in the story. Ask students also to consider how the characters in *The Giving Tree* communicate.

Elements of Poetry

Tell students that repetition, the repeating of words or phrases, is a poetic device. Discuss with students the repetition found in "Forgotten Language." Ask students to describe the emotions portrayed by the repetition and the way it provides a musical quality.

Teacher Tip **Writing** Encourage students who are writing a poem to include some of the elements of poetry that they reviewed in the previous activity.

Assessment Use the Poetry Writing Rubric on Appendix page 146 of the *Teacher's Edition* to assess students' expression of ideas.

$\mathcal{H}$ow the Alphabet Was Made

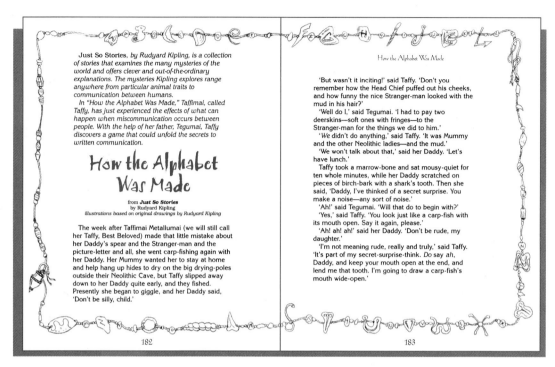

Student Anthology pp. 182–201

Selection Goals

- To appreciate the originality of the author's ideas
- To recognize the importance of written language as a means of communication

Selection Summary

What does a carp's mouth have to do with the Roman alphabet? According to Rudyard Kipling's story "How the Alphabet Was Made," that is where it all began. In this imaginative excerpt from Kipling's collection *Just So Stories*, the author explains how the alphabet originated from a child's game of "secret-surprise-think" during the Neolithic period.

Genre: Myth

Share with students some of the elements of a myth, which include

- ✦ an explanation of how something in nature looks or happens.

- ✦ characters who may be humans or gods and goddesses.

- ✦ an explanation of why people act as they do.

⊹ *Part 1* ⊹
Building Background

Activate Prior Knowledge

✦ Ask students why they think emphasis is placed on children learning the alphabet. Encourage them to discuss the benefits of understanding the letters and sounds of the alphabet.

✦ Ask students if they have read any other myths that explain how something came to be. Invite volunteers to share their stories with the rest of the class.

Background Information

✦ In addition to explaining how the alphabet was created, the tales in Kipling's *Just So Stories* explain such things as how camels got their humps, how leopards got their spots, and the origin of armadillos. Kipling's other books for children include *The Jungle Book* and *Rikki-Tikki-Tavi*.

✦ An *alphabet* is defined as "a series of letters or characters used to write a language, especially as arranged in a customary order." The alphabet used to write the English language and the alphabet that is described in the selection are called the Roman alphabet. Other major alphabets include the Greek, Arabic, Russian, and Hebrew alphabets.

✦ This selection is set in the Neolithic period, also called the New Stone Age. The Neolithic period began in the Middle East around 10,000 B.C. and was characterized by the development of agriculture and the use of tools and weapons made from shaped and polished stone.

Previewing the Literature

Browse the Selection

✦ Have students read aloud the title as well as the name of the author. Then have them browse the first couple of pages for clues that tell them something about the selection.

✦ Note on the board those things students mention as a result of their browsing and any questions they have about the selection.

> **Teacher Tip**
> Remind students that when reading a narrative text that covers a long period of time or a number of elements, it is helpful to summarize. Encourage students to use this strategy as they read "How the Alphabet Was Made."

Set Purposes for Reading

Have students set purposes for reading the selection. As they read, encourage students to focus on information from the selection that might be useful in their investigations of communication, evidence of Kipling's imagination and the imagination of each character, and Kipling's use of the illustrations.

Expanding Vocabulary

The words listed below can be found in the Glossary of the *Student Anthology.* Page numbers indicate where the words can be found in the selection.

hides, p. 182   The tough, thick skins of animals.

notion, p. 186   A belief.

flints, p. 188   Hard stones that produce sparks when struck. [Old High German *flins,* "pebble, stone."]

jostle, p. 197   To move and crash together as a result of being crowded together.

romps, p. 199   To play in a lively manner.

> **Teacher Tip**
> Students should be assuming the responsibility for determining the meanings of Expanding Vocabulary words. Instead of leading students to the definitions, encourage them to find the meanings of the words by using context clues, apposition, and word structure.

✦ Part 2 ✦

Reading the Selection

Read

✦ Have students silently read *Student Anthology* pages 182–201, stopping at the end of each page if they have any questions or need clarification.
✦ Encourage students to use summarizing or any other comprehension strategies that might help them read the selection.

Discuss

The following discussion suggestions can be carried out on different days, depending upon how much time you allot to each selection.

✦ Have students discuss their general reactions to the selection.

✦ Ask students what this selection adds to the theme that the other selection did not.

✦ Encourage students to review any questions they listed on the board before reading to see if the selection answered their questions.

✦ Ask students how their lives and ways of communicating would be different without written language. Have them discuss why they think alphabets were first invented and have continued to be used since ancient times.

✦ Have students discuss the importance of imagination and inventiveness. Encourage them to describe evidence of these qualities in both Kipling and his characters.

After students have discussed the selection, choose from **Responding to Literature** pages 82–87, and ask students to complete the assigned pages.

✦ Part 3 ✦
Knowledge-Building Project

Students should begin drafting the scripts for their plays as they continue their research for additional information about their topics. Before students start writing, discuss some of the differences between writing for a reading audience and writing for a viewing audience. Point out that students will have to communicate their information through the characters' dialogue and actions. Students will need to write dialogue that moves the story forward and informs the audience. In addition, students will need to write stage directions, which tell actors how to perform and how to move. The way an actor moves his or her body, the facial expressions an actor makes, and the tone of an actor's voice are all part of stage directions and communicate the writer's thoughts and feelings. These details help "show" the audience the story.

By the end of the next selection, students should have prepared the final drafts of the scripts for their plays.

> **Assessment**
> Use the Research Rubrics: Finding Needed Information on Appendix pages 148–149 of the *Teacher's Edition* to assess students' use of resources. Share with students the rubrics that will be used to evaluate them on their knowledge-building projects.

Objective

Students will formulate open-ended interview questions and write a book review.

Thinking Skills

✦ Formulating questions
✦ Evaluating the selection

Activity

Remind students that an open-ended question requires a thoughtful explanation and encourages a person to express his or her personal views. This type of question also generates further discussion and questioning. Tell students that a question that requires only a simple, brief response, such as yes or no, is usually used to help the subject recall information. As a class, generate examples of open-ended questions. Then have students formulate interview questions they would ask Rudyard Kipling about himself and the selection for their book reviews.

The Next Step

Ask students to brainstorm a list of devices that have been used for communicating. Then have students choose one item from their lists and research the history of that particular communication tool. Suggest that students create a time line to illustrate the major stages of the tool's development.

Name_____Date_____

Getting Started

What would you like to know about Rudyard Kipling and the characters in "How the Alphabet Was Made"? Think of questions you would like to ask the author about himself and his story. You will include the information you collect in a book review.

1. Make a list of *open-ended questions* to ask during your interview. An open-ended question cannot be answered with a simple "yes" or "no." Instead, this type of question requires thought and allows a person to respond according to his or her values.

Questions may vary.

_____

_____

_____

_____

_____

2. Find a classmate who has read "How the Alphabet Was Made." Take turns role-playing the part of the author to answer each other's questions. Remember to take good notes during your interview.

3. In your Personal Journal, write a book review of "How the Alphabet Was Made." Include information from your interview with the "author" to make the review more interesting to readers. Also include your personal responses to the author and the story.

See Appendix pages 122–123 for reviewing a fiction book.

82   How the Alphabet Was Made ✦ **Open Court Classics**

Responding to Literature p. 82

Teacher Tip As students complete the assigned *Responding to Literature* pages, be sure they continue finding needed information about the topic they selected for their knowledge-building projects.

I Can Do It, Too

In the selection "How the Alphabet Was Made," the characters make up "picture-sounds" that relate to things in their everyday lives. For example, the carp-fish's mouth and feeler represent the *ah* sound.

In the space below, or in your Personal Journal, create your own stories about the origins of some letters. You might choose to write about the letters in your name or the letters in your favorite activity. Include drawings to show how the forms of the letters evolved.

Letters and stories may vary.

Have a group discussion to share "picture-sounds" and the stories of how they evolved.

Responding to Literature p. 83

Teacher Tip Comprehension Strategies
Encourage students to tell where they paused in the selection to summarize and how it helped them understand what they read.

Assessment Use the Informal Comprehension Strategies Rubrics: Summarizing on Appendix page 145 of the *Teacher's Edition* to assess students' use of this strategy.

Objective

Students will create "picture-sounds" and record their original ideas in a story using the author's style as a model.

Thinking Skills

✦ Generating ideas
✦ Making connections

Activity

Tell students that the first known alphabet is thought to have developed along the eastern Mediterranean coast between 1700 and 1500 B.C. This alphabet evolved from other earlier writing systems. Then have students use their imaginations to brainstorm additional ideas about how letters of the Roman alphabet evolved. Tell students to use the selection as a model as they write their original stories. Encourage students to use a different time and place as the setting for their stories.

The Next Step

Have students conduct research to learn about the history of some alphabets, such as the Russian, Japanese, or Arabic alphabets, that are in use today. Students might also look for connections between modern alphabets and early writing systems, such as cuneiform and hieroglyphics.

UNIT 5

How the Alphabet Was Made
Lesson 3

Objective

Students will evaluate the selection based on specific standards.

Thinking Skills

✦ Evaluating the selection
✦ Drawing conclusions
✦ Proving with examples

Activity

Explain that the Nobel prize is an award given to individuals who make important innovations or advances for the interest of humanity. Tell students that the Nobel prize is comprised of six different categories—chemistry, physics, medicine, literature, promotion of peace, and economics. Then have students reread the selection and provide examples from the reading as they answer the questions.

The Next Step

Have students locate and read another story written by Kipling. As students read, ask them to look for the same qualities described in the quotation on *Responding to Literature* page 84. Then in their Personal Journals, have students write a book review of the story they selected.

Name_____ Date_____

A Closer Look

In 1907, Rudyard Kipling was awarded the Nobel Laureate in Literature. He received this prize "in consideration of the power of observation, originality of imagination, virility of ideas and remarkable talent for narration which characterize the creations of this world-famous author."

Reread "How the Alphabet Was Made" and look for examples of these qualities of writing. Then answer the questions below.

Possible answers below:

1. How does this selection show that Kipling was observant?
   The dialogue Kipling created for Taffy shows he was observant of how children speak.

2. What makes this story original and imaginative?
   Kipling's explanations for the origins of the letters in the alphabet are unique and creative.

3. What do you think is special about the way Kipling tells this story?
   Kipling's use of dialogue allows readers to follow Taffy's and Tegumai's thought process as they "invent" letters.

4. What other comments or questions do you have about Kipling's writing?
   Comments and questions may vary.

84   How the Alphabet Was Made ✦ Open Court Classics

Responding to Literature p. 84

> **Teacher Tip** Tell students that Rudyard Kipling was offered many awards for his talent as a writer; however, he declined most of them. Have students discuss why Kipling might have refused such honors as being made a knight and Poet Laureate, but accepted the Nobel Prize for Literature.

I Wonder

In "How the Alphabet Was Made," the author suggests that a child played a big part in developing the alphabet. The ideas and opinions of young children usually are not taken very seriously. How do you think life might be different if they were? Write a persuasive paragraph to express your ideas on the lines below. Be sure to follow the steps of the writing process.

Persuasive paragraphs may vary.

_____

_____

_____

_____

_____

_____

_____

_____

_____

_____

_____

See Appendix pages 120–121 for persuasive writing and Appendix pages 133–134 for writing a paragraph.

Extra Effort: Meet with a partner to debate how life might be different if the ideas and opinions of young children were taken seriously. Support your position with points raised in your persuasive paragraph.

Open Court Classics ✦ How the Alphabet Was Made　　**85**

Responding to Literature p. 85

Teacher Tip **Writing** Remind students to choose the most effective way to organize their persuasive paragraphs. Suggest that they begin with a question or organize their points by order of importance.

Assessment Use the Persuasive Writing Rubric on Appendix page 146 of the *Teacher's Edition* to assess how well students identify their positions and support their arguments.

Objective

Students will practice expressing and defending their ideas through persuasive writing.

Thinking Skills

✦ Generating ideas
✦ Proving with evidence

Activity

Ask students to recall a time they had an opinion or idea that was not taken seriously by others. Ask them what they think might have happened if their opinion or idea had been taken seriously. Then have students write a persuasive paragraph describing how they think life might be different if children's opinions and ideas had greater influence.

The Next Step

Have students conduct research about inventors who are children. Then have them select a subject and investigate ways the inventor and his or her invention affected the general population. Suggest students investigate organizations, such as Invention Convention, for information. (Be sure to review resources for appropriateness before suggesting them to students.) Have students write a news story about their chosen subject in their Personal Journals. Encourage students to select an invention that has affected communication.

Objective

Students will make inferences based on the selection and write from a scientist's perspective.

Thinking Skills

✦ Making inferences
✦ Describing characteristics of a family during the Neolithic period

Activity

Remind students that a paragraph should have a topic sentence followed by sentences that include supporting details. If students have more than one main idea to express, encourage them to write as many paragraphs as needed. Also remind students to check their work and correct any errors in spelling, grammar, punctuation, or capitalization.

The Next Step

Have students conduct research about family life during the Neolithic period. Then in their Personal Journals, have students create a graphic organizer to compare the information from their research to the Neolithic family in the selection. Encourage students to discuss their opinions about whether the fictional Neolithic family Kipling created was realistic.

Name_____ Date_____

Think like an Anthropologist

Anthropologists are scientists who are interested in finding out about the physical, cultural, and social development of people from prehistoric times to the present. Anthropologists learn about people by studying behaviors, physical traits, and artifacts.

Return to "How the Alphabet Was Made" and review how the author describes the characters. Consider what the characters say and the daily tasks each one performs. Then using this information from the text, write a paragraph about the family unit in the Neolithic period.

The Neolithic Family

Students might describe the characters as imaginative, playful, caring, and inquisitive. The daily tasks performed by the characters might include fishing, gathering, hanging hides, and cooking.

See Appendix pages 133–134 for writing a paragraph.

Extra Effort: When you have finished writing, investigate some of the ideas in your paragraph. How does your research support or contradict your ideas?

86 How the Alphabet Was Made ✦ **Open Court Classics**

Responding to Literature p. 86

Teacher Tip Write the word *Neolithic* on the board. Tell students that that the root word *lithic* comes from the Greek word *lithos,* which means "stone." Then explain that *neo* comes from the Greek word *neos,* which means "new." Point out that the Neolithic period is also referred to as the New Stone Age.

Name_____Date_____

Check It Out

Everything we use, even the alphabet, was invented or discovered at some point in time. Some inventions and discoveries have been so important that they changed the way people live. In "How the Alphabet Was Made" Tegumai tells his daughter, "I believe we've found out *the* big secret of the world." Throughout history, people, such as inventors of the typewriter, Morse code, and the telephone, probably have had the same thought about their innovations.

List some inventions and discoveries that you think have made an important difference in the way people communicate.
Inventions and discoveries may vary.

_____

_____

Choose one of these inventions or discoveries and research it. As you research, take notes in your Personal Journal.

Present your information in the form of a friendly letter addressed to the inventor or discoverer. Your letter should be from the point of view of a person whose way of communicating was changed by the invention or discovery.

On the lines below, write any new questions or ideas that you have about communication.
Questions or ideas may vary.

_____

_____

See Appendix page 130 for writing a friendly letter.

Open Court Classics ✦ How the Alphabet Was Made   87

Responding to Literature p. 87

> **Assessment** Use the *Responding to Literature* pages as an informal assessment of students' understanding of the selection and of their ability to make inferences and evaluate text.

Objective

Students will conduct research about an important communication tool and write a friendly letter.

Thinking Skills

✦ Identifying facts
✦ Determining relevance

Activity

Ask students what it would be like to be without many of the things they use in their daily lives. Then have students identify some communication tools that have had a great impact on people's lives and choose one to investigate. Encourage students to think creatively about methods of communicating. For example, ask them how artists and musicians convey meaning and how their works affect others. Remind students to write from the point of view of someone whose way of communicating was changed by the innovation.

The Next Step

Ask students to consider devices that they think would enhance the way we communicate today. Then have students invent a new communication tool and explain its benefits. Encourage students to create a drawing or model of their invention to share with the rest of the class.

Someday

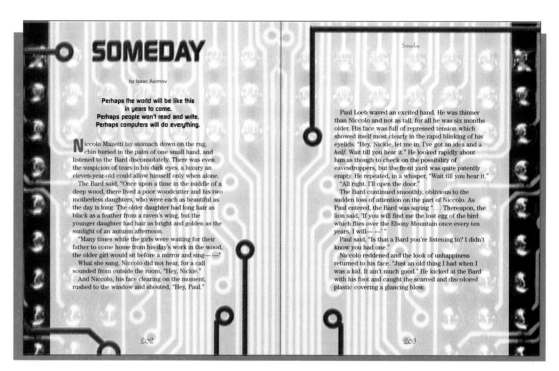

Student Anthology pp. 202–219

Selection Goals

- To recognize that science fiction addresses unrealistic situations in a realistic way

- To write an alternative ending corresponding to the genre

- To understand the author's vision of the future and the ways in which people will communicate

Selection Summary

Isaac Asimov loved writing stories about the impact of scientific advances upon human beings. Innovations in computer technology and robotics were of particular interest to Asimov. In the selection "Someday," the author considers a future in which people rely so heavily on computers that reading and writing have become obsolete forms of communication.

Genre: Science Fiction

Share with students some of the elements of science fiction, which include

- how characters solve problems in a futuristic setting anywhere in the universe.

- humans, extraterrestrials, or members of other species.

- the effects of science and technology on life.

⟶ *Part 1* ⟵
Building Background

Activate Prior Knowledge

✦ Ask students to share what they know about the science fiction genre. Invite them to discuss movies they have seen and books and stories they have read from this genre.

✦ Ask students to name some modern communication tools that are replacing or have replaced other forms of equipment. For example, ask students to consider what items are commonly used instead of a typewriter or a record player.

Background Information

✦ Works of science fiction have been written since ancient times. Greek and Roman myths often included tales of imaginary people and places. Stories about traveling to the moon date back as far as the seventeenth century.

✦ Isaac Asimov was a scientist, teacher, and writer. Asimov wrote more than 400 books on a variety of topics, but he is most well known for his works of science fiction.

✦ Tell students that the storytelling computer in this selection is called the Bard. Ask students if anyone is familiar with the term *bard.* Explain that a bard was a storyteller and poet who roamed from place to place to entertain people with stories and poems. In addition to science fiction, Isaac Asimov wrote about many other subjects, including the English playwright and poet William Shakespeare, perhaps the most famous bard of all time.

✦ Remind students that science fiction stories are often set in the future, as is the case with this selection.

Previewing the Literature

Browse the Selection

✦ Have students note the title as well as the name of the author. Then have students browse the first couple of pages of the selection to look for anything that catches their attention, such as unfamiliar words. Remind students to stop and clarify any new words or passages as they read the selection.

✦ Note on the board those things students mention as a result of their browsing and any questions they have about the selection.

Set Purposes for Reading

Have students set purposes for reading this selection. As they read, encourage students to focus on elements of science fiction found in the selection and the author's purpose.

Expanding Vocabulary

The words listed below can be found in the Glossary of the **Student Anthology.** Page numbers indicate where the words can be found in the selection.

bard, p. 202   A poet who wrote and narrated verses about leaders and heroes.

oblivious, p. 203   Not aware or mindful of.

winced, p. 204   Moved suddenly or involuntarily, as in pain or distress.

condescending, p. 204   Having a superior attitude.

begrudged, p. 206   Gave unwillingly and with displeasure.

censorship, p. 209   The act of examining books, films, or other material to remove what is considered morally, politically, or otherwise objectionable. [Latin *censor,* Roman *censor,* from *censere,* "to assess."]

random, p. 217   Made or done with no clear pattern; made or done by chance.

Teacher Tip
This selection has a large number of words that are likely to be unfamiliar to students. In addition to the vocabulary words listed above, encourage students to record in their Personal Journals any other words from the selection that they would like to learn and remember.

✥ *Part 2* ✥

Reading the Selection

Read

✦ Have students silently read **Student Anthology** pages 202–219, stopping at the end of each page if they have any questions or need clarification.

✦ Encourage students to use monitoring and clarifying or any other comprehension strategies that might help them read the selection.

Discuss

The following discussion suggestions can be carried out on different days, depending upon how much time you allot to each selection.

✦ Ask students what this selection adds to the theme that the other selections do not.

✦ Encourage students to review any questions they listed on the board before reading to see if the selection answered their questions.

✦ Have students discuss which elements of science fiction are in this selection.

✦ Have students discuss the author's purpose for writing this selection. Ask them to consider whether there is a lesson or message.

✦ Have students discuss Niccolo's ambivalent feelings about the Bard and how Asimov communicates to readers Niccolo's fondness for it.

After students have discussed the selection, choose from *Responding to Literature* pages 88–93, and ask students to complete the assigned pages.

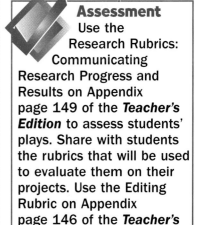

Teacher Tip
Writing During the editing stage of the writing process, encourage students to check for errors in spelling, punctuation, capitalization, usage, and grammar. Suggest that students ask a peer to help edit their scripts.

✧ *Part 3* ✧
Knowledge-Building Project

Students should begin reviewing and editing their plays. Emphasize the importance of reading scripts out loud. Explain that this will help students identify parts that sound awkward and need to be improved. You might also suggest that students have a peer or family member read their scripts out loud. This will provide students with the opportunity to listen to their own scripts and identify any errors or discrepancies. As students revise and edit their work, tell them to assess whether the mood they had intended to create is communicated through the characters and the setting and whether their intended message is effectively conveyed to the audience. Students should also focus on maintaining consistency in the characters' speech and actions to establish a clear personality for each character.

Assessment
Use the Research Rubrics: Communicating Research Progress and Results on Appendix page 149 of the *Teacher's Edition* to assess students' plays. Share with students the rubrics that will be used to evaluate them on their projects. Use the Editing Rubric on Appendix page 146 of the *Teacher's Edition* to assess students' revisions of their scripts.

Students' final drafts should include a description of the setting, a list of characters, and stage directions. Suggest that they also think about scenery, props, or costumes they could use to enhance their plays. Encourage students to rehearse their shows several times before making their final presentations.

By the end of this selection, students should be ready to perform their plays.

Someday

Lesson 1

Objective

Students will learn to use affixes to comprehend word meanings.

Thinking Skills

✦ Identifying affixes
✦ Defining and comprehending unfamiliar words

Activity

Reiterate to students that an *affix* is a syllable or group of syllables added to a word to change its meaning. Remind them that a *prefix* is added to the beginning of a word and a *suffix* is added to the end of a word. Tell students that for this activity they should try to comprehend the meanings of the words using only the word parts, but they may rely on context clues in the sentences if necessary. If students find it challenging to remember the meanings of some prefixes and suffixes, have them think about other words they know that have the same parts. For example, students might think about the meaning of the prefix *de-* in *defrost* to determine the meaning of the word *decode*.

The Next Step

Have students look up the words from the activity in a dictionary to compare the dictionary definitions with those they created.

Name_____ Date_____

Getting Started

"Someday" contains several technical terms and other words that might be new to you. You can often figure out the meaning of an unfamiliar word by looking at the root word and then its affix(es). Below are some sentences from the selection. Identify the affix(es) of each underlined word and write each affix's meaning. Then use the meaning of the affix(es) and the root word to write your own definition of the word. **Possible answers below:**

"He kicked at the Bard with his foot and caught the scarred and <u>discolored</u> plastic covering a glancing blow."

Affix(es): dis-: Not; -ed: Past tense.

My Definition: Definitions may vary.

"Mr. Daugherty says that, in olden days, everybody learned how to make squiggles when they were kids and how to <u>decode</u> them, too."

Affix(es): de-: Reverse.

My Definition: Definitions may vary.

"It was quietly taking in the slowly unreeling book, and the sound of the book's <u>vocalizations</u> was a dimly heard murmur."

Affix(es): -ize: To produce; -ation: Action; -s: Plural.

My Definition: Definitions may vary.

"But not in its usual voice somehow, in a lower tone that had a hint of <u>throatiness</u> in it."

Affix(es): -y: Like or full of; -ness: Quality or state.

My Definition: Definitions may vary.

88   Someday ✦ Open Court Classics

Responding to Literature p. 88

Teacher Tip Encourage students to make a list of prefixes and suffixes and their meanings. Suggest that students create an "Affix Dictionary" for their lists of affixes. Making the list will provide students with a good reference source and will reinforce the meanings of the affixes.

Name_____ Date_____

A Closer Look

The word *personality* describes the qualities or traits that are specific to a person. Personality traits distinguish one person's character or behavior from others. Some examples of personality traits are trustworthiness, respectfulness, and fairness. What are some of your personality traits?
Personality traits may vary.

_____

The two main characters in "Someday" are eleven-year-old boys who share some of the same interests, but seem to have very different personalities. List traits that describe each boy's personality, and support your descriptions with examples from the selection. **Possible answers below:**

	Personality Trait	Example from the Selection
Niccolo	**Sensitive**	**Niccolo's feelings are hurt when Paul criticizes the Bard.**
Paul	**Curious**	**Paul wants to learn more about the squiggles.**

How do you think each boy's personality traits would affect the way he communicated with others?
Answers may vary.

_____

_____

Responding to Literature p. 89

Teacher Tip Tell students to think about the reasons Asimov gave certain traits to each boy. Have students discuss whether Asimov wanted readers to be partial to one of the characters.

Lesson 2

Objective

Students will analyze characters and support their analyses with examples from the selection.

Thinking Skills

✦ Analyzing characters
✦ Proving with evidence

Activity

Encourage students to skim the selection to identify clues about Niccolo's and Paul's personality traits. Suggest to students that when considering the characters' personality traits, they look at what the characters say and do in addition to what the author says about them. Explain that readers can learn a lot about a character from his or her words and actions. Then have students complete the chart and answer the question with a thoughtful response.

The Next Step

Have pairs of students perform passages from the selection as a dramatic reading. To help students get in character for the reading, remind them to review the personality traits they identified for each boy and consider how the traits influence the way each boy communicates.

UNIT 5

Someday

Lesson 3

Objective

Students will make personal choices and explain their reasoning.

Thinking Skills

✦ Determining relevance
✦ Justifying choices

Activity

Have students choose works they would enter into the Bard. Encourage them to think about the pieces they choose from a variety of perspectives. Students should consider a work's historical and moral importance in addition to its entertainment and educational value. Some students might find it limiting to choose only four selections for the Bard. Encourage these students to expand this activity and create a "Top 10" list in their Personal Journals.

The Next Step

Have students choose a story, poem, book, or song from their lists and bring it to class. Encourage students to share the selection with classmates, discuss why they chose the selection, and explain its significance.

Name_____ Date_____

What Would You Do?

In the selection, Paul criticizes the outdated Bard at Niccolo's house and changes the Bard "so it'll know about computers and automation and electronics and real things about today. Then it can tell interesting stories, you know, instead of about princesses and things." What are your reactions to the changes Paul makes to the Bard?
Reactions may vary.

_____

Imagine that you could choose what would be entered into the Bard. What writings do you find entertaining, educational, and/or important? On the lines below, list four stories, poems, books, or songs that you would include when programming the Bard. Then explain why these works are important.

Answers may vary.

1. **Title:** _____

   Reason for Including: _____

   _____

2. **Title:** _____

   Reason for Including: _____

   _____

3. **Title:** _____

   Reason for Including: _____

   _____

4. **Title:** _____

   Reason for Including: _____

   _____

90   Someday ✦ Open Court Classics

Responding to Literature p. 90

Teacher Tip Comprehension Strategies Have students share any problems they encountered while reading "Someday." Ask them how they clarified any confusing ideas or passages.

Assessment Use the Informal Comprehension Strategies Rubrics: Monitoring and Clarifying on Appendix page 144 of the *Teacher's Edition* to assess students' use of this strategy as they read.

Name_____ Date_____

Lesson 4

I Wonder

Computers play a big role in our world. They make work easier and information more accessible. Computers have also changed the way we communicate. They allow people from all over the world to share information and send messages. Consider the different ways you communicate as you respond to the questions below.

Possible answers below:

1. What could happen if people become too dependent on computers for communication?

   Humans could forget the feeling of receiving a letter from a friend. People could lose their conversation skills.

2. How would the way people treat and respect each other change if they only used a computer to communicate?

   Communicating only by computer could make people less courteous to one another.

3. How would always communicating through a computer change your life and the way you communicate?

   Answers may vary.

Extra Effort: Research the history of computers. Investigate how computers and their effects on communication have changed throughout history. Record your discoveries on a time line to share with classmates.

Open Court Classics ✦ Someday   **91**

Responding to Literature p. 91

Teacher Tip As students complete the assigned *Responding to Literature* pages, be sure they are preparing for their final presentations.

Objective

Students will think reflectively and express their ideas through personal writing to answer questions.

Thinking Skills

✦ Making inferences
✦ Predicting

Activity

Encourage students to base their predictions on personal experiences and knowledge as they answer the questions on *Responding to Literature* page 91. Encourage students to focus on the character aspect of the questions. Ask them to consider what they value about their personal relationships with other people.

The Next Step

Ask students if they think computers will ever have the ability to feel emotion and whether this would change their ideas about the impact of computers on human communication. Then have students write a short story to show how another aspect of life might be affected if computers were the main source of communication. Encourage students to include elements of science fiction in their writing and share their thoughts with classmates.

UNIT 5

Someday

Lesson 5

Objective

Students will model the author's style to write an alternate ending to the selection.

Thinking Skills

✦ Adding to the selection

✦ Extrapolating information

Activity

Have students expand on the Bard's final sentence in the selection and then write an alternate ending. Emphasize to students the importance of writing an ending that is cohesive with the rest of the selection. Encourage them to return to the selection and take notes on aspects of the author's writing, such as tone and word choice. Remind students to incorporate these ideas in their writing.

The Next Step

Have a group discussion that allows students to exchange ideas about how they would like to see the selection end. Invite volunteers to share their concluding paragraphs with the class. Then encourage students to discuss their ideas about the future of modern communication and changes they predict might occur.

Name_____ Date_____

I Can Do It, Too

An *autobiography* is a story that a person tells about his or her own life. At the end of "Someday," the Bard is telling what seems to be an autobiographical story. The story also includes the Bard's predictions about future relationships between people and computers. The Bard, however, leaves the listeners in suspense as it simply repeats, "Someday-someday-someday."

Reread the last five paragraphs of the selection. Focus on the author's train of thought and elements of the science-fiction genre as you read. Record your observations in your Personal Journal. Next imagine what the Bard would have said if it had not become stuck. Finish the Bard's sentence on the lines below, then rewrite the final paragraph of the story.

"And the little computer knew then that computers would always grow wiser and more powerful until someday

Sentences may vary.

_____

_____

My Final Paragraph

Paragraphs may vary.

_____

_____

_____

_____

_____

_____

_____

See Appendix page 126 for tips for writing science fiction and Appendix pages 133–134 for writing a paragraph.

92 Someday ✦ Open Court Classics

Responding to Literature p. 92

Teacher Tip Writing Remind students that in narrative writing, a story has a clear beginning, middle, and end. Point out that by repeating the title, "Someday," Asimov ended the story the same way he began it. You might suggest to students that they also refer to an earlier part of the story in their conclusions. Have them review the selection for a significant line or passage that would contribute to a strong ending.

Name_____ Date_____

In My Opinion

François René de Chateaubriand (1768-1848), an important French author, said, "Take away the art of writing from this world, and you will probably take away its glory."

In "Someday," the art of writing *is* gone, and writing has become a science instead. Computers create stories with different combinations of "vocabulary, characters, plot lines, and climaxes." While all of these elements are part of a good story, what other elements does good writing require? How are stories manufactured by a computer different from stories written by people? Write your opinion in the form of a persuasive paragraph. Remember to follow the steps of the writing process.

My Opinion

Persuasive paragraphs may vary.

_____

_____

_____

_____

_____

_____

_____

_____

_____

_____

_____

See Appendix pages 120–121 for persuasive writing and Appendix pages 133–134 for writing a paragraph.

Open Court Classics ✦ Someday   **93**

Responding to Literature p. 93

Assessment Use the Narrative Writing Rubric on Appendix page 146 of the *Teacher's Edition* to assess students' narrative paragraphs.

Assessment Use the *Responding to Literature* pages as an informal assessment of students' understanding of the selection and of their ability to express personal ideas in writing.

Lesson 6

Objective

Students will formulate opinions and express them through persuasive writing.

Thinking Skill

Formulating an opinion

Activity

Tell students that Isaac Asimov was a prolific writer who loved his profession. They might find this information particularly interesting considering that Asimov wrote a story about a time when writers are no longer needed. Have students write a persuasive paragraph about writing as an art versus writing as a science. Remind them to support their opinions with reasons.

The Next Step

Have students meet with peers to discuss whether they agree or disagree with the quotation from French author de Chateaubriand. Encourage them to discuss what he means by *glory* and to consider what might happen to the art of reading if the art of writing were lost. For example, would listening to a computer tell a story provide the same feelings and emotions that reading a book provides?

𝒲rap-Up

Knowledge-Building Project

Students have completed their investigations and should now be ready to present their plays. Plays can be performed in small groups or before the entire class. Remind students to speak clearly and loudly. Encourage students to respond to each production by commenting on how the dialogue, facial expressions, character movement, and so on, were used to communicate information. Also have students tell what new facts they learned about communication. Use the Research Rubrics: Overall Assessment of Research on Appendix page 149 of the *Teacher's Edition* to assess students' knowledge-building projects as a whole.

Reviewing the Concepts

In this unit students investigated a variety of reasons and ways people communicate. With settings that range from the ancient past to the distant future, the selections underscore our basic need to exchange ideas and information. Students investigated some of the following key concepts in this unit:

✦ Communication exists between humans and nature and among elements of the natural world.

✦ Written language has been an important form of communication since ancient times.

✦ In the future computers might replace some form of human communication.

Evaluating the Unit

✦ Ask students to evaluate each selection on the basis of effectiveness of reading/vocabulary, literary value, interest of the subject matter, style of writing, application of theme, and the selection's personal value to the student.

✦ Ask students to evaluate the different activities in the unit, including the knowledge-building project. Have them consider these questions: Which activities made you think? Which ones did you find less challenging and why? Which ones seemed confusing? Which activities did you most enjoy and why? Which activities changed your opinions and offered new ideas? Which activities stimulated novelty and original thinking? What activities would you like to add to the unit?

✦ Ask students to evaluate this *Open Court Classics* unit. They can describe how the theme was explored in the unit. They can also compare and contrast the selections based on the genres and the authors' purposes.

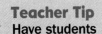

Teacher Tip
Have students record in their Personal Journals the forms of communication they use throughout the course of a day. Encourage students to discuss their lists with adults from different generations and compare the forms of communication used by people of different ages.

Assessment

Vocabulary Assessment

To assess students' understanding of the vocabulary words, you might want to do one of the following:

✦ Have students use the vocabulary words from the unit in the correct context to write a story.

✦ Have students create a game using the vocabulary words from the unit in the correct context.

✦ Administer an informal oral assessment. Have students supply the definition of the vocabulary words or use the words properly in sentences.

Informal Comprehension Strategies Rubrics

Use the Informal Comprehension Strategies Rubrics: Asking Questions, Summarizing, and Monitoring and Clarifying on Appendix pages 144–145 of the **Teacher's Edition** to determine whether a student is using a particular strategy or strategies as he or she reads the selections. Note these and any other strategies a student is using, instead of the degree to which a student might be using any particular strategy. In addition, encourage the student to tell of any strategies other than the ones being taught that he or she is using.

Research Rubrics

Use the Research Rubrics: Recognizing Information Needs, Finding Needed Information, Communicating Research Progress and Results, and Overall Assessment of Research on Appendix pages 148–149 of the **Teacher's Edition** to assess a student's performance throughout the investigation. The rubrics range from 1 to 4 in most categories, with 1 being the lowest score. In addition, you can use the rubrics to assess a group's collaborative work as well as an individual's participation in that group.

Writing Rubrics

Use the Genre Writing Rubric, the Poetry Writing Rubric, the Persuasive Writing Rubric, the Editing Rubric, and the Narrative Writing Rubric on Appendix page 146 of the **Teacher's Edition** to assess student writing. The rubrics range from 1 to 4 in most categories, with 1 being the lowest score.

$\mathcal{O}$verview

UNIT 6 • A Changing America

There is a New America every morning when we wake up.
—Adlai E. Stevenson—

Unit Goals

- To recognize the magnitude of Frederick Douglass's autobiography
- To consider how Douglass effected change in America
- To appreciate the challenges undertaken by workers who built America's first transcontinental railroad
- To evaluate how the transcontinental railroad changed America
- To identify qualities that characterize an American work
- To make connections between themes in literature and fine art
- To create a picture essay or photo-essay about a historical document

Introduction

This unit will take students on a historical journey from this country's period of slavery to a celebration of the industrious individuals who contributed to America's progress and success. Selection 1 is "Escape from Slavery: The Boyhood of Frederick Douglass in His Own Words" on page 222, accompanied by the poem "Frederick Douglass" on page 231; Selection 2 is "Rails Across the Country" on page 232; and Selection 3 is "I Hear America Singing" on page 242, accompanied by the painting *July Hay* on page 243. Students will examine how America has changed and how it has stayed the same.

Unit Discussion

Invite students to share their ideas about life in America during the 1800s. Discuss how early American life might have compared to living in modern America. Continue the discussion by asking questions such as the following:

✦ What does the quotation in the unit opener mean?

✦ How has this country changed for the better or worse throughout time?

✦ How do you think citizens of other countries viewed America in the 1800s? How do you think their views are different today?

Knowledge-Building Project

Residents of America have always had certain expectations for life in this country, such as independence and stability. Many important historical documents reveal how America's leaders have attempted to satisfy these needs of their fellow citizens. Have students list documents that have significantly affected the way of life in America. Lists might include documents, such as the Declaration of Independence and the Articles of Confederation. Students might also list important laws, speeches, and treaties, such as the Gettysburg Address and the Treaty of Paris. Encourage students to apply what they learn from the selections to their knowledge-building projects. As a final product, students will use the information they gathered from their research to prepare a picture essay or photo-essay that illustrates a historical document's influence on American life. Explain that a picture essay or photo-essay tells a story through images instead of words. Encourage students to consider a variety of ways that they might present their picture essays or photo-essays. For example, students might consider displaying their images on a poster board or creating a Web site to display their stories.

> **Teacher Tip**
> As an alternative to the outlined project, you might suggest that students write a biographical report about an important figure in American history.

	Unit 6 Project Overview
Unit Overview	Students brainstorm a list of significant documents in American history.
Selection 1	Students select a topic and make a conjecture about the document's influence on American life.
Selection 2	Students collect images that represent the meaning of the document and illustrate its effects.
Selection 3	Students compile and organize the images they have chosen and write captions describing them.
Unit Wrap-Up	Students present their picture essays or photo-essays.

Escape from Slavery

Escape from Slavery:
The Boyhood of
Frederick Douglass
in His Own Words

Chapter One from *Escape from Slavery*
edited by Michael McCurdy

Introduction

Frederick Douglass was born in a small cabin near Hillsborough (now spelled Hillsboro), in Talbot County, Maryland, probably in 1817. He spent his early childhood on one of the thirteen farms that made up Edward Lloyd's immense wheat-producing plantation. Lloyd's chief manager, Aaron Anthony, was Frederick's first owner.

The cabin where Frederick lived was built of rough slabs of bark, with a floor made from the clay of nearby Tuckahoe Creek. As a small boy, he had no privacy in the cramped cabin that he shared with several cousins, two younger sisters, his grandparents Betsey and Isaac Bailey, and his grandmother's little son. To enable her daughters to work on the plantation, Betsey was expected to care for their children. She was a slave, but Isaac was a freeman. The family may originally have been brought from the West Indies to be sold to Maryland tobacco farmers.

Frederick's early years were relatively carefree. He explored the woods and creek around the cabin and enjoyed a loving home life. All this was to change abruptly when at the age of six he was sent to live in his owner's house. He accompanied his grandmother on the long walk, unaware of what was about to happen. Soon after their arrival, she left quietly, without Frederick knowing, until one of the children at his new home cried, "Fed, Fed! Grandmammy gone, Grandmammy gone!"

Student Anthology pp. 222–231

Selection Goals

- To appreciate the historical significance of Frederick Douglass's autobiography
- To recognize the changes that transpired as a result of Douglass's ideas

Selection Summary

Frederick Douglass, born into a life of adversity, recalls the inhumanity that he and others endured as slaves. This selection is excerpted from a book by the same title, which is an edited version of Douglass's autobiography *Narrative of the Life of Frederick Douglass: An American Slave*. In addition to "Escape from Slavery," students will read the poem "Frederick Douglass" by Robert Hayden.

Genre: Autobiography

Share with students some of the elements of an autobiography, which include

- an account by a person about his or her life.

- details about how the person talks, feels, or thinks.

- the entirety of the person's life or only an important part of the person's life.

- the most important events in the person's life.

✧ *Part 1* ✧

Building Background

Activate Prior Knowledge

✦ Ask students what they know about slavery in the United States. Have them discuss how it contributed to the Civil War. Encourage students to recall what they have learned about this period in America's history in previous units.

✦ Have students discuss autobiographies they have read. Ask them why they think people write about challenges they have faced and how readers might benefit from reading about such challenges.

Background Information

✦ Frederick Augustus Washington Bailey, the son of a slave woman and an unnamed white man, was born into slavery in rural Maryland. At the age of six, Frederick traveled with his grandmother to the Lloyd Plantation where he was left to live and work for the next two years. Frederick was then sent to Baltimore to live and work with a shipbuilder named Hugh Auld. It was there that he learned to read and write, although it was against the law. Seven years later Frederick was sent to work on a farm, where he was cruelly beaten and nearly starved. He was later returned to Baltimore and, while working in a shipyard in September 1838, fled to freedom in New York. A few weeks later he moved to New Bedford, Massachusetts, under his new name, Frederick Douglass.

> **Teacher Tip**
> Tell students that the child mentioned in the introduction to the selection (the one who told Frederick his grandmother had left) is believed to be Frederick's sibling. A brother and two sisters were already at work on the plantation where Frederick was taken at the age of six.

✦ *Narrative of the Life of Frederick Douglass: An American Slave* was the first of three autobiographies by Frederick Douglass. Douglass published his first autobiography in 1845, then expanded it in his 1855 book *My Bondage and My Freedom. Life and Times of Frederick Douglass*, published in 1881, is Douglass's autobiography in its final form.

✦ In December 1865 the Thirteenth Amendment to the United States Constitution was ratified, officially abolishing slavery in all areas of the country.

Previewing the Literature

Browse the Selection

✦ Have students browse the entire selection for anything that catches their attention, such as unfamiliar words or clues that tell how this selection relates to the unit theme.

✦ Note on the board those things students mention as a result of their browsing and any questions they have about the selection.

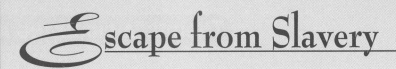

Set Purposes for Reading

Have students set purposes for reading the selection. As they read, encourage students to focus on the elements of an autobiography.

Expanding Vocabulary

The words listed below can be found in the Glossary of the **Student Anthology.** Page numbers indicate where the words can be found in the selection.

tidings, p. 225 — Information or news.

bushel, p. 226 — A measure for dry goods; a bushel is equal to 32 quarts.

esteemed, p. 228 — Thought highly of.

rude, p. 228 — Unpolished; primitive.

incoherent, p. 228 — Not clear.

testimony, p. 228 — A statement.

conceive, p. 228 — To imagine or to form an idea. [Middle English, from Latin *concipere,* "to take in."]

impose, p. 229 — To force or make unfair demands on a person.

→Part 2←
Reading the Selection

Read

✦ Have students silently read **Student Anthology** pages 222–231, stopping at the end of each page if they have any questions or need clarification.

✦ Encourage students to use visualizing or any other comprehension strategies that might help them read the selection.

Discuss

The following discussion suggestions can be carried out on different days, depending upon how much time you allot to each selection.

✦ Have students discuss their general reactions to the selection.

✦ Ask students how this selection relates to the theme.

✦ Encourage students to review any questions they listed on the board before reading to see if the selection answered their questions.

✦ Have students discuss the impact that Douglass's personal story might have had on people's perception of the institution of slavery.

✦ Ask students for what audience they think Douglass wrote his autobiography. Encourage them to discuss the similarities and differences between how his story might have been received in 1845 and how it is viewed today.

After students have discussed the selection, choose from **Responding to Literature** pages 94–101, and ask students to complete the assigned pages.

⤳ *Part 3* ⤝

Knowledge-Building Project

Have students review their list of important historical documents and conduct some preliminary research to help them narrow their choices and select a topic. Encourage students to utilize a variety of print and nonprint sources. For example, students might draw on community resources, such as museums or historical societies, or other reference sources, such as the Internet or films. Once students have selected a document to investigate, have them make conjectures about how the document influenced American society. Encourage students to consider not only the immediate effects of the document, but also how its impact is still felt or exhibited today.

Students should then begin researching their chosen document and recording their notes in their Personal Journals. Suggest that students look for information about events or conditions that led to the creation of the document. Students might also investigate the author(s) of the document and the people directly affected by the document.

By the end of the next selection, students should have begun to create or collect images for their picture essays or photo-essays.

> **Teacher Tip**
> Tell students that the Declaration of Independence, the Constitution, and the Bill of Rights are called the Charters of Freedom. These documents are on display at the National Archives Building in Washington, D.C.

> **Assessment**
> Use the Research Rubrics: Making Conjectures on Appendix page 148 of the *Teacher's Edition* to assess how well students make conjectures. Discuss with students the rubrics that will be used to evaluate them on their projects.

UNIT 6

Escape from Slavery

Lesson 1

Objective

Students will learn to identify a paradox, formulate related questions, and make comparisons between ideas.

Thinking Skills

✦ Comparing and contrasting ideas
✦ Formulating questions

Activity

Discuss with students the Declaration of Independence and its authors. If necessary, explain that the Declaration of Independence was drafted by Thomas Jefferson to proclaim the American colonists' independence from Great Britain. Next have students think about this selection and its author. Encourage students to consider Douglass's and Jefferson's circumstances as they complete the activity.

The Next Step

Read the following passage from Frederick Douglass's famous speech "The Meaning of July Fourth for the Negro": "The rich inheritance of justice, liberty, prosperity and independence, bequeathed by your fathers, is shared by you, not by me. The sunlight that brought light and healing to you, has brought stripes and death to me. This Fourth July is yours, not mine. You may rejoice, I must mourn." Then have students write a paragraph reacting to Douglass's thoughts regarding the Declaration of Independence.

Name_____ Date_____

UNIT 6 A Changing America • *Escape from Slavery*

Getting Started

In this selection you read Frederick Douglass' account of the poor treatment of slaves and the freedoms they were denied. However, the United States was founded on the belief that all people are equal. Why does that make the treatment of slaves particularly hard to understand?

Possible answer: The poor treatment of slaves goes against the statement that all people are equal; slaves and white people were not treated equally.

A *paradox* is a statement that has conflicting ideas and seems both true and false. For example, the expression "All is possible, the impossible too" is a paradox. Think about the paradox between the ideas expressed in the Declaration of Independence and what you read about in this selection. Then record questions and ideas that you have on the lines below.

Questions and ideas may vary.

_____

_____

_____

_____

_____

_____

_____

_____

_____

_____

94   Escape from Slavery ✦ Open Court Classics

Responding to Literature p. 94

> **Teacher Tip** Make available copies of the Declaration of Independence for students to read. Encourage students to identify specific phrases from this document and passages from the selection that appear to contradict one another.

94   **Unit 6** A Changing America ✦ **Escape from Slavery**

Making Connections

The selection "Escape from Slavery" can raise some interesting ideas about people's rights and about how people treat each other. What are some ideas and questions you thought about as you read the selection?

Ideas and questions may vary.

_____

_____

Recall what you know about nineteenth-century America. How was life during this time different from life today? How might our behavior toward each other have changed over time? Use the Venn diagram below to show the similarities and differences between the way Americans treated one another in the 1800s and the way they treat one another today.

Answers may vary.

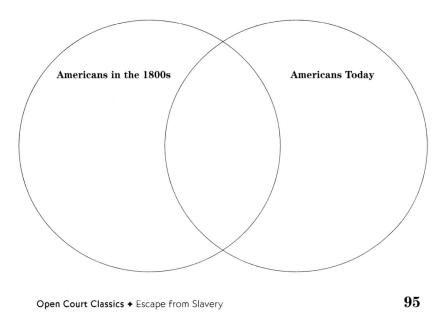

Americans in the 1800s   Americans Today

Open Court Classics ✦ Escape from Slavery   **95**

Responding to Literature p. 95

A CHANGING AMERICA

Lesson 2

Objective

Students will formulate questions and compare aspects of nineteenth-century America with modern American society.

Thinking Skills

✦ Formulating questions
✦ Comparing and contrasting behaviors
✦ Making connections

Activity

Before students begin this activity, suggest that they gather more information about nineteenth-century America. Have students consider how people's rights have changed from the nineteenth century to today. Encourage students also to consider more than relationships between the slaves and white Americans. For example, ask them to think about how women's rights and roles have changed and how the code of social behavior in general is different.

The Next Step

Have students research the Bill of Rights and other amendments to the Constitution. Encourage students to consider how the content of each amendment reflects on Americans' values at the time it was passed. Then have students write about ways in which Americans' values have changed over time.

Teacher Tip Tell students that at the time Douglass's autobiography was published, he was still considered an escaped slave under federal law. Encourage them to discuss why publishing his autobiography and risking his freedom might have been important to Douglass.

Objective

Students will learn to infer the significance of songs associated with a particular time and place.

Thinking Skills

✦ Making inferences
✦ Making connections

Activity

Explain to students that slaves sang songs as a means of communication. Tell students that slaves used song lyrics as a code to convey hidden messages. For example, the lyrics of a song might be used to warn an escaping slave of danger. Have students reflect on the selection and their prior knowledge as they respond to questions. You might consider providing students with some lyrics to songs so they can analyze the emotions and hidden messages.

The Next Step

Have students discuss how the power of music influences people's emotions. Encourage students to discuss with peers their ideas about music and its ability to promote change. In their Personal Journals have students list ideas that were generated from their discussions.

Name_____ Date_____

In My Opinion

In "Escape from Slavery" Frederick Douglass explains that it is a mistake to think of slaves' singing as a sign that they are satisfied with their lives. Douglass describes the deep sadness he feels while hearing, or even thinking about, the songs. Consider these ideas as you respond to the following questions. **Possible answers below:**

1. Why do you think slaves sing?
   They sing to express their feelings.
   _____
   _____

2. What do you think are the meanings of their songs?
   The songs describe the sadness they feel and the hardships they experience.
   _____

3. Think about the lyrics to a song that you think expresses grievance or protest. Explain what this song has in common with the slaves' songs of the mid 1800s. Use the lyrics of the song you choose to support your answer.
   Answers may vary.
   _____
   _____
   _____

Extra Effort: Investigate the changes music has undergone throughout history. What can account for these changes? How do the lyrics and rhythm of music relate to the events of a specific time period? Write about your ideas in your Personal Journal.

96   Escape from Slavery ✦ Open Court Classics

Responding to Literature p. 96

Teacher Tip Comprehension Strategies Encourage students to tell what they visualized as they were reading. Then have them explain how visualizing helped them better understand the selection.

Assessment Use the Informal Comprehension Strategies Rubrics: Visualizing on Appendix page 145 of the *Teacher's Edition* to assess students' use of this strategy.

Name_____Date_____

Reality Check

Reflect on what you know about the Civil War. Then record the causes of the war on the lines below.

Possible answer: In the North most people wanted

to outlaw slavery, and in the South most people

wanted the right to own slaves.

This selection is set in Maryland, which was a border state during the Civil War. What do you think it meant to be a "border state"? What other states were considered "border states"?

A border state was a state that allowed slavery but

did not withdraw from the Union. Other border

states included Delaware, Kentucky, and Missouri.

What questions do you have about Maryland and the changes occurring in America during the Civil War?

Questions may vary.

List some sources in which you might find answers to your questions.

Sources may vary.

Examine your sources and record the information you find in your Personal Journal. Then choose a way to present the information. For example, you might create a map of the border states or a map illustrating important cities during the war. As you prepare your presentation, consider how these states and cities played a role in the changing of America.

Open Court Classics ✦ Escape from Slavery

97

Responding to Literature p. 97

> **Teacher Tip** As students complete the assigned *Responding to Literature* pages, be sure they progress with making conjectures about a potential research topic for their knowledge-building projects.

Objective

Students will formulate and examine questions about the roles various states played in the Civil War.

Thinking Skills

✦ Formulating questions
✦ Accessing sources

Activity

Although slavery was the primary cause, other complicated issues were factors in the Civil War. Explain that the South's economic system was based upon slavery, and southerners feared the effect abolition would have on their economy. The North wanted to prevent slavery from spreading because they wanted to control southern political power. Most people viewed slavery as a socioeconomic issue rather than a moral one. Have students consider this as they evaluate the Civil War and border states.

The Next Step

It was not uncommon for families to have members in the Union army and in the Confederate army. Ask students to consider the circumstances that might have led to this type of situation. Then have students investigate encyclopedias, films, and so on, to understand more about how and why families were divided by the war.

UNIT 6

Escape from Slavery

Lesson 5

Objective

Students will write an expository essay about a writer's influence in the campaign to end slavery.

Thinking Skills

✦ Evaluating written works
✦ Determining significance
✦ Drawing conclusions

Activity

Explain to students that abolitionists used several tactics to publicize their ideas. Tell them that abolitionists used such methods as public meetings and debates, mass mailings, speeches, and newspaper articles to spread their message. Have students identify an abolitionist author they would like to learn more about. Then encourage students to investigate their chosen author's works, and write an expository essay about his or her role in abolishing slavery.

The Next Step

Encourage students to think about a writer, such as Langston Hughes, who they think has influenced modern American society. Have students choose pieces of this person's writing to investigate. Then in their Personal Journals, have students write a persuasive paragraph describing how this writer has effected change in today's society.

Name_____ Date_____

Read All about It

In addition to his autobiography, Frederick Douglass wrote other books and many speeches and articles. Important works have also been written by other *abolitionists*, people who wanted to end slavery, such as Harriet Beecher Stowe and Thomas Paine. How do you think writers influenced the movement to abolish slavery?

1. Look at sources for information about abolitionist writing. List the names of some authors and works that you would like to investigate.
   Authors and works may vary.
   _____
   _____
   _____
   _____
   _____
   _____

2. Choose an author from your list. Then locate one or more pieces, such as autobiographies or journals, written by that person. Take notes in your Personal Journal.

3. In your Personal Journal, write an expository essay about the writer and his or her work. Include your ideas about the writer's role in the fight to end slavery. Remember to follow the steps of the writing process.

See Appendix page 138 for writing an expository essay.

98   Escape from Slavery ✦ **Open Court Classics**

Responding to Literature p. 98

Teacher Tip **Writing** Encourage students to publish their writing. You might suggest that students bind their expository essays into a book, or that they include illustrations or photographs of their subjects.

Assessment Use the Publishing Writing Rubric on Appendix page 146 of the *Teacher's Edition* to assess the presentation of students' written works.

Name_____ Date_____

Speak Your Mind

Frederick Douglass was a talented writer and speaker who cared about many human rights causes in addition to slavery. For example, he spoke in favor of women's right to vote, better conditions for prisoners, free education in public schools, and world peace. Through his emotional speeches, Douglass was able to influence his listeners. How do you think Douglass achieved these results?

Possible answer: He appealed to the feelings of

his listeners.

Think about a cause or issue that is meaningful to you. It might be something that affects your life directly or something that you have read or heard about. List your ideas on the lines below. Then in your Personal Journal, write your opinion in the form of a speech that you will deliver to the class. Try to include points that will appeal to your audience's emotions.

Ideas may vary.

_____

_____

_____

_____

_____

_____

_____

_____

See Appendix page 136 for writing a speech.

Extra Effort: Investigate another powerful speaker who has impacted listeners with his or her speeches. In your Personal Journal, write about the techniques the speaker used to influence listeners.

Open Court Classics ✦ Escape from Slavery   **99**

Objective

Students will learn to write a persuasive speech that appeals to listeners' emotions.

Thinking Skills

✦ Generating information
✦ Prioritizing personal concerns

Activity

Explain to students that Frederick Douglass believed strongly in the right of freedom for all people and that many of his ideas are still prominent issues today. Then have students complete ***Responding to Literature*** page 99. When they have finished, ask students to discuss what they think Douglass would say about issues in our world today, such as world peace and education.

The Next Step

Provide students with copies of Abraham Lincoln's famous Gettysburg Address and the Emancipation Proclamation. Have students compare the two documents, considering the audience and purpose of each, and then record their comparisons in their Personal Journals.

Responding to Literature p. 99

Teacher Tip **Writing** Encourage students to select a topic they feel passionately about and that is meaningful to them. Remind students to conclude their speeches with a summary of the main points and an appeal to the audience.

Assessment Use the Persuasive Writing Rubric on Appendix page 146 of the *Teacher's Edition* to assess the development and support of students' arguments.

UNIT 6

Frederick Douglass

Lesson 1

Poetry

Vocabulary

The following words are from the poem and might be unfamiliar to students: *diastole, systole, mumbo jumbo, exiled, alien,* and *rhetoric.* Encourage students to locate each word and its meaning in the Glossary of the **Student Anthology** before they read. You might also suggest that students record the words and definitions in their Personal Journals.

Activity

Encourage students to reread "Frederick Douglass" before they respond to questions about the techniques used by the poet. Then have students write poems to express their ideas about freedom. Encourage students to include the elements of poetry they have learned about in their writing.

The Next Step

Have students share their poems with the rest of the class. Encourage listeners to provide feedback after each poem is read. For example, listeners might comment on the effectiveness of the poet's word choice and tone. Listeners might also describe images and feelings that were formed as a result.

Think like a Poet

The poem "Frederick Douglass" is about the author of the selection "Escape from Slavery." Reflect on how the poem, like the selection, refers to some of the cruelty Douglass suffered as a slave. Think about how the poem also honors Douglass as a courageous leader. Refer to the poem as you answer the questions below. **Possible answers below:**

1. How does Robert Hayden use punctuation for effect in this poem? Notice that the first sentence does not end until Line 21.
   Running thoughts together one line after another creates a sense of urgency.

2. The poet uses many adjectives to describe freedom. Why do you think he calls it *beautiful, terrible,* and *needful?*
   Freedom has different meanings to different people.

3. What impact does Hayden's word choice have on the poem?
   Hayden provides readers with strong images and ideas.

What does freedom mean to you? On the lines below, write some ways you would describe freedom. Then in your Personal Journal, include these ideas in a poem of your own.
Responses may vary.

See Appendix page 125 for tips for writing poetry.

100   Escape from Slavery/Frederick Douglass ✦ **Open Court Classics**

Responding to Literature p. 100

> **Teacher Tip** Tell students that in 1976 Robert Hayden became the first African American to be named Consultant in Poetry to the Library of Congress. This position later became known as Poet Laureate.

Name_____ Date_____

A Closer Look

Robert Hayden wrote the poem "Frederick Douglass" in 1962, when many Americans were fighting for civil rights. The goal of the Civil Rights movement was equal rights for African Americans. How might the events of this time period have inspired Hayden to write a poem about Frederick Douglass?

Possible answer: Frederick Douglass had

fought for the same thing; Hayden wanted

people to remember Douglass and his fight.

Reread the poem. Then write a paragraph describing what you think is meant by "equal rights." Include your ideas about whether Americans today have equal rights. Use your Personal Journal to plan and organize your thoughts.

Paragraphs may vary.

_____

_____

_____

_____

_____

_____

_____

_____

_____

_____

See Appendix pages 133–134 for writing a paragraph.

Open Court Classics ✦ Escape from Slavery/Frederick Douglass   **101**

Responding to Literature p. 101

Activity

Explain that *civil rights* refers to the rights, such as fair treatment by the law and the right to vote, that all citizens are guaranteed to receive. Then ask students to complete ***Responding to Literature*** page 101. Encourage students to use examples and reasons to support their opinions about the current state of equal rights in America.

The Next Step

Tell students that many activists, such as Martin Luther King, Jr., Thurgood Marshall, and Rosa Parks, took part in the Civil Rights movement. Encourage students to read more about this era. Then have them make a list of people whom they think were influential in this effort and choose one person to investigate. Encourage students to write about how the efforts of this person created changes in America.

Elements of Poetry

Tell students that "Frederick Douglass" is a free verse poem. Explain that free verse poetry conveys the poet's thoughts or feelings with carefully chosen words, instead of techniques such as rhythm or rhyme. Ask students to identify words in the poem that powerfully communicate the thoughts or feelings of Robert Hayden. Then ask how Hayden's word choice influenced their thoughts and feelings.

Teacher Tip This activity might raise sensitive issues for some members of your class. Encourage all students to express their emotions through writing rather than by confronting one another.

Assessment Use the *Responding to Literature* pages as an informal assessment of students' understanding of the selection and of persuasive writing and evaluating ideas.

Rails Across the Country

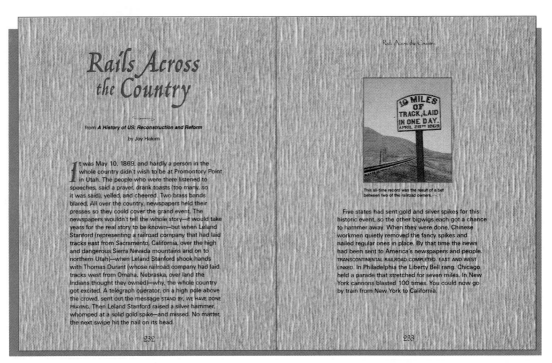

Student Anthology pp. 232–241

Selection Goals

- To identify the elements of expository text
- To recognize how the first transcontinental railroad changed America

Selection Summary

In 1869 a significant change occurred in transportation when it became possible to travel by train from one coast of America to another. This expository selection by author Joy Hakim describes the extraordinary efforts, as well as the corrupt deals, that led to the completion of the United States' first transcontinental railroad.

Genre: Expository Text

Share with students some of the elements of an expository text, which include

- ✦ factual and verifiable information about a specific subject.

- ✦ events presented in the order in which they occurred.

- ✦ writing organized by topics.

- ✦ diagrams, photographs, maps, or illustrations.

❖ *Part 1* ❖
Building Background

Activate Prior Knowledge

✦ Ask students to describe how people traveled across the country before the railroad was built and ways in which the railroad changed travel and the lifestyles of Americans.

✦ Ask students what songs they have heard or books they have read about trains or railroads. Encourage students to share information and ideas from these sources.

Background Information

✦ Both northerners and southerners wanted the transcontinental railroad to connect their regions of the country with the West. However, when the South withdrew from the government, the North was free to choose the route. In 1862 Congress passed the Pacific Railroad Act, which mapped out a route from Omaha, Nebraska, to Sacramento, California.

✦ Losing their land was not the only negative effect the railroad had on Native Americans. The transcontinental railroad also contributed to the devastation of buffalo herds. Native Americans relied on these animals for nutritious food and warm hides that helped them survive harsh winters. Some of the earliest settlers of the West were trappers and traders who sold meat and hides, many thousands of which they shipped back East on trains. In addition, some railroad companies offered tourists the chance to shoot buffalo from train windows.

✦ Joy Hakim received the 1997 James Michener Prize in Writing for her 11-book series A History of US. The Michener Prize, presented by the National Council for the Social Studies, was subsequently discontinued due to a lack of qualified nominations.

Previewing the Literature

Browse the Selection

✦ Because this piece is nonfiction, have students browse the entire selection. Discuss with them what they think the selection conveys about a changing America.

✦ Note on the board those things students mention as a result of their browsing and any questions they have about the selection.

> **Teacher Tip**
> Tell students that before the railroad was built, it took about six months to travel by stagecoach across the United States from coast to coast. The same trip, traveling by train, took only ten days.

Rails Across the Country

Set Purposes for Reading

Have students set purposes for reading, such as to add to their personal knowledge. As they read, encourage students to focus on ways the railroad brought change to America, risks that were taken to build the railroad, and elements of expository writing.

Expanding Vocabulary

The words listed below can be found in the Glossary of the **Student Anthology.** Page numbers indicate where the words can be found in the selection.

contempt, p. 236 — A feeling of disrespect or scorn toward a person.

undertaking, p. 239 — A task or venture.

regulate, p. 239 — To manage or control. [Middle English, from Latin *regula*, "rule."]

foresight, p. 240 — Good judgment in planning for the future.

⟡ Part 2 ⟡
Reading the Selection

Read

✦ Have students silently read **Student Anthology** pages 232–241, stopping at the end of each page if they have any questions or need clarification.

✦ Encourage students to use monitoring and adjusting reading speed or any other comprehension strategies that might help them read the selection.

Discuss

The following discussion suggestions can be carried out on different days, depending upon how much time you allot to each selection.

✦ Have students discuss their general reactions to the selection.

✦ Ask students what this selection adds to the theme that the other selection did not.

✦ Encourage students to review any questions they listed on the board before reading to see if the selection answered their questions.

✦ Ask students whether the selection left them with a positive or negative feeling about America's first transcontinental railroad. Encourage them to discuss the reasons for their feelings.

✦ Have students discuss how rail travel helped to develop the West and why settlers wanted to go there.

After students have discussed the selection, choose from ***Responding to Literature*** pages 102–107, and ask students to complete the assigned pages.

✧ *Part 3* ✧
Knowledge-Building Project

Students should continue to research a selected historical document for additional information about its impact on America and its people. Remind them to focus on information that describes the document's effects on America and its people. Tell students that they will need to make inferences and draw conclusions about the document's influence when considering how it has made a difference in the lives of Americans today.

Remind students that a picture essay or photo-essay tells a story through images instead of words. Tell students that the images they display could include photos they take, pictures they draw or paint, pictures cut from magazines, photocopies made from resource books, and so on. Explain that while captions provide some explanation of the illustrations, the message should be conveyed primarily through pictures or photos. Then have students return to the information they recorded in their Personal Journals. Students should begin making a list of ideas they have about images that represent the significance of the document they are researching. Then have them begin to collect or create the images.

By the end of the next selection, students should have completed their picture essays or photo-essays.

Teacher Tip
If students wish to create their own photo-essays, suggest that they ask a parent or guardian to provide a disposable camera for them to use.

Assessment
Use the Research Rubrics: Revising Problems and Conjectures on Appendix page 149 of the *Teacher's Edition* to assess how well students identify and develop their conjectures. Review with students the rubrics that will be used to evaluate them on their knowledge-building projects.

Objective

Students will identify cause-and-effect relationships from the selection.

Thinking Skills

✦ Distinguishing causes from effects
✦ Identifying relationships

Activity

Ask students to explain how identifying cause-and-effect relationships in expository writing will help their comprehension of a selection. Encourage them to tell how these relationships can help them better understand the events occurring in the selection and the circumstances surrounding the events. Then have students review the selection and identify cause-and-effect relationships. Encourage students also to consider the long-term effects associated with the causes they identify.

The Next Step

Have students investigate how subsequent developments in transportation, the transcontinental railroad in particular, changed train travel. Have students record their findings in their Personal Journals.

Name_____ Date_____

Getting Started

Most accounts of history show how certain actions lead to certain results. These are called *cause-and-effect relationships*. What cause-and-effect relationships can you identify in the selection "Rails Across the Country"?

Reread the selection and look for these relationships. Then in the space below, create a graphic organizer to show connections among events. Answer the question below when you have finished.

Possible graphic organizer and answers below:

Cause		Effect
President Lincoln signs the Pacific Railroad Act.	→	Building of the transcontinental railroad begins.
Government gives subsidies for railway track that is laid.	→	The railroad companies race each other to lay more track.
Thomas Durant owes his workers money.	→	Workers chain his train car to a track.
People can buy things from other states.	→	The United States seems smaller.

How did laying tracks across the country cause a change in America?
People could travel more freely.

102

Rails Across the Country ✦ **Open Court Classics**

Responding to Literature p. 102

Teacher Tip **Comprehension Strategies** Remind students that when a selection contains a large amount of information, good readers slow down or reread certain passages to make sure they understand the text. Ask students where they slowed their reading speed or reread passages to make sure they understood all of the information. Have students tell how using this strategy helped them better understand the selection.

Name_____Date_____

Rails Across the Country • A Changing America **UNIT 6**

In My Opinion

"Rails Across the Country" is from one of many history books written by Joy Hakim. When Hakim was writing her books, she sent copies to schools in several different cities and asked students to read them and give their opinions. In the margins, students wrote a *B* for parts that were boring, *G* for parts that were good, and *NC* for parts that were not clear. She also asked the students to tell her anything else they wanted to know.

Reread the selection as if you were giving feedback to Hakim. In your Personal Journal, write whether you think each paragraph is boring, good, not clear, or a combination of these things. Explain the reasons for the rating you give each paragraph. Then complete the rest of this page.

Other questions or things I would like to know about the railroad:
Responses may vary.

_____

_____

_____

_____

_____

_____

_____

_____

_____

_____

Extra Effort: Research to find answers to your questions. You might also want to investigate changes that have taken place along the railroad route since 1869.

Open Court Classics ✦ Rails Across the Country   **103**

Responding to Literature p. 103

Assessment Use the Informal Comprehension Strategies Rubrics: Monitoring and Adjusting Reading Speed on Appendix page 144 of the *Teacher's Edition* to assess students' use of this strategy.

Teacher Tip Explain that an honest reaction from a reader is a valuable tool for a writer and is an important part of the writing process.

Lesson 2

Objective

Students will learn to evaluate the selection and provide constructive feedback.

Thinking Skills

✦ Evaluating text
✦ Judging content
✦ Formulating questions

Activity

Discuss with students what they think makes writing boring, good, or unclear. Help students develop some guidelines for using the ratings described on ***Responding to Literature*** page 103. Next create a list with students of tips for making writing more interesting and easier to understand. Then have students use the ratings B, G, and NC to evaluate each paragraph of the selection.

The Next Step

Have students refer to a paragraph from the selection that they rated as "boring" or "not clear." Ask students to think about what evidence or additional support could be included to enhance the paragraph. Then in their Personal Journals, have students use their ideas to rewrite the paragraph from the selection.

Objective

Students will formulate and express opinions about the transcontinental railroad's effect on Native Americans.

Thinking Skills

✦ Judging effects
✦ Formulating opinions

Activity

Encourage students to consult sources, such as encyclopedias, documentaries, or the Internet, for additional information about the transcontinental railroad, the people who helped build it, and its effects on Native Americans. Explain that using a variety of print and nonprint sources will help students write more thorough responses as they complete the activity.

The Next Step

Have students organize a debate. One group can argue that it was necessary to use Native American lands for the railroad, and the other group can argue the importance of honoring the treaties. Remind students that a debate requires research and that their ideas should be communicated through supporting details. Tell students that a well-supported and logical argument is crucial to the effectiveness of a debate. Encourage students to read more about the formal rules of debating before they begin.

Name_____ Date_____

UNIT 6 A Changing America • *Rails Across the Country*

Speak Your Mind

Although this selection describes the great celebration that took place when the transcontinental railroad was completed, not everyone in the United States was happy. What do you think were the causes of this displeasure?
Possible answer: Railroad workers were unhappy that they were treated badly while the railroad owners became rich.

The government had promised different groups of Native Americans certain areas of land; however, promises were broken when the government allowed railroads to be built on Native American property.

1. Explain how the railroad changed Native American lifestyles.
   Possible answer: They had to move off the land they once lived on and owned.

2. Explain whether the railroad could or could not have been built without using Native American land. You might want to refer to a map to support your explanation.
   Answers may vary.

3. Explain whether you think that having a railroad across the country was or was not more important than honoring an agreement.
   Answers may vary.

104 Rails Across the Country ✦ **Open Court Classics**

Responding to Literature p. 104

Teacher Tip Provide students with examples of treaties between the United States government and various Native American groups. Many of these documents are available on the Internet. Then ask students how the treaties influenced their opinions.

Rails Across the Country • A Changing America **UNIT 6**

Picture This

Once the tracks were laid, the Central Pacific and Union Pacific railroad companies had to sell their services to customers. Think about the advantages of the railroad as you answer the questions below.

1. What kind of information do you think the railroad companies would have included in their advertisements?

   They would have told people how comfortable

   traveling by train was compared to riding in a

   wagon.

2. What were the benefits of traveling by railroad? How was it different from other forms of transportation available at that time?

   Railroad travel was faster than other forms of

   transportation.

Create a poster as an advertisement for railroad travel in 1869. It can be for one of the railroad companies mentioned in the selection or another company that you create. Use the lines below to make a list of ideas for your poster, such as the information you want to include and the types of illustrations you will use.

Ideas may vary.

See Appendix page 124 for tips for writing an advertisement.

Open Court Classics ✦ Rails Across the Country

105

Responding to Literature p. 105

Teacher Tip Explain to students that it is especially important for advertisers to know their audience and the audience's needs. Encourage students to consider these things before they start to design their posters.

Teacher Tip As students complete the assigned *Responding to Literature* pages, be sure they progress with revising problems and conjectures about a topic for their projects.

Objective

Students will create an advertisement that identifies and illustrates positive aspects of railroad travel.

Thinking Skills

✦ Determining importance and appeal
✦ Generating ideas

Activity

Ask students what the West symbolized to the American people at this time. Explain that advertisers for the railroad industry often glorified the West by describing the land as picturesque and the lifestyle in the region as adventurous. Have students create a poster as an advertisement for a railroad company that offered transcontinental passage.

The Next Step

Have students use the Internet and other sources to investigate actual railroad artifacts from this era, such as posters, historical papers, and iron or steel rails. Then in their Personal Journals, have students record information about the artifact, such as its purpose or significance. Encourage students to provide pictures or illustrations of their artifacts. This activity provides a good opportunity to discuss with students the difference between primary sources and secondary sources.

UNIT 6

Rails Across the Country
Lesson 5

Objectives

✦ Students will make inferences about the impact of the railroad on the towns through which it passed.

✦ Students will design a map and write a friendly letter.

Thinking Skills

✦ Identifying facts
✦ Making inferences

Activity

Have students create a map that shows the route of America's first transcontinental railroad, including several stations and towns on the route. Tell students to make inferences about how the railroad affected life in one of these towns. Then have them write a friendly letter from the perspective of a person living in the town they chose. Encourage students to share their maps and friendly letters with classmates.

The Next Step

Have students conduct research to find out what happened to the towns on the route when railroad stations closed. Then in their Personal Journals, have students write a paragraph about one of the towns and the changes it experienced. You might suggest that students read more about life before the transcontinental railroad to more accurately depict changes.

UNIT 6 A Changing America • *Rails Across the Country*

Reality Check

On May 10, 1869, it became possible to travel by train all the way from New York to California. Railroad track had been laid for 1,776 miles across the United States. You know from the selection that one of the places through which the track passed was Promontory Point, Utah.

Look in reference sources to find out more about the route of the first transcontinental railroad. Use the information you collect to create a map that shows the route of the railroad as well as important stations and towns along the way.

Maps may vary.

Investigate a town shown on your map. Then in your Personal Journal, write a letter to a friend from the point of view of a person living in that town. In your letter, describe how life in the town has changed since the construction of the railroad.

See Appendix page 130 for writing a friendly letter.

106   Rails Across the Country ✦ **Open Court Classics**

Responding to Literature p. 106

Teacher Tip **Writing** Remind students to include the five parts of a friendly letter—the heading, salutation, body, closing, and signature.

Assessment Use the Personal Writing Rubric on Appendix page 146 of the *Teacher's Edition* to assess how well students express their thoughts.

Name_____Date_____

Rails Across the Country • A Changing America **UNIT 6**

Make It Happen

A *documentary* is a type of movie that addresses a subject in a factual and informative way. The topics of documentaries often deal with politics, society, or history. One of the ways that documentary filmmakers present information is through interviews with people who were directly involved with the subject or are experts on the subject.

Imagine that you are going to make a documentary about the building of America's first transcontinental railroad. Review the selection to choose people whom you want to interview for your documentary. Try to include as many different points of view as possible to give a more complete picture of your topic. On the lines below, make a list of people to interview and questions to ask each one. Then work with family members, classmates, and friends to create your documentary.

People I want to interview:
Answers may vary.

_____

_____

Questions I will ask during the interviews:
Questions may vary.

_____

_____

_____

_____

_____

_____

_____

Open Court Classics ✦ Rails Across the Country

107

Responding to Literature p. 107

Teacher Tip Create a rubric with students that will be used to evaluate their documentaries. A rubric might evaluate such components as purpose, appropriate choice of subjects and in-depth questions, smooth transitions, length of documentary, and so on.

Assessment Use the *Responding to Literature* pages as an informal assessment of students' understanding of the selection and of their ability to identify relationships and evaluate text.

Objective

Students will recognize informational sources and formulate interview questions to create a documentary.

Thinking Skills

✦ Identifying and accessing sources
✦ Formulating interview questions
✦ Generating information

Activity

Familiarize students with the format and elements of a documentary by showing one or two short documentary films to the class. Then tell students that a documentary uses many carefully selected sources. Explain that interviews are a good source for information because they provide both historical facts and personal thoughts. Emphasize to students the importance of clearly stating their intentions in their documentaries. Explain that the points students are trying to make should be clear to the audience as they watch the movie.

The Next Step

Set aside time for a film festival at which students can show their documentaries. After each presentation, encourage students to ask the "director" any questions they have about his or her film or to share how the film affected their understanding of the unit theme.

I Hear America Singing

Student Anthology pp. 242–243

Selection Goals

- To recognize qualities that characterize an American work
- To identify common themes in literary and visual arts

Selection Summary

Students conclude the unit with two classic American works, one of poetry and one of art. Walt Whitman's poem "I Hear America Singing" honors individual citizens whose collective efforts contributed to the success and progression of our country. Following this theme, Thomas Hart Benton's painting *July Hay* depicts two farmers at work in the field.

Genre: Poetry

Share with students some of the elements of poetry, which include

- ✦ words that rhyme.
- ✦ incomplete sentences, each on its own line.
- ✦ lines with rhythm or meter.
- ✦ repeated words.

⊹ Part 1 ⊹
Building Background

Activate Prior Knowledge

✦ Ask students to name American poets. Encourage students to share any details they can recall about the poets' works.

✦ Ask students to name some occupations that they think were common when the United States was a developing country. Have students think about the types of services that would have been needed during that period and how those needs have changed. Ask students what occupations of today did not exist in the mid-1800s.

Background Information

✦ Walt Whitman is considered to be one of the greatest American poets of all time. Whitman focused much of his creative energy on capturing and conveying the spirit of his country and fellow citizens. Taking inspiration from the young nation where he was born, Whitman broke from traditional forms and styles of poetry to create something new and original.

✦ Whitman's book *Leaves of Grass* was first published in 1855 as a collection of 12 poems. Whitman revised the work throughout his life, producing many more editions with additional poems. *Leaves of Grass* has been described as a "subjective epic." The poems present the experiences of one man in such a way that they include an entire population.

✦ Thomas Hart Benton was born in the American Midwest, which is the setting for most of his paintings. Benton's interest in American politics, history, and folklore are reflected in his paintings, which include several large murals. Two of Benton's famous murals were commissioned for the Missouri State Capitol in Jefferson City, Missouri, and the Truman Library in Independence, Missouri.

Teacher Tip
Walt Whitman's father was a carpenter and a farmer, and Whitman himself also worked as a carpenter. The carpenter and the farmer, or "ploughboy," are both honored in "I Hear America Singing."

Previewing the Literature

Browse the Selection

✦ Have students note the title of the poem as well as the author's name. Encourage them to skim the poem for unfamiliar terms.

✦ Note on the board those things students mention as a result of their browsing and any questions they have about the selection.

UNIT
6

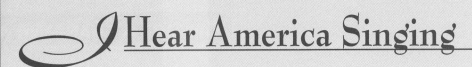

I Hear America Singing

Set Purposes for Reading

Have students set purposes for reading the selection. As they read, encourage students to consider the following questions: Why did Whitman choose to include the particular occupations mentioned in this poem? How do the ideas in Whitman's poem relate to the unit theme?

Expanding Vocabulary

The words listed below can be found in the the poem "I Hear America Singing," and in the Glossary of the *Student Anthology.*

blithe   Lighthearted and happy.

mason   A person who builds with bricks, stones, or cement.

intermission   A breaking or stopping point between activities.

robust   Having strength and energy. [Latin *robustus*, "oaken, strong."]

Teacher Tip
Point out to students that word choice is an especially important aspect of poetry because poets try to communicate their messages in a limited number of lines. Poets carefully select words that create vivid images and convey a certain feeling or mood.

✦ Part 2 ✦
Reading the Selection

Read

✦ Have students silently read **Student Anthology** pages 242–243, stopping at the end of each line if they have any questions or need clarification.

✦ Encourage students to use making connections or any other comprehension strategies that might help them read the selection.

✦ If students in a group prefer reading the poem aloud to each other, remind them to do this quietly to prevent disturbing others.

108C **Unit 6** A Changing America ✦ **Selection 3 Overview**

Discuss

The following discussion suggestions can be carried out on different days, depending upon how much time you allot to each selection.

✦ Have students discuss their general reactions to the selection.

✦ Ask students what this selection adds to the theme that the other selections do not.

✦ Encourage students to review any questions they listed on the board before reading to see if the selection answered their questions.

✦ Have students discuss how the workers portrayed in Whitman's poem and Benton's painting might have felt about their work. Encourage students to compare the reality of the tasks with the way they are presented by the author and the artist.

✦ Ask students to identify the elements of the poem and the painting that characterize them as American.

After students have discussed the selection, choose from ***Responding to Literature*** pages 108–113, and ask students to complete the assigned pages.

⭢ *Part 3* ⭠
Knowledge-Building Project

Students should be making final selections of the images they will include in their picture essays or photo-essays. Tell students to focus on the organization of images to make sure they are presented in a logical sequence.

Once students have sequentially arranged their images, they should write a caption for each one. Explain that a caption is a title for or description of an image. Because captions will be the only text provided in their picture essays or photo-essays, students should write descriptions rather than merely titles. Share the following tips for writing captions:

✦ Describe what is happening without telling readers what they can see for themselves. For example, do not tell readers that a person in the picture is smiling. However, if the reason for the smile is not obvious, you should explain that to readers.

✦ Explain unusual or prominent objects in the picture.

✦ Do not express opinions in your captions.

✦ Write your captions in complete sentences.

By the end of this selection, students should be ready for their presentations. Encourage them to provide a copy of the document that is the subject of their picture essay or photo-essay.

> **Assessment**
> Use the Research Rubrics: Communicating Research Progress and Results on Appendix page 149 of the **Teacher's Edition** to assess students' presentations of their picture essays or photo-essays. Discuss with students the rubrics that will be used to evaluate them on their knowledge-building projects.

UNIT 6

I Hear America Singing

Lesson 1

Objectives

◆ Students will identify adjectives.
◆ Students will make inferences from the poem.

Thinking Skills

◆ Identifying adjectives
◆ Making inferences
◆ Determining relevance

Activity

Have students identify the adjectives in the poem, and then answer the questions. Encourage students to use a dictionary to determine the parts of speech of words that might be unfamiliar or new to them.

The Next Step

Have students read another poem about America that was written in a different era. Then have students compare how America is represented in that poem with how it is portrayed in "I Hear America Singing." Suggest that students create a Venn diagram or other graphic organizer in their Personal Journals to compare the two poems.

Name_____ Date_____

Getting Started

Some of the adjectives Walt Whitman uses in "I Hear America Singing" create strong images and ideas. Make a list of adjectives from the poem. Then answer the questions below.
Possible answers below:

Adjectives

varied	young
blithe	robust
strong	friendly
delicious	melodious

1. Based on the adjectives Whitman chose, how do you think he felt about the people in his poem?
He respected and admired the people for

working hard at their occupations.

_____

_____

_____

2. Explain whether you think the same words used by Whitman to describe America in 1860 could be used to describe America today.
Answers may vary.

_____

_____

_____

_____

Responding to Literature p. 108

Teacher Tip As students complete the assigned *Responding to Literature* pages, be sure they continue with the necessary preparations for their knowledge-building projects.

Name_____ Date_____

A Closer Look

The title "I Hear America Singing" refers to the group of people who form this country. However, in the lines of his poem, Whitman stresses the importance of individuals. Read the poem again. Then answer the questions below. Support your ideas with examples from the poem.
Possible answers below:

1. How does this poem honor the people of America as individuals?

   Whitman names specific occupations and the

   unique "song" each worker sings.

   _____

   _____

2. How does the poem show connections among individual American people?

   Whitman suggests that at the end of the day,

   individuals come together to sing their "strong

   melodious songs."

   _____

3. Why do you think Whitman portrays both a sense of individuality and of unity in this poem?

   Whitman wants to show that America is a strong

   country due to the efforts and talents of

   individual citizens.

   _____

Responding to Literature p. 109

Teacher Tip Walt Whitman and his poetry have inspired many musical compositions. Locate one of these recordings, such as *A Sea Symphony* or *When Lilacs Last in the Dooryard Bloom'd,* and play it for students.

Objective

Students will learn to analyze poetry and draw conclusions to comprehend the author's purpose.

Thinking Skills

✦ Analyzing poetry
✦ Drawing conclusions
✦ Understanding author's purpose

Activity

As they respond to the questions, have students consider how Whitman pays tribute to individuals, yet also celebrates them as a group. Remind students to support their answers with examples from the poem.

The Next Step

Tell students that this poem mentions jobs that were common in America in 1860. Explain that people still have these occupations, but now there are many more opportunities in our country. Ask students what comes to mind when they think about people working in America today. Then have them make a list of their ideas. Have students use their lists to write a poem that celebrates the work of modern Americans. You might suggest that students develop a list of survey questions to ask adults about their work and use the responses in their poems.

UNIT 6

I Hear America Singing

Lesson 3

Objectives

✦ Students will examine a metaphor from the poem.
✦ Students will practice using metaphors in their writing.

Thinking Skills

✦ Applying a poetic device
✦ Making connections

Activity

Have students consider how the metaphor Whitman uses in his poem might relate to their lives. Then have students write poems in which they include metaphors for their daily activities. As students write their poems, encourage them to use poetic devices, such as alliteration, imagery, repetition, and so on. Have students share their finished poems with the class.

The Next Step

In their Personal Journals have students create a list of metaphors for various aspects of modern American life. Encourage students to discuss how the metaphors they identified would compare to metaphors used to describe American life in the 1860s.

I Wonder

A *metaphor* is a figure of speech that suggests a similarity between two things that are not alike. Metaphors are often used in writing, especially in poems. In "I Hear America Singing" Walt Whitman uses singing as a metaphor for work. Think about metaphors as you complete this page.

How can the daily routines of people be reflected in music?
Possible answer: Just like music, daily routines can be rhythmic and repetitive.

What would a song expressing the activities of your day sound like? Include a description of the *rhythm*, or beat, that would best represent your daily routine.
Answers may vary.

Write a poem describing your daily routine. Include metaphors for your activities.
Poems may vary.

See Appendix page 125 for tips for writing poetry.

Extra Effort: Find another poem that uses metaphors, and share it with a partner. Discuss the use and effectiveness of metaphors in the poem you chose.

110   I Hear America Singing ✦ **Open Court Classics**

Responding to Literature p. 110

Teacher Tip **Writing** Students should revise their poems until they have captured the feelings or ideas they wanted to convey; achieved a good match of rhythm, tone, and message; and selected the best words to express their ideas.

Assessment Use the Poetry Writing Rubric on Appendix page 146 of the *Teacher's Edition* to assess students' poems.

Name_____ Date_____

Big Ideas

Walt Whitman once wrote that his goal was "to give something to our literature which will be our own; with neither foreign spirit, nor imagery, nor form . . . strengthening and intensifying the national soul . . ." Consider why Whitman believed this was important as you answer the questions below.

1. Why do you think Americans needed a strong national identity when the country was younger? Support your answer with reasons or evidence.

    Possible answer: Many people had immigrated to

    America from other countries, and they needed

    to feel they belonged in their new country.

    People needed to remember that the United

    States was one country, not just the North or the

    South.

2. Explain why you think national identity is or is not important in modern America. Provide support for your answer.

    Answers may vary.

    _____

    _____

3. In addition to literature, what symbols can help to create a nation's identity?

    Possible symbols: Liberty Bell, bald eagle, White

    House, and American flag.

    _____

Choose one of your ideas to make into a presentation about "the national soul." You might create a collage, write a poem or song, or put together a slide show.

Open Court Classics ✦ I Hear America Singing   **111**

Responding to Literature p. 111

Teacher Tip Tell students that Whitman's dedication to his country was further demonstrated during the Civil War, when he tended to wounded Union soldiers in army hospitals in Washington, D.C. Encourage students to discuss what Whitman's presence and help might have meant to these soldiers.

Objective

Students will think critically and reflectively about the need for a national identity.

Thinking Skills

✦ Understanding author's purpose
✦ Extrapolating information

Activity

Ask students to imagine that they are citizens of the United States in 1860. Encourage them to reflect on their feelings about their country and its future. Then have students answer the questions and produce an original piece, such as a poem, a collage, or a song, that illustrates their ideas about "the national soul." When they have finished, ask students to compare and contrast the pride and patriotism of today with the time in which Whitman's poem was written.

The Next Step

Have students, with a partner or on their own, compile a list of other American writers. Students should write a brief explanation of why each person is included on the list and how he or she influenced change in America. For example, students might list a writer who is responsible for an economic or social change in America. Encourage students to consider writers from a variety of genres as they generate their lists.

Objective

Students will learn to analyze fine art.

Thinking Skills

+ Analyzing fine art
+ Formulating an opinion
+ Understanding artist's purpose

Activity

Tell students that although Walt Whitman and Thomas Hart Benton were from different generations and worked with different tools, their work had similar themes. Explain that both Whitman and Benton became well known for presenting and praising America and its people. Encourage students to think about these themes as they complete the activity.

The Next Step

Have students imagine that Whitman asked Benton to illustrate his poem "I Hear America Singing." What ideas and images might the two share? Encourage students to write in their Personal Journals a description of the images they think Benton would compose and to share their thoughts with classmates.

Name_____ Date_____

Think like an Artist

The artist Thomas Hart Benton was considered by some to be an American Regionalist painter. That means his work represented a particular place. The region in which most of Benton's work is set is the American Midwest. However, Benton did not want to be labeled as a regional painter, because he wanted Americans from all over the country to make a connection to his artwork. Benton's painting *July Hay* has been described as "distinctly American." Consider this as you answer the questions below.

Possible answers below:

1. The part of a painting that draws viewers' eyes to it is called the focal point. What do you think is the focal point of this painting?
   I think the two workers are the focal point.

2. Which do you think is more important in this composition—people or nature? Explain your answer.
   I think they are both important because they are working together.

3. What aspects of Benton's style makes this painting "distinctly American"?
   The portrayal of farmers hard at work makes it "distinctly American."

4. How do you think Americans who live in cities relate to this painting?
   They appreciate the painting's representation of the country's "heartland."

112   I Hear America Singing/July Hay ✦ **Open Court Classics**

Responding to Literature p. 112

Teacher Tip Comprehension Strategies Ask students what connections they made between what they already know and the ideas presented in the painting. Have students explain how making connections helped them understand the artwork in a new way.

Assessment Use the Informal Comprehension Strategies Rubrics: Making Connections on Appendix page 144 of the *Teacher's Edition* to assess students' use of this strategy.

Name_____ Date_____

I Hear America Singing/July Hay • A Changing America **UNIT 6**

In My Opinion

One meaning of the word *classic* is "having lasting significance or worth." Walt Whitman's poem "I Hear America Singing" was written in 1860, and Thomas Hart Benton's painting *July Hay* was created in 1943. Both works are considered to be classics.

Determine whether you agree with this evaluation. Then write a letter to the editor expressing your opinion about whether these works have lasting significance. Support your opinion with details and examples. Remember to follow the steps involved in the writing process as you compose your letter to the editor.

Letters to the editor may vary.

_____

_____

_____

_____

_____

_____

_____

_____

_____

_____

_____

_____

_____

See Appendix page 131 for writing a letter to the editor.

Open Court Classics ✦ I Hear America Singing/July Hay   **113**

Responding to Literature p. 113

Objectives

✦ Students will evaluate the meaning of *classics* in relation to the poem and art.
✦ Students will express their opinions in a letter to the editor.

Thinking Skills

✦ Evaluating classics
✦ Judging significance
✦ Formulating opinions

Activity

Before students begin the writing portion of this activity, encourage them to locate and read an actual letter to the editor. Then have students write a letter to the editor about whether the works in this selection qualify as *classic*. Remind students to support their opinions with details and examples.

The Next Step

Have students write a line about the workers in *July Hay* that could be added to Whitman's poem "I Hear America Singing." Remind students to use Whitman's poem as a model for the line they add.

Teacher Tip Encourage students to discuss their impressions of the painting *July Hay* and how it relates to the unit theme.

Assessment Use the *Responding to Literature* pages as an informal assessment of students' understanding of the selection and of their ability to recognize an author's or artist's purpose.

*W*rap-Up

Knowledge-Building Project

Students have completed their investigations and should be ready to present their picture essays or photo-essays. Presentations may be done in small groups or before the entire class. Encourage students to respond to each presentation, offering constructive feedback. Also have students share the new facts they learned, new questions that were generated about changes in America, and what they found to be most interesting. After the presentations, designate an area for students to display their work. Use the Research Rubrics: Overall Assessment of Research on Appendix page 149 of the ***Teacher's Edition*** to assess students' knowledge-building projects as a whole.

Teacher Tip
• Suggest that students read a biography of Abraham Lincoln and focus on the issues and challenges of his presidency.
• Have students create a time line illustrating important events of their home state and the changes that consequently occurred.

Reviewing the Concepts

In this unit students investigated life in America when the country was young. The selections feature various aspects of early American life and portray the spirit of determination for which this nation is known. Students investigated some of the following key concepts in this unit:

✦ Frederick Douglass's precise memory and skill as a storyteller resulted in an autobiography that revealed to Americans the harsh reality of life as a slave.

✦ The first transcontinental railroad made the country both bigger and smaller—it expanded development in the West and made communication between the two coasts much easier.

✦ Works by some writers and artists contain elements and themes that characterize them as American.

Evaluating the Unit

✦ Ask students to evaluate each selection on the basis of effectiveness of reading/vocabulary, literary value, interest of the subject matter, style of writing, application of theme, and the selection's personal value to the student.

✦ Ask students to evaluate the different activities in the unit, including the knowledge-building project. Have them consider these questions: Which activities made you think? Which ones did you find less challenging and why? Which ones seemed confusing or challenging? Which activities did you most enjoy and why? Which activities best contributed to your growth intellectually? Which activities changed your opinions and offered new ideas? Which activities stimulated novelty and original thinking? What activities would you like to add to the unit?

✦ Ask students to evaluate this ***Open Court Classics*** unit. They can describe how the theme was explored in the unit. They can also compare and contrast the selections based on their tone and their representation of America.

Assessment

Vocabulary Assessment

To assess students' understanding of the vocabulary words, you might want to do one of the following:

✦ Have students write a sentence for each vocabulary word, incorporating apposition or context clues.

✦ Have students identify synonyms and/or antonyms for the vocabulary words.

✦ Administer an informal oral assessment. Have students supply the definition of the vocabulary word or use the word properly in a sentence.

Informal Comprehension Strategies Rubrics

Use the Informal Comprehension Strategies Rubrics: Visualizing, Monitoring and Adjusting Reading Speed, and Making Connections on Appendix pages 144–145 of the **Teacher's Edition** to determine whether a student is using a particular strategy or strategies as he or she reads the selections. Note these and any other strategies a student is using, instead of the degree to which a student might be using any particular strategy. In addition, encourage the student to tell of any strategies other than the ones being taught that he or she is using.

Research Rubrics

Use the Research Rubrics: Making Conjectures, Revising Problems and Conjectures, Communicating Research Progress and Results, and Overall Assessment of Research on Appendix pages 148–149 of the **Teacher's Edition** to assess a student's performance throughout the investigation. The rubrics range from 1 to 4 in most categories, with 1 being the lowest score. In addition, you can use the rubrics to assess a group's collaborative work as well as an individual's participation in that group.

Writing Rubrics

Use the Publishing Writing Rubric, the Persuasive Writing Rubric, the Personal Writing Rubric, and the Poetry Writing Rubric on Appendix page 146 of the **Teacher's Edition** to assess student writing. The rubrics range from 1 to 4 in most categories, with 1 being the lowest score.

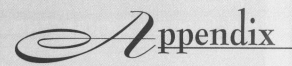

Appendix

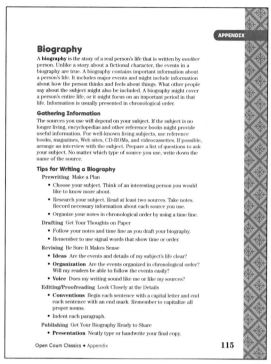

Biography

A **biography** is the story of a real person's life that is written by *another* person. Unlike a story about a fictional character, the events in a biography are true. A biography contains important information about a person's life. It includes major events and might include information about how the person thinks and feels about things. What other people say about the subject might also be included. A biography might cover a person's entire life, or it might focus on an important period in that life. Information is usually presented in chronological order.

Gathering Information

The sources you use will depend on your subject. If the subject is no longer living, encyclopedias and other reference books might provide useful information. For well-known living subjects, use reference books, magazines, Web sites, CD-ROMs, and videocassettes. If possible, arrange an interview with the subject. Prepare a list of questions to ask your subject. No matter which type of source you use, write down the name of the source.

Tips for Writing a Biography

Prewriting Make a Plan
- Choose your subject. Think of an interesting person you would like to know more about.
- Research your subject. Read at least two sources. Take notes. Record necessary information about each source you use.
- Organize your notes in chronological order by using a time line.

Drafting Get Your Thoughts on Paper
- Follow your notes and time line as you draft your biography.
- Remember to use signal words that show time or order.

Revising Be Sure It Makes Sense
- **Ideas** Are the events and details of my subject's life clear?
- **Organization** Are the events organized in chronological order? Will my readers be able to follow the events easily?
- **Voice** Does my writing sound like me or like my sources?

Editing/Proofreading Look Closely at the Details
- **Conventions** Begin each sentence with a capital letter and end each sentence with an end mark. Remember to capitalize all proper nouns.
- Indent each paragraph.

Publishing Get Your Biography Ready to Share
- **Presentation** Neatly type or handwrite your final copy.

Open Court Classics ✦ Appendix

115

Responding to Literature p. 115

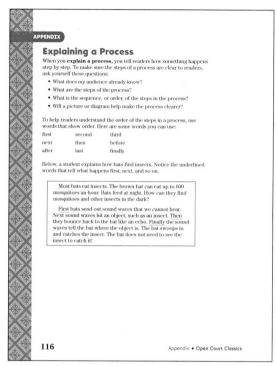

Explaining a Process

When you **explain a process,** you tell readers how something happens step by step. To make sure the steps of a process are clear to readers, ask yourself these questions:
- What does my audience already know?
- What are the steps of the process?
- What is the sequence, or order, of the steps in the process?
- Will a picture or diagram help make the process clearer?

To help readers understand the order of the steps in a process, use words that show order. Here are some words you can use:

first	second	third
next	then	before
after	last	finally

Below, a student explains how bats find insects. Notice the underlined words that tell what happens first, next, and so on.

> Most bats eat insects. The brown bat can eat up to 600 mosquitoes an hour. Bats feed at night. How can they find mosquitoes and other insects in the dark?
>
> First bats send out sound waves that we cannot hear. Next sound waves hit an object, such as an insect. Then they bounce back to the bat like an echo. Finally the sound waves tell the bat where the object is. The bat swoops in and catches the insect. The bat does not need to see the insect to catch it!

116

Appendix ✦ Open Court Classics

Responding to Literature p. 116

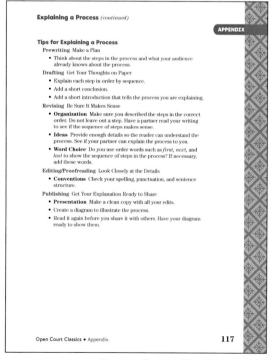

Explaining a Process *(continued)*

Tips for Explaining a Process

Prewriting Make a Plan
- Think about the steps in the process and what your audience already knows about the process.

Drafting Get Your Thoughts on Paper
- Explain each step in order by sequence.
- Add a short conclusion.
- Add a short introduction that tells the process you are explaining.

Revising Be Sure It Makes Sense
- **Organization** Make sure you described the steps in the correct order. Do not leave out a step. Have a partner read your writing to see if the sequence of steps makes sense.
- **Ideas** Provide enough details so the reader can understand the process. See if your partner can explain the process to you.
- **Word Choice** Do you use order words such as *first, next,* and *last* to show the sequence of steps in the process? If necessary, add these words.

Editing/Proofreading Look Closely at the Details
- **Conventions** Check your spelling, punctuation, and sentence structure.

Publishing Get Your Explanation Ready to Share
- **Presentation** Make a clean copy with all your edits.
- Create a diagram to illustrate the process.
- Read it again before you share it with others. Have your diagram ready to show them.

Open Court Classics ✦ Appendix

117

Responding to Literature p. 117

News Story

A **news story** is an accurate report about a person or an event that is happening now. The writer must report a news story in a way that makes readers care about it. Its purpose is to inform readers. A news story should include only facts, not opinions. Readers count on news stories to be accurate and not take sides. Many people form opinions based on news stories, but if the facts are not accurate, readers cannot make the best decisions. For example, a news story might report on a new toy so parents can decide if it is safe for their children.

Parts of a News Story
- The **headline** is a short title that gives readers an idea of what the story is about.
- The **byline** tells who wrote the story.
- The **lead** (first paragraph) answers the five Ws and convinces readers to keep reading.
- The **body** comes after the lead, gives more details about the five Ws, and may include quotations from people.
- The **ending** summarizes the news story.

Five Ws

Who?	Who was involved or whom does it affect?
What?	What did he or she do? What happened?
When?	When did the event take place?
Where?	Where did the event take place?
Why?	Why did the person do what he or she did? Why did the event happen?

How to Get Answers for the Five Ws
- **Observation** If you were there, you can report what you saw and heard.
- **Interviews** If you were not there, you can talk to people who were. Remember, a news story must be accurate, so stick to the facts. If someone tells you what he or she thinks about the events, make sure you present the information as an opinion so readers will know it is not a fact.

118

Appendix ✦ Open Court Classics

Responding to Literature p. 118

News Story *(continued)*

APPENDIX

Tips for Writing a News Story

Prewriting Make a Plan
- Do you have the answers for the five Ws?

Drafting Get Your Thoughts on Paper
- Start with the lead.
- Write down all the important information quickly.
- Write a headline that lets your readers know the subject of the news story.

Revising Be Sure It Makes Sense
- **Organization** Is your story accurate? Did you stick to the facts? Did you make it clear which things were facts and which were opinions?
- Did you cover the five Ws in the lead?
- **Voice** Did you convince your audience they wanted to read your news story?
- **Sentence Fluency** Did you tell your news story quickly and simply?

Editing/Proofreading Look Closely at the Details
- **Conventions** Check your spelling. If you are unsure of a word, look it up in the dictionary.
- Check capitalization and punctuation.

Publishing Get Your News Story Ready to Share
- **Presentation** Make a clean copy of your news story so it is easy to read and appealing to your readers. Publish it in your school or classroom newspaper, or submit it to your local newspaper for publication.

Open Court Classics ✦ Appendix   119

Responding to Literature p. 119

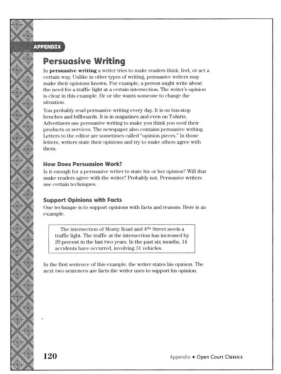

APPENDIX

Persuasive Writing

In **persuasive writing** a writer tries to make readers think, feel, or act a certain way. Unlike in other types of writing, persuasive writers may make their opinions known. For example, a person might write about the need for a traffic light at a certain intersection. The writer's opinion is clear in this example. He or she wants someone to change the situation.

You probably read persuasive writing every day. It is on bus-stop benches and billboards. It is in magazines and even on T-shirts. Advertisers use persuasive writing to make you think you *need* their products or services. The newspaper also contains persuasive writing. Letters to the editor are sometimes called "opinion pieces." In those letters, writers state their opinions and try to make others agree with them.

How Does Persuasion Work?

Is it enough for a persuasive writer to state his or her opinion? Will that make readers agree with the writer? Probably not. Persuasive writers use certain techniques.

Support Opinions with Facts

One technique is to support opinions with facts and reasons. Here is an example.

> The intersection of Monty Road and 4th Street needs a traffic light. The traffic at the intersection has increased by 20 percent in the last two years. In the past six months, 14 accidents have occurred, involving 31 vehicles.

In the first sentence of this example, the writer states his opinion. The next two sentences are facts the writer uses to support his opinion.

120   Appendix ✦ Open Court Classics

Responding to Literature p. 120

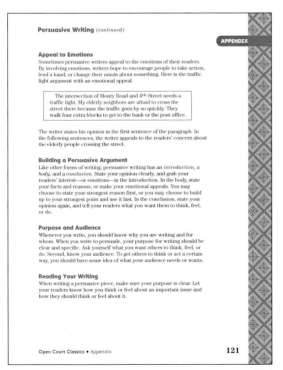

Persuasive Writing *(continued)*

APPENDIX

Appeal to Emotions

Sometimes persuasive writers appeal to the emotions of their readers. By involving emotions, writers hope to encourage people to take action, lend a hand, or change their minds about something. Here is the traffic light argument with an emotional appeal.

> The intersection of Monty Road and 4th Street needs a traffic light. My elderly neighbors are afraid to cross the street there because the traffic goes by so quickly. They walk four extra blocks to get to the bank or the post office.

The writer states his opinion in the first sentence of the paragraph. In the following sentences, the writer appeals to the readers' concern about the elderly people crossing the street.

Building a Persuasive Argument

Like other forms of writing, persuasive writing has an *introduction*, a *body*, and a *conclusion*. State your opinion clearly, and grab your readers' interest—or emotions—in the introduction. In the body, state your facts and reasons, or make your emotional appeals. You may choose to state your strongest reason first, or you may choose to build up to your strongest point and use it last. In the conclusion, state your opinion again, and tell your readers what you want them to think, feel, or do.

Purpose and Audience

Whenever you write, you should know why you are writing and for whom. When you write to persuade, your purpose for writing should be clear and specific. Ask yourself what you want others to think, feel, or do. Second, know your audience. To get others to think or act a certain way, you should have some idea of what your audience needs or wants.

Reading Your Writing

When writing a persuasive piece, make sure your purpose is clear. Let your readers know how you think or feel about an important issue and how they should think or feel about it.

Open Court Classics ✦ Appendix   121

Responding to Literature p. 121

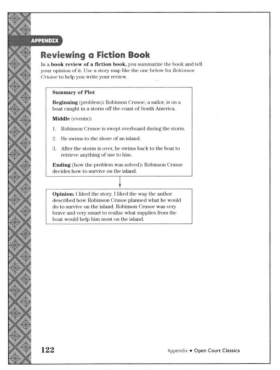

APPENDIX

Reviewing a Fiction Book

In a **book review of a fiction book,** you summarize the book and tell your opinion of it. Use a story map like the one below for *Robinson Crusoe* to help you write your review.

> **Summary of Plot**
>
> **Beginning** (problem): Robinson Crusoe, a sailor, is on a boat caught in a storm off the coast of South America.
>
> **Middle** (events):
> 1. Robinson Crusoe is swept overboard during the storm.
> 2. He swims to the shore of an island.
> 3. After the storm is over, he swims back to the boat to retrieve anything of use to him.
>
> **Ending** (how the problem was solved): Robinson Crusoe decides how to survive on the island.

> **Opinion:** I liked the story. I liked the way the author described how Robinson Crusoe planned what he would do to survive on the island. Robinson Crusoe was very brave and very smart to realize what supplies from the boat would help him most on the island.

122   Appendix ✦ Open Court Classics

Responding to Literature p. 122

Appendix

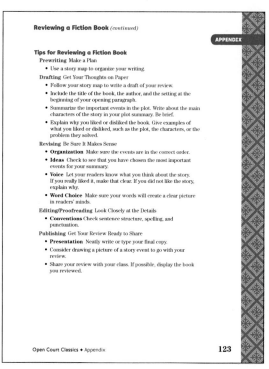

Reviewing a Fiction Book *(continued)*

APPENDIX

Tips for Reviewing a Fiction Book

Prewriting Make a Plan
- Use a story map to organize your writing.

Drafting Get Your Thoughts on Paper
- Follow your story map to write a draft of your review.
- Include the title of the book, the author, and the setting at the beginning of your opening paragraph.
- Summarize the important events in the plot. Write about the main characters of the story in your plot summary. Be brief.
- Explain why you liked or disliked the book. Give examples of what you liked or disliked, such as the plot, the characters, or the problem they solved.

Revising Be Sure It Makes Sense
- **Organization** Make sure the events are in the correct order.
- **Ideas** Check to see that you have chosen the most important events for your summary.
- **Voice** Let your readers know what you think about the story. If you really liked it, make that clear. If you did not like the story, explain why.
- **Word Choice** Make sure your words will create a clear picture in readers' minds.

Editing/Proofreading Look Closely at the Details
- **Conventions** Check sentence structure, spelling, and punctuation.

Publishing Get Your Review Ready to Share
- **Presentation** Neatly write or type your final copy.
- Consider drawing a picture of a story event to go with your review.
- Share your review with your class. If possible, display the book you reviewed.

Open Court Classics ✦ Appendix   123

Responding to Literature p. 123

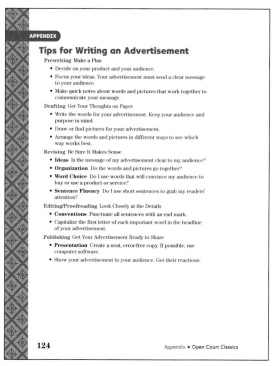

APPENDIX

Tips for Writing an Advertisement

Prewriting Make a Plan
- Decide on your product and your audience.
- Focus your ideas. Your advertisement must send a clear message to your audience.
- Make quick notes about words and pictures that work together to communicate your message.

Drafting Get Your Thoughts on Paper
- Write the words for your advertisement. Keep your audience and purpose in mind.
- Draw or find pictures for your advertisement.
- Arrange the words and pictures in different ways to see which way works best.

Revising Be Sure It Makes Sense
- **Ideas** Is the message of my advertisement clear to my audience?
- **Organization** Do the words and pictures go together?
- **Word Choice** Do I use words that will convince my audience to buy or use a product or service?
- **Sentence Fluency** Do I use short sentences to grab my readers' attention?

Editing/Proofreading Look Closely at the Details
- **Conventions** Punctuate all sentences with an end mark.
- Capitalize the first letter of each important word in the headline of your advertisement.

Publishing Get Your Advertisement Ready to Share
- **Presentation** Create a neat, error-free copy. If possible, use computer software.
- Show your advertisement to your audience. Get their reactions.

124   Appendix ✦ Open Court Classics

Responding to Literature p. 124

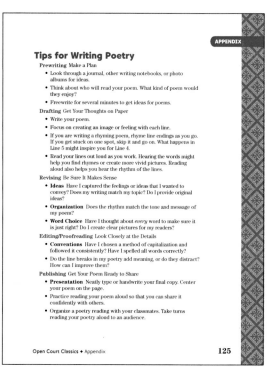

APPENDIX

Tips for Writing Poetry

Prewriting Make a Plan
- Look through a journal, other writing notebooks, or photo albums for ideas.
- Think about who will read your poem. What kind of poem would they enjoy?
- Freewrite for several minutes to get ideas for poems.

Drafting Get Your Thoughts on Paper
- Write your poem.
- Focus on creating an image or feeling with each line.
- If you are writing a rhyming poem, rhyme line endings as you go. If you get stuck on one spot, skip it and go on. What happens in Line 5 might inspire you for Line 4.
- Read your lines out loud as you work. Hearing the words might help you find rhymes or create more vivid pictures. Reading aloud also helps you hear the rhythm of the lines.

Revising Be Sure It Makes Sense
- **Ideas** Have I captured the feelings or ideas that I wanted to convey? Does my writing match my topic? Do I provide original ideas?
- **Organization** Does the rhythm match the tone and message of my poem?
- **Word Choice** Have I thought about *every* word to make sure it is just right? Do I create clear pictures for my readers?

Editing/Proofreading Look Closely at the Details
- **Conventions** Have I chosen a method of capitalization and followed it consistently? Have I spelled all words correctly?
- Do the line breaks in my poetry add meaning, or do they distract? How can I improve them?

Publishing Get Your Poem Ready to Share
- **Presentation** Neatly type or handwrite your final copy. Center your poem on the page.
- Practice reading your poem aloud so that you can share it confidently with others.
- Organize a poetry reading with your classmates. Take turns reading your poetry aloud to an audience.

Open Court Classics ✦ Appendix   125

Responding to Literature p. 125

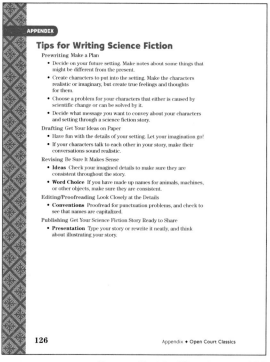

APPENDIX

Tips for Writing Science Fiction

Prewriting Make a Plan
- Decide on your future setting. Make notes about some things that might be different from the present.
- Create characters to put into the setting. Make the characters realistic or imaginary, but make true feelings and thoughts for them.
- Choose a problem for your characters that either is caused by scientific change or can be solved by it.
- Decide what message you want to convey about your characters and setting through a science fiction story.

Drafting Get Your Ideas on Paper
- Have fun with the details of your setting. Let your imagination go!
- If your characters talk to each other in your story, make their conversations sound realistic.

Revising Be Sure It Makes Sense
- **Ideas** Check your imagined details to make sure they are consistent throughout the story.
- **Word Choice** If you have made up names for animals, machines, or other objects, make sure they are consistent.

Editing/Proofreading Look Closely at the Details
- **Conventions** Proofread for punctuation problems, and check to see that names are capitalized.

Publishing Get Your Science Fiction Story Ready to Share
- **Presentation** Type your story or rewrite it neatly, and think about illustrating your story.

126   Appendix ✦ Open Court Classics

Responding to Literature p. 126

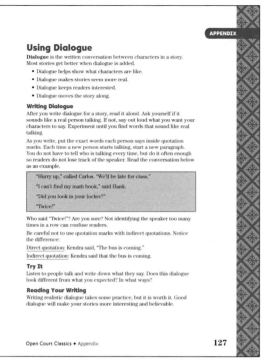

APPENDIX

Using Dialogue

Dialogue is the written conversation between characters in a story. Most stories get better when dialogue is added.

- Dialogue helps show what characters are like.
- Dialogue makes stories seem more real.
- Dialogue keeps readers interested.
- Dialogue moves the story along.

Writing Dialogue

After you write dialogue for a story, read it aloud. Ask yourself if it sounds like a real person talking. If not, say out loud what you want your characters to say. Experiment until you find words that sound like real talking.

As you write, put the exact words each person says inside quotation marks. Each time a new person starts talking, start a new paragraph. You do not have to tell who is talking every time, but do it often enough so readers do not lose track of the speaker. Read the conversation below as an example.

> "Hurry up," called Carlos. "We'll be late for class."
>
> "I can't find my math book," said Hank.
>
> "Did you look in your locker?"
>
> "Twice!"

Who said "Twice!"? Are you sure? Not identifying the speaker too many times in a row can confuse readers.

Be careful not to use quotation marks with indirect quotations. Notice the difference:

Direct quotation: Kendra said, "The bus is coming."

Indirect quotation: Kendra said that the bus is coming.

Try It

Listen to people talk and write down what they say. Does this dialogue look different from what you expected? In what ways?

Reading Your Writing

Writing realistic dialogue takes some practice, but it is worth it. Good dialogue will make your stories more interesting and believable.

Open Court Classics ◆ Appendix   **127**

Responding to Literature p. 127

APPENDIX

Writing a Description

A **description** tells how something looks, sounds, smells, tastes, and feels. If you write good descriptions, your readers can almost experience the things you have written.

Sensory Details

Sensory details describe how something looks, sounds, smells, tastes, and/or feels. Using sensory details will make the object or place you describe seem more real, as in this example:

> As I blew up the rubber raft, I could taste the salt of last year's trip to the ocean. The raft smelled like the moldy garden hose stored in our basement.

Select the Right Word

Colorful adjectives such as *bumpy, spongy,* and *shrill* are examples of good descriptive details. Specific nouns such as *Big Ben, cicada,* and *No. 2 pencil* add interest, also. Precise action verbs such as *plunge, slammed,* and *pleaded* add energy to your writing. Be creative and exact with your words. For example, the sentence *I shut the door and spoke to him* becomes much more interesting when you add descriptive words, such as *I gently fastened the door and whispered to my brother.*

Organize a Description

Writers can help readers see the person, place, or object being described by organizing sensory details and ideas in a logical way. The subject you choose to describe can help you decide which type of organization to use.

Imagine you are looking at a totem pole. Your eyes would probably start at the top and follow the pole all the way to the bottom. If you were to describe that totem pole, that would be a way to organize the description—from top to bottom.

If you walk into a room or a place you have never been before, you might look at every object and in every corner, turning your head from left to right. As a writer, you can do the same for your readers by using left-to-right organization.

Whether you organize your description from top to bottom or left to right, a graphic organizer can help you get started.

128   Appendix ◆ Open Court Classics

Responding to Literature p. 128

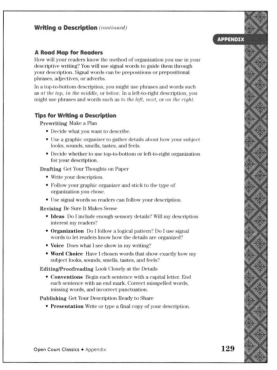

Writing a Description *(continued)*

APPENDIX

A Road Map for Readers

How will your readers know the method of organization you use in your descriptive writing? You will use signal words to guide them through your description. Signal words can be prepositions or prepositional phrases, adjectives, or adverbs.

In a top-to-bottom description, you might use phrases and words such as *at the top, in the middle,* or *below.* In a left-to-right description, you might use phrases and words such as *to the left, next,* or *on the right.*

Tips for Writing a Description

Prewriting Make a Plan

- Decide what you want to describe.
- Use a graphic organizer to gather details about how your subject looks, sounds, smells, tastes, and feels.
- Decide whether to use top-to-bottom or left-to-right organization for your description.

Drafting Get Your Thoughts on Paper

- Write your description.
- Follow your graphic organizer and stick to the type of organization you chose.
- Use signal words so readers can follow your description.

Revising Be Sure It Makes Sense

- **Ideas** Do I include enough sensory details? Will my description interest my readers?
- **Organization** Do I follow a logical pattern? Do I use signal words to let readers know how the details are organized?
- **Voice** Does what I see show in my writing?
- **Word Choice** Have I chosen words that show exactly how my subject looks, sounds, smells, tastes, and feels?

Editing/Proofreading Look Closely at the Details

- **Conventions** Begin each sentence with a capital letter. End each sentence with an end mark. Correct misspelled words, missing words, and incorrect punctuation.

Publishing Get Your Description Ready to Share

- **Presentation** Write or type a final copy of your description.

Open Court Classics ◆ Appendix   **129**

Responding to Literature p. 129

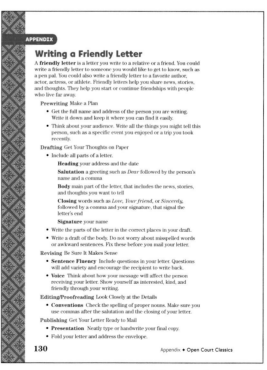

APPENDIX

Writing a Friendly Letter

A **friendly letter** is a letter you write to a relative or a friend. You could write a friendly letter to someone you would like to get to know, such as a pen pal. You could also write a friendly letter to a favorite author, actor, actress, or athlete. Friendly letters help you share news, stories, and thoughts. They help you start or continue friendships with people who live far away.

Prewriting Make a Plan

- Get the full name and address of the person you are writing. Write it down and keep it where you can find it easily.
- Think about your audience. Write all the things you might tell this person, such as a specific event you enjoyed or a trip you took recently.

Drafting Get Your Thoughts on Paper

- Include all parts of a letter.

   Heading your address and the date

   Salutation a greeting such as *Dear* followed by the person's name and a comma

   Body main part of the letter, that includes the news, stories, and thoughts you want to tell

   Closing words such as *Love, Your friend,* or *Sincerely,* followed by a comma and your signature, that signal the letter's end

   Signature your name

- Write the parts of the letter in the correct places in your draft.
- Write a draft of the body. Do not worry about misspelled words or awkward sentences. Fix these before you mail your letter.

Revising Be Sure It Makes Sense

- **Sentence Fluency** Include questions in your letter. Questions will add variety and encourage the recipient to write back.
- **Voice** Think about how your message will affect the person receiving your letter. Show yourself as interested, kind, and friendly through your writing.

Editing/Proofreading Look Closely at the Details

- **Conventions** Check the spelling of proper nouns. Make sure you use commas after the salutation and the closing of your letter.

Publishing Get Your Letter Ready to Mail

- **Presentation** Neatly type or handwrite your final copy.
- Fold your letter and address the envelope.

130   Appendix ◆ Open Court Classics

Responding to Literature p. 130

Appendix

Writing a Letter to the Editor

A **letter to the editor** is written to a newspaper or magazine to influence the way readers think, feel, or act about a problem or issue. When you write a letter to the editor, you do not write to an individual. You write with the goal of getting your letter printed so you can influence anyone who reads it.

In a letter to the editor, state your viewpoint, and support it with one or any combination of the following techniques:

- Appeal to your readers' sense of reason by providing facts and reasons that support your opinion.
- Use examples to prove your point.
- Provide a solution to the problem.

Remember to write your letter using the standard letter format (*heading, salutation, body, closing,* and your *signature*).

Prewriting Make a Plan

- What is your purpose? State your opinion clearly.
- Who will read your letter? Make sure you know your audience.
- Write down the facts or examples that support your opinion.
- Check to see where and to whom to address the letter.

Drafting Get Your Thoughts on Paper

- Write your facts or examples in the order of importance.
- Include all parts of a letter—the heading, the salutation, the body, the closing, and your signature.

Revising Be Sure It Makes Sense

- **Ideas** Is my opinion clear and supported by facts or examples? Did I refer to the article or letter to which I am responding?
- **Organization** Are my facts or examples in a logical order?
- **Word Choice** Are the words I use precise enough to convince readers that my opinion is one they should hold?
- **Sentence Fluency** Did I use different lengths and styles of sentences for variety and for emphasis?

Editing/Proofreading Look Closely at the Details

- **Conventions** Make sure that the parts of your letter to the editor are correctly formatted. Check that each proper name begins with capital letter.

Publishing Get Your Letter to the Editor Ready to Mail

- **Presentation** Neatly write or type your letter.
- Fold your letter and address the envelope.

Open Court Classics ✦ Appendix **131**

Responding to Literature p. 131

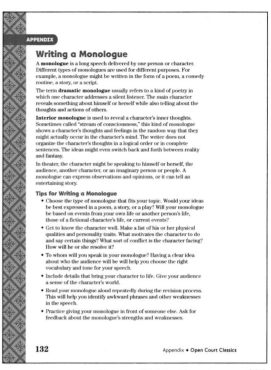

Writing a Monologue

A **monologue** is a long speech delivered by one person or character. Different types of monologues are used for different purposes. For example, a monologue might be written in the form of a poem, a comedy routine, a story, or a script.

The term **dramatic monologue** usually refers to a kind of poetry in which one character addresses a silent listener. The main character reveals something about himself or herself while also telling about the thoughts and actions of others.

Interior monologue is used to reveal a character's inner thoughts. Sometimes called "stream of consciousness," this kind of monologue shows a character's thoughts and feelings in the random way that they might actually occur in the character's mind. The writer does not organize the character's thoughts in a logical order or in complete sentences. The ideas might even switch back and forth between reality and fantasy.

In theater, the character might be speaking to himself or herself, the audience, another character, or an imaginary person or people. A monologue can express observations and opinions, or it can tell an entertaining story.

Tips for Writing a Monologue

- Choose the type of monologue that fits your topic. Would your ideas be best expressed in a poem, a story, or a play? Will your monologue be based on events from your own life or another person's life, those of a fictional character's life, or current events?
- Get to know the character well. Make a list of his or her physical qualities and personality traits. What motivates the character to do and say certain things? What sort of conflict is the character facing? How will he or she resolve it?
- To whom will you speak in your monologue? Having a clear idea about who the audience will be will help you choose the right vocabulary and tone for your speech.
- Include details that bring your character to life. Give your audience a sense of the character's world.
- Read your monologue aloud repeatedly during the revision process. This will help you identify awkward phrases and other weaknesses in the speech.
- Practice giving your monologue in front of someone else. Ask for feedback about the monologue's strengths and weaknesses.

132 Appendix ✦ Open Court Classics

Responding to Literature p. 132

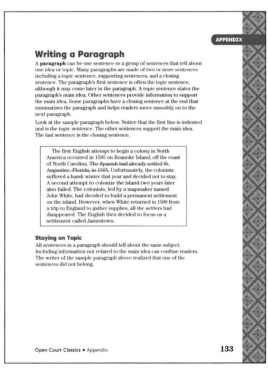

Writing a Paragraph

A **paragraph** can be one sentence or a group of sentences that tell about one idea or topic. Many paragraphs are made of two or more sentences including a topic sentence, supporting sentences, and a closing sentence. The paragraph's first sentence is often the topic sentence, although it may come later in the paragraph. A topic sentence states the paragraph's main idea. Other sentences provide information to support the main idea. Some paragraphs have a closing sentence at the end that summarizes the paragraph and helps readers move smoothly on to the next paragraph.

Look at the sample paragraph below. Notice that the first line is indented and is the topic sentence. The other sentences support the main idea. The last sentence is the closing sentence.

> The first English attempt to begin a colony in North America occurred in 1585 on Roanoke Island, off the coast of North Carolina. The Spanish had already settled St. Augustine, Florida, in 1565. Unfortunately, the colonists suffered a harsh winter that year and decided not to stay. A second attempt to colonize the island two years later also failed. The colonists, led by a mapmaker named John White, had decided to build a permanent settlement on the island. However, when White returned in 1590 from a trip to England to gather supplies, all the settlers had disappeared. The English then decided to focus on a settlement called Jamestown.

Staying on Topic

All sentences in a paragraph should tell about the same subject. Including information not related to the main idea can confuse readers. The writer of the sample paragraph above realized that one of the sentences did not belong.

Open Court Classics ✦ Appendix **133**

Responding to Literature p. 133

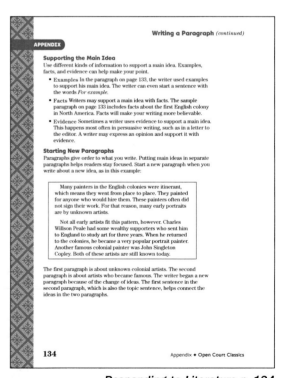

Writing a Paragraph *(continued)*

Supporting the Main Idea

Use different kinds of information to support a main idea. Examples, facts, and evidence can help make your point.

- **Examples** In the paragraph on page 133, the writer used examples to support his main idea. The writer can even start a sentence with the words *For example.*
- **Facts** Writers may support a main idea with facts. The sample paragraph on page 133 includes facts about the first English colony in North America. Facts will make your writing more believable.
- **Evidence** Sometimes a writer uses evidence to support a main idea. This happens most often in persuasive writing, such as in a letter to the editor. A writer may express an opinion and support it with evidence.

Starting New Paragraphs

Paragraphs give order to what you write. Putting main ideas in separate paragraphs helps readers stay focused. Start a new paragraph when you write about a new idea, as in this example:

> Many painters in the English colonies were itinerant, which means they went from place to place. They painted for anyone who would hire them. These painters often did not sign their work. For that reason, many early portraits are by unknown artists.
>
> Not all early artists fit this pattern, however. Charles Willson Peale had some wealthy supporters who sent him to England to study art for three years. When he returned to the colonies, he became a very popular portrait painter. Another famous colonial painter was John Singleton Copley. Both of these artists are still known today.

The first paragraph is about unknown colonial artists. The second paragraph is about artists who became famous. The writer began a new paragraph because of the change of ideas. The first sentence in the second paragraph, which is also the topic sentence, helps connect the ideas in the two paragraphs.

134 Appendix ✦ Open Court Classics

Responding to Literature p. 134

Writing a Press Release

A **press release** is a written notice issued to the media with information to be distributed at a particular time. Individuals and companies issue press releases for a number of reasons. For example, a press release might be used to promote a person, product, or event; to inform the public; or to tell about a new or improved product.

The standard elements of a press release are explained below in the order that they should appear on the page.

1. FOR IMMEDIATE RELEASE These words appear in the upper left-hand corner, printed in all capital letters.

2. Contact Information The name, title, address, and telephone number of the organization's representative who will answer questions about the press release appear two spaces below the release statement.

3. Headline The headline appears in boldface type two spaces below the contact information.

4. Dateline The dateline includes the city where the press release is issued and the date it is mailed.

5. Lead Paragraph The first paragraph should grab readers' attention and answer the five Ws (*who, what, when, where,* and *why*).

6. Text The message is developed more fully in the body of the press release.

7. Summary In the lower left-hand corner, the central message is restated in one or two sentences. A summary includes any important dates, such as when a new product will be released or when an event will take place.

Tips for Writing a Press Release

- A press release should be no longer than one page. Provide enough details to be accurate but not so much information that readers will lose interest.

- Make your press release interesting to readers. Attract their attention with an engaging headline, and keep their interest by using active rather than passive verbs. Include information you think will be important to them.

- Focus on the facts. Provide current and appropriate data.

- Include as much contact information (name, address, telephone and fax number, e-mail address) as possible.

- Proofread your writing to check for errors in spelling, grammar, and style. A press release with mistakes will not make a good impression on your audience.

Responding to Literature p. 135

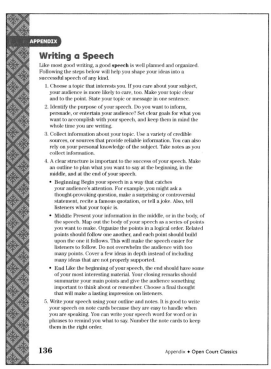

Writing a Speech

Like most good writing, a good **speech** is well planned and organized. Following the steps below will help you shape your ideas into a successful speech of any kind.

1. Choose a topic that interests you. If you care about your subject, your audience is more likely to care, too. Make your topic clear and to the point. State your topic or message in one sentence.

2. Identify the purpose of your speech. Do you want to inform, persuade, or entertain your audience? Set clear goals for what you want to accomplish with your speech, and keep them in mind the whole time you are writing.

3. Collect information about your topic. Use a variety of credible sources, or sources that provide reliable information. You can also rely on your personal knowledge of the subject. Take notes as you collect information.

4. A clear structure is important to the success of your speech. Make an outline to plan what you want to say at the beginning, in the middle, and at the end of your speech.

   - Beginning Begin your speech in a way that catches your audience's attention. For example, you might ask a thought-provoking question, make a surprising or controversial statement, recite a famous quotation, or tell a joke. Also, tell listeners what your topic is.

   - Middle Present your information in the middle, or in the body, of the speech. Map out the body of your speech as a series of points you want to make. Organize the points in a logical order. Related points should follow one another, and each point should build upon the one it follows. This will make the speech easier for listeners to follow. Do not overwhelm the audience with too many points. Cover a few ideas in depth instead of including many ideas that are not properly supported.

   - End Like the beginning of your speech, the end should have some of your most interesting material. Your closing remarks should summarize your main points and give the audience something important to think about or remember. Choose a final thought that will make a lasting impression on listeners.

5. Write your speech using your outline and notes. It is good to write your speech on note cards because they are easy to handle when you are speaking. You can write your speech word for word or in phrases to remind you what to say. Number the note cards to keep them in the right order.

Responding to Literature p. 136

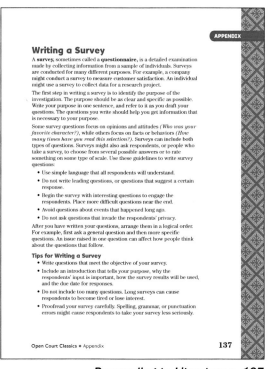

Writing a Survey

A **survey**, sometimes called a **questionnaire**, is a detailed examination made by collecting information from a sample of individuals. Surveys are conducted for many different purposes. For example, a company might conduct a survey to measure customer satisfaction. An individual might use a survey to collect data for a research project.

The first step in writing a survey is to identify the purpose of the investigation. The purpose should be as clear and specific as possible. Write your purpose in one sentence, and refer to it as you draft your questions. The questions you write should help you get information that is necessary to your purpose.

Some survey questions focus on opinions and attitudes (*Who was your favorite character?*), while others focus on facts or behaviors (*How many times have you read this selection?*). Surveys can include both types of questions. Surveys might also ask respondents, or people who take a survey, to choose from several possible answers or to rate something on some type of scale. Use these guidelines to write survey questions:

- Use simple language that all respondents will understand.

- Do not write leading questions, or questions that suggest a certain response.

- Begin the survey with interesting questions to engage the respondents. Place more difficult questions near the end.

- Avoid questions about events that happened long ago.

- Do not ask questions that invade the respondents' privacy.

After you have written your questions, arrange them in a logical order. For example, first ask a general question and then more specific questions. An issue raised in one question can affect how people think about the questions that follow.

Tips for Writing a Survey

- Write questions that meet the objective of your survey.

- Include an introduction that tells your purpose, why the respondents' input is important, how the survey results will be used, and the due date for responses.

- Do not include too many questions. Long surveys can cause respondents to become tired or lose interest.

- Proofread your survey carefully. Spelling, grammar, or punctuation errors might cause respondents to take your survey less seriously.

Responding to Literature p. 137

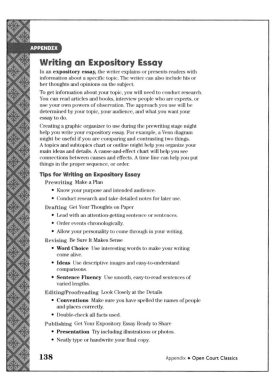

Writing an Expository Essay

In an **expository essay**, the writer explains or presents readers with information about a specific topic. The writer can also include his or her thoughts and opinions on the subject.

To get information about your topic, you will need to conduct research. You can read articles and books, interview people who are experts, or use your own powers of observation. The approach you use will be determined by your topic, your audience, and what you want your essay to do.

Creating a graphic organizer to use during the prewriting stage might help you write your expository essay. For example, a Venn diagram might be useful if you are comparing and contrasting two things. A topics and subtopics chart or outline might help you organize your main ideas and details. A cause-and-effect chart will help you see connections between causes and effects. A time line can help you put things in the proper sequence, or order.

Tips for Writing an Expository Essay

Prewriting Make a Plan

- Know your purpose and intended audience.

- Conduct research and take detailed notes for later use.

Drafting Get Your Thoughts on Paper

- Lead with an attention-getting sentence or sentences.

- Order events chronologically.

- Allow your personality to come through in your writing.

Revising Be Sure It Makes Sense

- **Word Choice** Use interesting words to make your writing come alive.

- **Ideas** Use descriptive images and easy-to-understand comparisons.

- **Sentence Fluency** Use smooth, easy-to-read sentences of varied lengths.

Editing/Proofreading Look Closely at the Details

- **Conventions** Make sure you have spelled the names of people and places correctly.

- Double-check all facts used.

Publishing Get Your Expository Essay Ready to Share

- **Presentation** Try including illustrations or photos.

- Neatly type or handwrite your final copy.

Responding to Literature p. 138

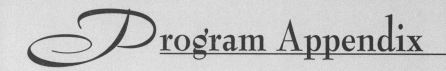

Program Appendix

Open Court Classics

Table of Contents

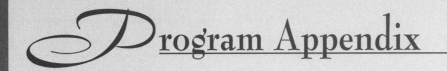

Program Appendix

Student Anthology

The ***Student Anthology*** gives students the opportunity to read and enjoy classic literature—both old standards and newer favorites. Each ***Student Anthology*** has six thematic units and an average of three selections per unit. In addition to the main selections, poetry can also be found in the anthologies. The selections were chosen using E. D. Hirsch's Core Knowledge™ series, Accelerated Reader® lists, and input from teachers of gifted and talented students. The unit themes match those found in *Open Court Reading* and can be found on the next page.

From historical fiction and plays to biographies and essays, the ***Student Anthology*** exposes students to a broad array of genres and writing styles. The anthologies include entire stories or selections, such as "John Henry," Hans Christian Andersen's "The Silver Penny," and "Arachne the Weaver," or excerpts from larger works such as *Little Women*, *The Hobbit*, and Booker T. Washington's autobiography *Up from Slavery*. As students will spend roughly two weeks on each selection, including the workbook activities and the knowledge-building projects, students will need to balance their reading time with that spent on the accompanying activities. Excerpts were chosen precisely for this reason. These excerpts will give students a taste of classic literature and entice them to read the larger works.

At the end of most selections in the ***Student Anthologies*** is a biography of the author of the selection. Students can learn more about the ways authors work by reading these features.

Open Court Classics Themes

Level 2
- **Unit 1** Sharing Stories
- **Unit 2** Kindness
- **Unit 3** Look Again
- **Unit 4** Fossils
- **Unit 5** Courage
- **Unit 6** Our Country and Its People

Level 3
- **Unit 1** Friendship
- **Unit 2** City Wildlife
- **Unit 3** Imagination
- **Unit 4** Money
- **Unit 5** Storytelling
- **Unit 6** Country Life

Level 4
- **Unit 1** Risks and Consequences
- **Unit 2** Dollars and Sense
- **Unit 3** From Mystery to Medicine
- **Unit 4** Survival
- **Unit 5** Communication
- **Unit 6** A Changing America

Level 5
- **Unit 1** Cooperation and Competition
- **Unit 2** Astronomy
- **Unit 3** Heritage
- **Unit 4** Making a New Nation
- **Unit 5** Going West
- **Unit 6** Journeys and Quests

Level 6
- **Unit 1** Perseverance
- **Unit 2** Ancient Civilizations
- **Unit 3** Taking a Stand
- **Unit 4** Beyond the Notes
- **Unit 5** Ecology
- **Unit 6** A Question of Value

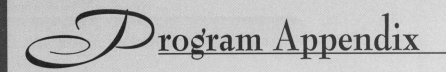
Program Appendix

Responding to Literature Workbook

After students have read a corresponding selection in the ***Student Anthology,*** they will work on the activities in the ***Responding to Literature*** workbook. Each selection averages six pages of activities in the workbook; poems average two pages. You might want to have students use any or all of the activities, depending on their needs and the available time. For example, students who have a firm grasp of the vocabulary in "Bambi" in Grade 2 might not need to do the Getting Started page that deals with unfamiliar words the students encountered in the story. They might, however, find the remainder of the activities challenging.

The activities in the ***Responding to Literature*** workbook use cognitive thinking skills as their basis. Each workbook activity for a particular selection starts with concrete skills, such as Identifying or Defining and then moves on to more complex skills, such as Adapting or Evaluating by the end of the selection. Having students move from the concrete to the abstract allows them to build logically on a foundation of skills. For a complete listing of the Thinking Skills, see the Scope and Sequence on Appendix pages 150–152.

The workbook contains a variety of activities for students to complete. A short description of these activities and the possible accompanying Thinking Skills follows.

✦ **Big Ideas:** Students answer questions or conduct research about the big issues or theme in a selection. (Thinking Skills: Drawing Conclusions, Extrapolating Information)

✦ **Break It Down:** Students identify the causes and effects of situations found in the selections. (Thinking Skills: Cause and Effect, Identifying)

✦ **A Closer Look:** Students choose a character or an aspect of a selection to investigate in more detail. (Thinking Skills: Evaluating, Describing)

✦ **Getting Started:** Often the first activity in a unit, students work on increasing their comprehension of the text, usually in the form of questions that can be answered from the text. (Thinking Skills: Recalling Details, Formulating Questions)

✦ **Going Deep:** Students might formulate or answer questions that make them think in depth about the characters, the situations in the story, the theme, and so on. (Thinking Skills: Drawing Conclusions, Extrapolating Information)

✦ **I Can Do It, Too:** Students create material that will fit before, after, or alongside the selection, such as additional dialogue, description, explanations, and so on. (Thinking Skills: Adding to, Elaborating)

✦ **I Wonder:** Students may write or perform a reflective piece, such as an essay, poem, or song, on something the selection has caused them to consider. (Thinking Skills: Interpreting, Synthesizing)

✦ **In My Opinion:** Students state and support an opinion about a related subject, about the work itself, an issue, or other pertinent topic. (Thinking Skills: Making Connections, Formulating Opinions)

✦ **Life Lessons:** Students identify and examine the lesson or moral of a selection or reflect on how events in a story mirror real life. (Thinking Skills: Making Connections, Evaluating)

✦ **Making Connections:** Students connect the plot, characters, or motivations to their own lives or to other selections. (Thinking Skills: Making Connections, Contrasting)

✦ **Picture This:** Students use their imaginations to create something based on the selection. (Thinking Skills: Adapting, Redesigning)

✦ **Quite a Character:** Students explore character traits. (Thinking Skills: Analyzing Information, Comparing)

✦ **Reality Check:** Students verify factual information found in the text or examine the believable or unbelievable parts of a selection. (Thinking Skills: Determining, Proving with Evidence)

✦ **Speak Your Mind:** Slightly different from In My Opinion, this section begins by posing a debatable issue and provides an opportunity for students to express and support their opinions in the form of a speech. (Thinking Skills: Formulating Opinions, Interpreting)

✦ **Think Like a(n) _____:** Students respond to text-specific questions, in which they must place themselves in a particular discipline related to the selection and think like a writer, an archaeologist, a doctor, and so on, to answer questions or create works as if they were established practitioners. (Thinking Skills: Making Inferences, Author's Purpose)

✦ **What Would You Do?:** Students place themselves in a character's situation. (Thinking Skills: Making Inferences, Interpreting)

✦ **Word Wise:** Found in the lower grade levels, this activity gives students an opportunity to study vocabulary. (Thinking Skills: Defining, Classifying)

The listed activities provide students with the opportunity to do extensive research and writing. The Appendix in the *Responding to Literature* workbook gives students a structure for some of the more specific assignments. In addition, Appendix pages 133–135 of this *Teacher's Edition* give an overview of the writing process and some guidelines about what to expect from good writers. Rubrics for assessing students' work can be found on Appendix pages 146–147 of this *Teacher's Edition.*

Program Appendix

Teacher's Edition

The *Teacher's Edition* outlines the process for progressing through the selections in the *Student Anthology* and for working on the activities in the *Responding to Literature* workbook. The *Teacher's Edition* also traces the knowledge-building project from start to finish.

Unit Overview

The first step for each unit lies in the Unit Overview of the *Teacher's Edition.* The unit overview introduces the theme, goals, discussion ideas, and the knowledge-building project. The unit overview outlines the project, and then each step is delineated further in the selection overview. It is important to discuss with students the information about the unit theme and goals, so that they know how all of the selections are related.

Selection Overview

During the selection overview, share with students the selection goals and genre before activating their prior knowledge about the selection. Give any or all of the background information to students before they browse the selection. After they browse, have them set their purposes for reading. While you may wish to set purposes for them initially, it is important that by the end of the third unit students are at least attempting to set their own purposes for reading. They will gain more from their reading if they do.

Next, alert students to any challenging vocabulary in the selection, and have them write the definitions in their Personal Journals. See the Vocabulary section on pages 128–129 of this Appendix for a more complete description. Students can then read the selection from the *Student Anthology* independently. If you find that students are having any difficulties understanding the selection, you might want to meet in small groups or as a class to read the selection together and determine what kinds of comprehension strategies students are using and how to improve their comprehension. Refer to the Reading Comprehension section on pages 130–131 of this Appendix for a more detailed description.

Discuss the selections with students after they have completed their reading. The reading itself might take a couple of days. After discussing the selection, have students work on the activities you have chosen in the *Responding to Literature* workbook. Note that most selections have an average of six workbook pages; poems average two pages. Poems usually complement a selection, rather than stand alone.

For your convenience, the *Responding to Literature* pages have been reduced in the *Teacher's Edition,* and specific features have been included beside the reduced pages to help you guide students through the activity. As noted earlier, each activity targets two or three cognitive thinking skills. In addition, one or two objectives have been included so you can see at a glance what the primary goal or goals of the activity are. Teacher support for the activity itself is also provided. A feature called "The Next Step" will challenge students to move beyond the activity as they delve into additional writing or research about the topic.

Finally, four assessment features have been provided for each selection: Vocabulary, Informal Comprehension Strategies, Writing, and Research. Except for the Vocabulary assessment, rubrics found in the Assessment portion of this Appendix will be used to assess what students have learned.

As students work on the workbook activities, they will also be conducting independent research to complete their knowledge-building projects for the unit. Students begin work on their projects following the unit overview. A chart in the overview outlines the part of the project students will be working on in each lesson. The selection overview also has suggestions to guide students toward the completion of their projects. For a more complete description of the project and of knowledge building, refer to Appendix pages 136–142 of this *Teacher's Edition.*

Unit Wrap-Up

The unit concludes with the unit wrap-up. Here students present their project findings and review the concepts they have learned about in the unit. They also evaluate the activities, the knowledge-building project, the selections, and the ways in which the theme was explored in the unit.

Assessment is the last feature in the unit wrap-up. The assessment in place for *Open Court Classics* is more informal than formal. That is, instead of having students take a test at the end of each selection and unit, you will be assessing what they have learned using the following methods.

✦ The various activities in the *Responding to Literature* workbook to evaluate what students have learned about a particular selection or skill

✦ Vocabulary tests and/or games to evaluate students' vocabulary knowledge

✦ Informal Comprehension Strategies rubrics to assess whether students are using comprehension strategies as they read

✦ Writing rubrics to assess students' written work

✦ Research rubrics to assess what students have learned from their knowledge-building projects

Vocabulary

Vocabulary is closely connected to comprehension. The amount of reading a person does affects vocabulary development. In fact, considerable vocabulary growth can occur incidentally during reading. Therefore, it is important to expose students to challenging words that will increase their vocabulary and their general knowledge about a subject. Learning vocabulary will help students not only in reading the anthology selections, but in any future assignments as well.

Each selection in **Open Court Classics** has vocabulary words that are included in the selection overview. These vocabulary words are usually related to the theme, occur with relatively high frequency, or interrupt the selection in a way that seriously hinders understanding of a sentence or passage unless defined beforehand. These words are included in the glossary of the **Student Anthology,** in addition to other words that did not fit the criteria but that students might not know.

The vocabulary words for a selection may be divided into a General Vocabulary list and a list with a heading specific to that selection, such as Weaving Vocabulary for "Arachne the Weaver" or Medical Vocabulary for James Herriot's "A Spot or Two of Bother." The words have been grouped together because students effectively learn new words by relating them to words they already know. An understanding of different word relationships will enable students to quickly and efficiently secure new vocabulary words.

Additional strategies are listed below to help you give students more support for expanding their vocabularies. You can use one or more of these strategies with students if they have problems with the vocabulary words.

✦ **Synonyms:** Words with similar meanings. *(cup, mug, glass)*

✦ **Antonyms:** Words with opposite or nearly opposite meanings. *(hot/cold)*

✦ **Multiple Meanings:** Words that have more than one meaning. *(run, dressing, bowl)*

✦ **Shades of Meaning:** Words that express degrees of a concept or quality. *(like, love, worship)*

✦ **Levels of Specificity:** Words that describe at different levels of precision. *(living thing, plant, flower, tulip)*

✦ **Analogies:** Pairs of words that have the same relationship. *(ball is to baseball as puck is to hockey)*

✦ **Compound Words:** Words comprised of two or more words. *(daylight, houseboat)*

✦ **Homographs:** Words that are spelled the same but have different meanings and come from different roots. *(bear, count)*

✦ **Homophones:** Words that sound alike but have different spellings and meanings. *(mane/main, to/two/too)*

+ **Base Word Families:** Words that have the same base word. *(preview, viewing, review, viewed)*

+ **Prefix:** An affix attached to the beginning of a base word that changes the meaning of the word. *(disappear, reappear)*

+ **Suffix:** An affix attached to the end of a base word that changes the meaning of the word. *(thoughtless, thoughtful)*

+ **Concept Vocabulary:** Words that help develop understanding of a concept. *(space, sun, Earth, satellite, planet, asteroid)*

+ **Derivational Word Lists:** Words derived from a particular language or with specific roots or affixes. *(duo/dual/double/duplicate, biology/archaeology/psychology)*

+ **Key Word:** A mnemonic clue created to help one remember unfamilar vocabulary. (A *mole* in chemistry is a "gram molecule." Have students relate *mole* to *molecule.*)

+ **Apposition:** The definition appears directly before or after the word and is set off by a comma. *(She is a bibliophile, or a person who loves books.)*

+ **Context Clues:** Words, phrases, or sentences surrounding an unknown word that may provide a clue to its meaning.

After introducing the vocabulary words to students and using any of the strategies listed above, have students write the new words and the definitions in their Personal Journals. This will provide them with an easy-to-reference personal dictionary of vocabulary words. You might wish to have students use the words in sentences and write the sentences in their Personal Journals.

Program Appendix

Reading Comprehension

Good readers use a variety of strategies to help them make sense of the text and get the most out of what they read. Experienced readers generally understand most of what they read, but just as importantly, they recognize when they do not understand, and they have at their command an assortment of strategies for monitoring and furthering their understanding.

The following are some reading strategies that students can use to help them comprehend a selection. Share these strategies with students. For more difficult selections, you might want to model the strategies for students by thinking aloud as you read a short passage from the selection. Keep in mind that the goal for students reading selections from *Open Court Classics* is not simply comprehension. The goal is what students are able to do with what they have read. Of course, students will need to comprehend a text before moving on to the workbook activities in *Responding to Literature* or before they complete their knowledge-building projects. The strategies will help them do so.

Setting Reading Goals

Even before they begin reading and using comprehension strategies, good readers set reading goals and expectations. Readers who have set goals and have definite expectations about the text they are about to read are more engaged in their reading and notice more in what they read. Having determined a purpose for reading, they are better able to evaluate a text and determine whether it meets their needs. Even when the reading is assigned, the reader's engagement is enhanced when he or she has determined ahead of time what information might be gathered from the selection or how the selection might interest him or her.

Comprehension Strategies

Descriptions of strategies good readers use to comprehend the text are listed below.

✦ **Summarizing**   Good readers summarize to check their understanding as they read. Sometimes they reread to fill in gaps in their understanding. Good readers use the strategy of summarizing to keep track of what they are reading and to focus their attention on important information. The process of putting the information in one's own words not only helps good readers remember what they have read, but also prompts them to evaluate how well they understand the information. Sometimes the summary reveals that one's understanding is incomplete, in which case it might be appropriate to reread the previous section to fill in the gaps. Good readers usually find that the strategy of summarizing is particularly helpful when they are reading long or complicated texts.

✦ **Monitoring and Clarifying**   Good readers constantly monitor themselves as they read in order to make sure they understand what they are reading. They note the characteristics of the text, such as whether it is difficult to read or whether some sections are more challenging or more important than others are. In addition, when good readers become aware that they do not understand, they take appropriate action, such as rereading, in order to understand the text better. As they read, good readers stay alert for signs of problems such as loss of concentration, unfamiliar vocabulary, or lack of sufficient background knowledge to comprehend the text. This ability to self-monitor and identify aspects of the text that hinder comprehension is crucial to becoming a proficient reader.

✦ **Asking Questions**   Good readers ask questions that might prepare them for what they will learn. If their questions are not answered in the text, they might try to find answers elsewhere and thus add even more to their store of knowledge. Certain kinds of questions occur naturally to a reader. For example, good readers ask questions that might clear up confusion or they might wonder why something in the text is as it is. Intentional readers take this somewhat informal questioning one step further by formulating questions with the specific intent of checking their understanding. They literally test themselves by thinking of questions a teacher might ask and then by determining answers to those questions.

✦ **Predicting**   Good readers predict what will happen next. They make predictions about what they are reading and then confirm or revise those predictions as they go.

✦ **Making Connections**   Good readers make connections between what they are reading and what they already know from past experience or previous reading.

✦ **Visualizing**   Good readers visualize what is happening in the text. They form mental images as they read. They picture the setting, the characters, and the action in a story. Visualizing helps readers understand descriptions of complex activities or processes. Visualizing can also be helpful when reading expository text. When a complex process or an event is being described, the reader can follow the process or the event better by visualizing each step or episode. Sometimes an author or an editor helps the reader by providing illustrations, diagrams, or maps. If no visual aids have been provided, it might help the reader to create one.

✦ **Monitoring and Adjusting Reading Speed**   Good readers understand that not all text is equal. As a result, good readers continuously monitor what they are reading and adjust their reading speed accordingly. They skim parts of the text that are not important or relevant to their reading goals, and they purposely slow down when they encounter difficulty in understanding the text.

In order to have students practice reading comprehension strategies, you might want to model the use of the strategies at some point. Even if modeling the strategies is not necessary for your particular classroom situation, you will at some point need to confer individually with students to learn the strategies they are using, the types of problems they are encountering in the text, and how their use of one or more strategies helped them to understand a selection better.

Writing

Writing requires the ability to use a variety of skills to create and structure an idea and the ability to manipulate words and sentences for effect. Familiarity with writing genres, structures, traits, audiences, and purposes, as well as with the writing process, will help students as they become more proficient and skilled writers.

Share any or all of the information below with students. Note that additional information about specific types of writing can be found in the Appendix of the **Responding to Literature** workbook.

Writing Genres

Students typically write within several different genres, including the following:

✦ **Narrative Writing** Story with a beginning, middle, and end. It includes myth, realistic fiction, historical fiction, biography, science fiction, folktale, and legend.

✦ **Expository Writing** Informational writing. It includes research reports, scientific investigation, summaries, and explanations of a process.

✦ **Descriptive Writing** Observational writing that includes details. It includes descriptive paragraphs that may be part of narrative or expository writing.

✦ **Poetry** Involves particular attention to word choice and rhythm. Poetry may be free form, ballad, rhyming, or a variety of other forms.

✦ **Personal Writing** Functional writing to record ideas, thoughts, or feelings or to communicate with others, such through as e-mail, journal writing, lists, or messages.

✦ **Persuasive Writing** Involves the development of a persuasive argument. It includes persuasive essays, advertisements, and posters.

Writing Traits

Writing traits enhance the effectiveness of the writing and include the following:

✦ **Ideas/Content** Not only the quality of the idea, but the development, support, and focus of the idea make a strong composition.

✦ **Organization** The organization develops the central idea. The order and structure easily move the reader through the text.

✦ **Voice** Voice is the overall tone of a piece of writing. Good writers choose a voice appropriate for the topic, purpose, and audience.

✦ **Word Choice** Words convey the intended message in an interesting, precise, and natural way, appropriate to audience and purpose.

✦ **Sentence Fluency** Sentence fluency enhances the flow and rhythm of a composition and varying sentence patterns contribute to ease in oral reading.

✦ **Conventions** Good writers demonstrate consistent use and awareness of English language conventions.

✦ **Presentation** A quality piece of writing includes an impressive presentation with attention to format, style, illustration, and clarity.

The Writing Process

The better a writer is, the *harder* he or she works at writing. Usually the best writers are the best because they work the hardest and they take *more* time in planning and revising their writing, not because they are naturally talented. Providing a routine or process for students to follow will help them learn a systematic approach to writing and help them write with purpose and thought. Students will learn that there are steps they can take to make their writing clear, coherent, and appealing to their audience.

Prewriting/Organizing

Prewriting is the first phase of the writing process when students think through an idea they want to write about. Students should take time to plan before writing. Prewriting is the most time-consuming phase of the process, but it is crucial.

Good writers

✦ listen to advice about time requirements and plan time accordingly.

✦ spend time choosing, thinking about, and planning the topic.

✦ determine the purpose for writing.

✦ consider the audience and what readers already know about the topic.

✦ conduct research before writing, using many different sources.

✦ organize the resource information.

✦ make a plan for writing that shows how the ideas will be organized.

✦ elaborate on a plan and evaluate and alter ideas as writing proceeds.

Drafting

During this phase students shape their planning notes into main ideas and details. They devote their time and effort to getting words down on paper or on computer screens. Provide a writing environment with the expectation that there will be revision to the draft and to the original plan. Share these points with students:

✦ Drafting is putting your ideas down on paper for your own use. Do not worry about spelling or exact words.

✦ Write on every other line so that you will have room to make revisions.

✦ Write on only one side of a page so you can see all of your draft when you revise.

✦ Keep in mind your purpose for writing and your intended audience.

✦ Use your plan and your notes from research to add details.

Good writers

✦ express all their ideas in the first draft.

✦ think about what is being written, and evaluate and alter ideas while drafting.

✦ change or elaborate on original plans while drafting.

✦ are able to identify when they need more information about their writing.

✦ learn more about the topic while drafting.

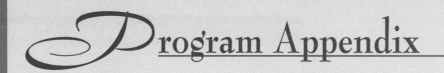

Revising

The purpose of revising is to make sure that ideas are expressed completely and clearly. It has been said that there is no good writing, just good rewriting. A distinction between good writers and poor writers is the amount of time they put into revision.

Good writers

✦ reread and evaluate what they have written.

✦ think of solutions to problems and understand which solutions will not work.

✦ recognize when text needs to be reorganized and unnecessary details eliminated.

✦ eliminate sentences or paragraphs that do not support the main idea.

✦ identify ideas that need elaboration and do more research to support ideas.

✦ take advantage of classroom and outside resources.

✦ check accuracy of facts and details and credit ideas from other people or sources.

✦ present and support personal points of view and ideas.

As students revise, have them ask themselves the following questions.

- Does each sentence belong in the paragraph and connect smoothly with the next?
- Have I combined sentences that were too short or broken sentences that were too long?
- Have I varied the beginnings of the sentences and changed words that were repeated too often?
- Have I used transition words to connect ideas?

Model asking questions such as the following when revising various kinds of writing.

1. About a Narrative
   - Does my first sentence get my readers' attention?
   - Are events in the story told in an order that makes sense?
   - Have I included dialogue to help move the story along?
   - Have I described my characters and setting and used descriptive details?
   - Does the plot include a problem, a climax, and a resolution of the problem?

2. About an Explanation
   - Will readers understand what I am saying?
   - Are the steps of the explanation in a clear order?
   - Have I made effective use of signal words?
   - Have I included enough information?

3. About Persuasive Writing
   - Have I made my position clear?
   - Does my evidence support my position?
   - Have I used opinions as well as facts?
   - Have I directed my writing to my audience?

Editing

After writing has been revised for content and style, students must read it carefully to make sure that it contains no errors. This fourth phase of the writing process is called *editing*, or *proofreading*, and must occur before a piece of writing can be published.

Good writers

✦ edit the work to allow the reader to understand and enjoy the words.

✦ correct most errors in English language conventions.

✦ use resources to address questions about English language conventions.

Editing Checklist

Have students use an editing checklist like the one shown below.

✦ Does each sentence begin with a capital letter and end with correct punctuation?

✦ Are there any sentence fragments or run-on sentences?

✦ Are any words missing from the sentence?

✦ Is any punctuation or capitalization missing from within the sentence?

✦ Is there any incorrect grammar or incorrect word usage in the sentence?

✦ Are there any misspelled words?

✦ Are the paragraphs indented?

✦ Can long paragraphs be shortened, or can short paragraphs be combined?

Presentation/Publishing

Presentation brings writing to an audience. This helps students learn about themselves and others and provides an opportunity for them to take pride in their work. Students need to decide how to prepare the piece for publication, what form the published work should take, whether to illustrate their writing, and where to place text in relation to the art.

Good writers

✦ present the work in a way that makes it easy to read and understand.

✦ consider format, style, illustration, and clarity in the presentation of the work.

✦ show pride in the finished work.

Presentation/Publishing Checklist

The following checklist will help students when they are presenting their work. Not every question applies to every form of presenting.

✦ Have I carefully edited my work?

✦ Have I carefully recopied my piece and illustrated it?

✦ Have I numbered the pages?

✦ Have I made a cover that includes the title and my name?

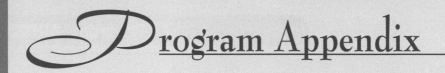

Knowledge Building

Cultivating students' love of knowledge and learning forms the core of the ***Open Court Classics*** program. This enrichment program encourages students to understand how reading classic literature can enhance their lives and help them become mature, thinking adults. Students will use what they learn in each unit as a basis for further inquiry and exploration. The units are based either on universal topics such as friendship, survival, and taking a stand or on more research-based topics such as astronomy, medicine, and money. Each unit provides a solid foundation of information upon which students can base their own inquiry and research. Students are invited to become true researchers by choosing definite areas of interest—problems or questions to research independently or in small groups. Students then present the results of their research to their classmates. In this way, they gain much more knowledge of the subject than they would have simply by reading the selections in the unit.

There is a suggested knowledge-building project in each unit overview of the ***Teacher's Edition.*** Also, a chart outlines what students will be doing in each selection as they work on their projects. Suggestions are then given at the beginning of each selection to guide students toward the completion of this project. An alternative project is also given. Students do not have to follow any of the suggestions for the knowledge-building projects in the ***Teacher's Edition.*** They can and should be encouraged to work on a project of their own choosing. The suggested projects are only in place as models for the type of projects that students might try.

There is a conventional approach to school research papers that can be found, with minor variations, in countless textbooks. It consists of a series of steps such as the following: select a topic, narrow the topic, collect materials, take notes, outline, and write. By following these steps, a student might produce a presentable paper, but the procedure does not constitute research in a meaningful sense. Instead, it gives students a distorted notion of what research is about, which should be the building of knowledge, not the presentation of a paper.

To build knowledge, students are encouraged to take the inquiry/exploration approach. This approach is based on the assumption that students can do research that will result in the construction of deeper knowledge. The procedure presents research as a never-ending, recursive cycle. Like real-world researchers, students produce their own questions, develop ideas or conjectures about why something is the way it is, and then pursue the answers. The answers, as for real researchers, might never come. What will come are more questions. Developing the questions, pursuing the answers, developing conjectures, revising ideas, and setting off on new avenues of research and exploration are the stuff of which strong, deep knowledge and expertise are made. The web of knowledge expands in ways that no teacher or student can predict easily.

In the classroom the inquiry/exploration procedure takes students through a recursive cycle that involves many steps. Students may go through these steps several times before they come to the end of their research. In real research the cycle can go on for years, and in some cases for lifetimes.

The steps in the recursive cycle of research are outlined below. As students work on their projects, they should follow these steps:

1. Decide on a problem or question to research.
2. Formulate an idea or conjecture about the problem.
3. Identify needs and make plans.
4. Reevaluate the problem or question based on what has been learned.
5. Revise the idea or conjecture.
6. Make presentations.
7. Identify new needs and make new plans.

Step 1: Decide on a problem or question to research. Students generate problems and questions after some discussion. They might or might not choose to consult reference materials before the discussion. If they do not conduct research prior to discussion of the question or problem, they might identify ideas that they truly wonder about or wish to understand. If students do consult reference sources before discussion, they might formulate questions that the reference source already has answered or problems in which they have no real interest.

The questions that have the greatest appeal or hold the most interest for students might differ from standard questions. Furthermore, these questions are more challenging to research. For example, standard questions related to the concept of astronomy include those such as "How were the planets formed?" or "Will we be able to travel to other planets?" Students might formulate an astronomy-related question such as "Why are the planets round?" They will not readily find a direct answer to this question. Instead, they will need to investigate several different sources that describe how the planets were formed. As they encounter references to "whirling balls of molten material" and find meteorites described as "pieces of material thrown off by spinning planets as they were forming," students might begin to formulate an explanation of why planets are round. As their explanations begin to form, they are led to ask new questions and follow new lines of inquiry, and possibly even to conduct experiments that involve spinning bodies.

Program Appendix

Having students generate problems or questions before consulting sources has the advantage of bringing their own conjectures into play and of revealing any theories they might possess. Young students often ask questions that show their naïve understanding of how things work. Questions such as "What is gravity made of?" and "What keeps the gravity inside Earth?" reveal the belief that gravity is a *substance*—something that can be seen and touched. Because these questions are based on false premises, they are unanswerable. However, encouraging students to investigate their questions can bring their beliefs in line with the scientific understanding of what gravity is—that it is not a substance; indeed, it is not an identifiable *thing* at all. They might be pleased to learn that this bothered Isaac Newton just as it bothers them.

If students are exploring a concept that they already know something about, they can start immediately to discuss aspects they question, things they want to understand, and so on. If the concept is unfamiliar and students have little related prior knowledge, then some teacher-directed introduction is needed to stimulate and provide a basis for questions. The kind of introduction to use depends on the students as well as the concept. In some classes, students already will have a good deal of information and many ideas that are relevant to the concept. If this is the case, they should begin with discussion and problems right away. It does not matter that their information and ideas might not be based on fact. What does matter is that students have *enough* accurate information to start their thinking.

Occasionally students might select problems that are too challenging for them. This is sure to happen if being "too challenging" means that students cannot find definitive answers to their questions. Given this definition, most real research questions are too challenging. When this occurs, teachers should remind students that the criterion of success is not finding answers but making progress. Shifting the criterion of success from answers to progress is an important move toward building knowledge and, in turn, a community of scholars.

How to Choose a Problem to Research

1. Discuss with students the nature of the unit. Explain to them that they will produce and publish in some way the results of their explorations, however preliminary. They are free to decide what problems or questions they wish to explore, how they wish to work (independently, with a partner, or in a small group), and how they want to present their findings.

2. Discuss with students the schedule you have planned for their investigations: how long the project is expected to take, how much time will be available for research, and when the first presentation will be due. In ***Open Court Classics,*** the average amount of time for a given unit from start to finish is six weeks. This schedule will partly determine the nature of the problems that students will work on and the depth of the inquiry students can pursue.

3. Have students talk about things they wonder about that are related to the unit subject. For example, in the Level 3 Money unit, students might wonder where money in the cash machine comes from or how prices are determined. Conduct a free-flowing discussion of questions about the unit subject.

4. Brainstorm possible questions for students to think about as a *starting point* for their questions. It is essential that students' own ideas and questions be the basis of all inquiry.

5. Using their wonderings, model for students the difference between a research topic and a research problem or question. For example, have them consider the difference between the topic *California* and the problem *Why do so many people move to California?* Explain that if students choose to research the topic *California*, everything they look up under the subject heading or index entry *California* will be related in some way to their topic. Choosing a specific question or problem, one that particularly interests students, helps them narrow their exploration and advance their understanding. Possible ideas for research topics are listed in each unit overview.

6. A good research problem or question not only requires students to consult a variety of sources but is engaging and adds to their knowledge of the concepts. Furthermore, good problems generate more questions. As students begin formulating conjectures, have them elaborate on their reasons for wanting to research their stated problems. They should go beyond simple expressions of interest or liking and indicate what is puzzling, important, or potentially informative about the problems they have chosen.

7. This initial problem or question serves only as a guide for research. As students begin collecting information and collaborating with classmates, their ideas will change, and they can revise their conjectures.

Step 2: Formulate an idea or conjecture about the problem. How can students judge their progress in researching a problem? Progress should not be judged by how close students are to identifying the answer, because this assumes they already know what the answer is. Progress is better demonstrated when a student can say, "Here is what I thought when I started, and here is what I think now. What I think now is more accurate than what I thought before in the following ways . . ." and then provide some reasons. Thus, conjectures—initial conjectures and revised conjectures—play a central role in inquiry/exploration research. In fact, the purpose of research is to improve conjectures.

Why is the term *conjecture* used? It seems to be an unnecessarily difficult term to use with young students. Why not use *theory, idea, belief, opinion,* or *hypothesis? Conjecture* is used because (1) it is the most precise term in the inquiry/exploration procedure; (2) it has a respectable place in science; and (3) it is good to use technical vocabulary with students when certain terms are going to be used frequently and when everyday language does not offer entirely adequate substitutes. The term *theory* implies something more elaborate and formal. *Idea* is too broad and covers too many possibilities. Further, it is possible to entertain a conjecture without holding it as a *belief* or an *opinion* (an important point to convey to students). *Hypothesis* is the most closely related term for this concept, but it implies a well-founded conjecture that already is based on evidence. It is not expected that students' initial conjectures be well founded, but it is expected that their later conjectures be better founded and thus evolve toward hypotheses or theories.

Students sometimes resist making initial conjectures, arguing legitimately that they do not know enough about a concept to make good conjectures. The appropriate response to this is "Make the best conjecture that you can. If you already have an idea of what is wrong with your conjecture, so much the better. That will give you a head start on improving it." The point to emphasize is that the goal of the research is to improve conjectures. For this process to be successful, there must be an initial conjecture.

Step 3: Identify needs and make plans. At this step, students identify the knowledge and resources they will need to address their conjectures. Then they make plans about how to obtain the needed knowledge, information, and understanding.

Identifying needs and making plans can proceed in two ways, depending upon the students. Younger students might be encouraged to discuss questions that are related to the research problem. Discussion can keep students from focusing on one key word and alert them to a wider range of relevant information. Older students, however, should begin by asking themselves what they need to know.

Make sure students take sufficient time in assessing their needs—both knowledge needs and physical needs in relation to their research. Careful preplanning can help the research progress smoothly with great results.

Step 4: Reevaluate the problem or question based on what has been learned. At this step students gather new information, guided by their research problem, conjectures, information needs, and plans. Depending on the kind of research a student is conducting, she or he may obtain new information from all kinds of sources: print materials, videos, electronically stored data, experiments, observations, interviews, and consultations with experts. This is an exciting part of the research procedure, but it can easily drift away from its purpose.

The best way to keep the information search purposeful is through frequent reevaluation steps. Students should use the new information they obtain to change their conjectures or reformulate their problems. This step may occupy most of the time and effort in the inquiry/exploration cycle of research. In order for this step to serve its purpose, it must alternate continually with the other steps in the cycle, allowing the new information to be processed as new knowledge, new conjectures, and new questions for further investigation.

The word *new* is a major factor in the reevaluation step of the procedure. When students report their findings, they must be prepared to respond to the question "What does this tell us that we didn't know?" or "How does this information help us?" Such questions should not be thought of as negative criticisms but as legitimate queries. Conventional school practices encourage students to recite information, even though it duplicates what others have said, simply to demonstrate what they have learned. It is important, therefore, to get students to think about what their information can contribute to the objectives of their research and to that of their classmates.

Step 5: Revise the idea or conjecture. In research, unlike most other activities, everything is open to revision: problems, conjectures, plans, methods, and even previously accepted facts. Accordingly, the revision step of the cycle has no specific agenda. It is wide open to anything that needs to be changed. However, revision should not be impulsive. Students should have a reason for making changes. New facts, new insights, or new inferences may be a basis for revisions of various kinds. Because there is no specific agenda, it is difficult to provide much structure for the revision step. The important thing is that individual students, partners, and research teams have opportunities to meet and consider possible revisions. This is where most of the real thinking and knowledge building will occur. Knowledge does not come simply from the acquisition of new information. It comes from reconsidering current beliefs and conjectures in light of the new information and trying to make sense of them in combination.

Given its importance, what can teachers do to make the revision step of the research cycle successful? What can they do if it isn't working? This step is largely a discussion phase, so the principles for making it successful are the same as those for discussions in general: constructive commenting, refocusing, seeding, and participant modeling. Beyond that, success of the revision-step discussions will depend on how well the cycle of research as a whole is progressing. If students are pursuing interesting and interrelated problems and are finding out significant new information, productive discussions should be easy to sustain. Students will be eager to contribute, and new problems and conjectures will arise spontaneously.

Discussions need to be focused in ways that will promote revision. If research has been going well, students will be eager for a chance to report their findings and not so eager to dwell on what others have found.

Step 6: Make presentations. In conventional research projects, all efforts are directed toward the final product—usually a written or oral report, but sometimes a presentation in some other medium, such as videocassette, demonstration, model, or poster. Presentations play an important role in the professional research world as well, but they are not limited by the presentation itself. Instead, the presentation is meant to produce feedback and criticism from peers that may change the research or modify conjectures. Presentations are occasions for the presenters to think about their research and its implications. A formal research publication has been shaped by its earlier presentations, as well as by the thinking that accompanied them. Most of these values are lost in the conventional school approach, where presentation occurs as the final step of research, after the thinking and learning about a topic are complete.

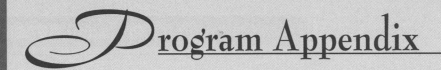

In the inquiry/exploration research cycle, presentations are an offshoot of the revision step. Because revision steps are expected to occur frequently, ample opportunities arise for presentations of all kinds. Students can give quick, informal presentations to keep the rest of the class informed about their progress. While they are expected to complete their research and turn in a project, the ultimate objective is not the project itself but the knowledge gained from the project.

Step 7: Identify new needs and make new plans. As stated earlier, the inquiry/exploration procedure views research as a recursive, never-ending process. Students should be encouraged to pursue problems or questions that interest them long after a unit of study is over.

Learning to read empowers students. Learning to learn enables them to use that power intelligently to direct their own learning process and to take charge of their own lives. *Open Court Classics* recognizes that for students to become more self-directed and purposeful in their learning, they must have opportunities to learn how to make connections between their existing knowledge and the new knowledge they encounter in reading and through discussions. Students must learn how to identify problems, ask different kinds of questions, confirm understandings, predict outcomes, interpret text, wonder about meaning, and compare ideas. In short, they must have opportunities to engage in the kind of inquiry and exploration that will prepare them for real-world thinking, decision making, and problem solving.

Assessment: Vocabulary

The assessment ideas below will help you evaluate your students' understanding of the vocabulary words for each selection. You may choose to do one or more of the following for each selection or at the end of a unit:

✦ Give students a standard vocabulary test in which you provide the words either orally or in writing, and have students define the words on paper. You might also consider doing the reverse by providing the definition and having students supply the correct vocabulary word.

✦ Distribute a written test at the end of the unit in which the vocabulary words are in one column and the definitions are in another column. Instead of having two very long columns, group the words and the definitions from one selection into separate sections, so that students are less likely to mix up words and definitions from different selections. Students can then match the definitions to the vocabulary words for each selection.

✦ Allow students the opportunity to design a test to exchange with a partner. They might come up with a matching test, a fill-in-the-blank test, or they might even want their partners to create a unique sentence for each vocabulary word.

✦ Have students create a game using the vocabulary words in the correct context. For example, have students begin by listing on the board all the words from the unit. Students will create an oral story, taking turns supplying sentences of the story using the vocabulary words correctly. Students could also do this individually by writing the story on paper.

✦ Administer a written test to students in which they must supply a synonym or an antonym for each vocabulary word.

✦ Let students find the derivation of each word and write the derivations in their Personal Journals. Have students explain how knowing the derivations can help them learn the vocabulary word.

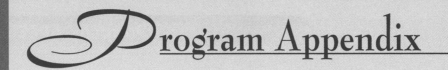

Program Appendix

Assessment: Informal Comprehension Strategies Rubrics

The Informal Comprehension Strategies Rubrics will help determine whether or not a student is using any of the strategies listed below. Discuss with students (individually or in small groups) the strategies they are using, instead of the degree to which they are using a strategy. Ask why they chose a particular strategy, and have them tell of any strategies they are using besides those listed below. If students are not using strategies, ask them why they are not doing so. You might need to monitor their comprehension more closely, either by observation or by administering short comprehension quizzes.

Asking Questions

✦ The student asks questions about ideas or facts presented in the text and attempts to answer these questions by reading the text.

Making Connections

✦ The student activates prior knowledge and related knowledge.

✦ The student uses prior knowledge to explain something encountered in text.

✦ The student connects ideas presented later in the text to ideas presented earlier.

✦ The student notes ideas in the text that are new to him or her or conflict with what he or she thought previously.

Monitoring and Adjusting Reading Speed

The student changes reading speed in reaction to the text, exhibiting such behavior as

✦ skimming parts of the text that are not important or relevant.

✦ purposely reading more slowly because of difficulty in comprehending the text.

Monitoring and Clarifying

✦ The student notes characteristics of the text, such as whether it is difficult to read or whether some sections are more challenging or more important than others.

✦ The student shows awareness of whether he or she understands the text and takes appropriate action, such as rereading, in order to understand the text better.

✦ The student rereads to reconsider something presented earlier in the text.

✦ The student recognizes problems during reading, such as unfamiliar vocabulary, loss of concentration, or lack of sufficient background knowledge to comprehend the text.

Predicting

✦ The student makes predictions about the text.

✦ The student updates predictions during reading, based on information in the text.

Summarizing

✦ The student paraphrases the text, reporting main ideas and a summary of what is in the text.

✦ The student decides which parts of the text are important in his or her summary.

✦ The student draws conclusions from the text.

✦ The student makes global interpretations of the text, such as recognizing the genre.

Visualizing

✦ The student visualizes ideas or scenes described in the text.

Writing Rubrics

Use the following writing rubrics to assess students' writing. The categories for evaluation are Genre, Writing Process, and Writing Traits. Share the rubrics with students before they begin their writing assignments, so that they can see how their writing will be evaluated. The points in the rubrics range from 1 to 4, with 4 being the highest. Assign a point value for each category or subcategory that you use to assess a student's writing. The total point value will vary for each assignment, depending on the categories or subcategories chosen.

Genre	1 Point	2 Points	3 Points	4 Points
Descriptive Writing	Includes little or no description of setting, character, or motivations.	Includes minimal description.	Includes adequate detail description.	Includes sensory details, motivations, and scenery details.
Expository Structure	Composition consists of statements with no evident order/organization. Extraneous material present.	Statements are related to a topic and have an evident purpose (to describe, explain, argue, etc.)	Main points and supportive details can be identified but they are not clearly marked.	Composition is clearly organized around main points with supportive facts or assertions.
Genre	Writing does not reflect any particular genre. A story is indistinguishable from a persuasive or expository composition.	Writing has minimal elements of genre.	Writing adequately reflects structure of a particular genre.	Writing develops around elements and structure of a specific genre.
Narrative	Narrative is missing elements (characterization, plot, setting). Logical order is not apparent.	Narrative includes plot outline but does not elaborate on details of character, plot, or setting.	Narrative adequately develops plot, character, and setting.	Narrative fully develops and elaborates on plot, character, and setting.
Persuasive	Position absent or confusing. Insufficient writing to show that criteria are met.	Position is vague or lacks clarity. Unrelated ideas or multiple positions are included.	Opening statement identifies position. Focus might be too broad. Fewer or more points than delineated in opening.	Introduction sets scope and purpose. Position maintained. Arguments supported. Includes effective closing.
Personal	Personal writing seen as task rather than as an aid. Minimal effort made. Does not reflect writer's ideas.	Some elements of personal writing reflect writer's thoughts and ideas.	Writer uses personal writing to record or develop thoughts.	Writer relies on personal writing to record, remember, develop, or express writer's thoughts.
Poetry	Little effort made to select/ arrange words to express a thought or idea. Main idea is not evident.	Some effort is made to work with word choice and arrangement to develop a thought in poetry form.	Writer has a clear idea to express in a poem and has attempted to use poetic form to express it.	Writer expresses idea in original or established poetic form. Words carefully selected/arranged for effect.
The Writing Process				
Getting Ideas	Shows little awareness that own ideas are the material of writing.	Consciously calls on own experience and knowledge for ideas in writing.	Is aware that writing requires thinking about content and ideas.	Evaluates and alters ideas as writing proceeds.
Prewriting/ Organizing Writing	Makes little or no attempt to develop a plan for writing.	Uses model to plan.	Elaborates on the model for planning.	Develops own plan based on the model.
Drafting	Writes without attention to plan or is unable to write.	Writes a minimal amount with some attention to plan.	Uses plan to draft.	Elaborates on plan in drafting.
Revising	Quickly finishes assignments and does not seek feedback.	Pays attention as teacher provides feedback about written work.	Welcomes feedback and advice from teacher or other students.	Actively seeks feedback from teacher and other students.
Editing	Demonstrates no attention to correcting grammar, usage, mechanics, or spelling errors.	Corrects some errors in English language conventions. Many are not corrected.	Corrects many errors in English language conventions.	Corrects most English language convention errors. Uses resources or seeks assistance when uncertain.
Presentation/Publishing	Presents revised and edited draft as final.	Recopies final draft with no extra presentation.	Adequate presentation efforts with illustration, format, and style.	Impressive presentation with attention to format, style, illustration, and clarity.

Writing Traits	1 Point	2 Points	3 Points	4 Points
Audience	Displays little or no sense of audience.	Displays some sense of audience.	Writes with audience in mind throughout.	Displays a strong sense of audience. Engages audience.
Elaboration (supporting details and examples that develop main idea)	States ideas or points with minimal detail to support them.	Includes sketchy, redundant, or general details; some might be irrelevant. Support for key ideas is very uneven.	Includes mix of general statements and specific details/examples. Support mostly relevant but might be uneven or lack depth.	Includes specific details and supporting examples for each key point/idea. Might use compare or contrast to support ideas.
Focus	Topic is unclear or wanders and must be inferred. Extraneous material might be present.	Topic/position/direction is unclear and must be inferred.	Topic/position is stated and direction/purpose is previewed and maintained. Mainly stays on topic.	Topic/position is clearly maintained. Details maintain central theme/purpose.
Ideas/Content	Superficial and/or minimal content is included.	Main ideas understandable, yet overly simplistic or broad; results might not be effective. Support is limited, insubstantial, overly general, or off topic.	The writing is clear and focused. The reader can easily understand the main ideas. Support is present but might be limited or somewhat general.	Writing is exceptionally clear, focused, and interesting. Main ideas stand out and are developed by strong support and rich details.
Organization	Writing lacks coherence; organization seems haphazard and disjointed. No evident plan. Facts are presented randomly. No transitions are included. Beginning is weak and ending is abrupt. No awareness of paragraph structure or organization.	Attempt made to organize the writing, but overall structure is skeletal or inconsistent. Plan evident but loosely structured, or writer overuses a pattern. Writing might be listing of facts/ideas with a weak beginning or ending. Awkward or nonexistent transitions. Has beginning use of paragraphs.	Organization is clear and coherent. Order and structure are present but might seem formulaic. Plan is evident. Reasons for the order or key concepts might be unclear. Includes beginning or conclusion but might lack impact. Transitions present. Uses paragraphs appropriately.	Organization enhances the development of central idea. Order and structure move the reader easily along. Plan is evident. Key concepts logically sequenced. Beginning grabs attention. Conclusion adds impact. Variety of transitions used to enhance meaning. Paragraphs used appropriately.
Sentence Fluency	Writing is choppy, rambling, or hard to follow. Incomplete sentences or awkward constructions force reader to slow down or reread.	The writing tends to be mechanical rather than fluid. Occasional awkward constructions might force the reader to slow down.	Writing flows, but some connections might not be fluid. Sentence patterns vary somewhat, contributing to ease in oral reading.	Writing has an effective flow and rhythm. Sentences carefully crafted, with consistently strong and varied structure.
Voice	The writing provides little sense of involvement or commitment. There is no evidence that the writer has chosen a suitable voice. Does not engage audience.	Writer's commitment to the topic seems inconsistent. A sense of the writer might emerge at times; however, voice is either inappropriately personal or impersonal.	Writer shows commitment to topic. A voice is present. In places, writing is expressive, engaging, or sincere. Words and expressions are clear and precise.	Strong commitment to the topic, with voice appropriate for the topic, purpose, and audience. Unique style is evident. Writing is engaging, expressive, or sincere.
Word Choice	Exhibits less than minimal word usage. Writing shows extremely limited vocabulary and frequent misuse of words. Monotonous language includes no interesting words. Words and expressions are simple and may be repetitive, inappropriate, or overused.	Exhibits minimal word usage. Ordinary language lacks interest, precision, or variety and might not always be appropriate to audience and purpose. Writing has few interesting words. Words are clear but more general than specific.	Exhibits adequate word usage. Words effectively convey intended message. Writing has a variety of words that are functional and appropriate to audience and purpose. Contains some interesting words and some vivid descriptive language.	Exhibits exceptional word usage. Words convey intent in a precise, natural, and interesting way appropriate to audience and purpose. Words carefully chosen and placed for impact. Often contains interesting words. Literary devices used effectively.

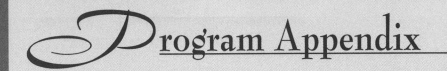

Assessment: Research Rubrics

The Research Rubrics that follow can be used to assess a student's performance during the stages of investigation for each unit. The rubrics range from 1 to 4 in most categories, with 1 being the lowest score. Most lessons in the *Teacher's Edition* have one or two Research Rubrics categories listed. Find the appropriate rubric from the list to assess how well a student's research is progressing. If students are working in groups, use the Collaborative Group Work Rubric to assess the group as a whole, and the Participation in Collaborative Inquiry Rubric to assess an individual's participation in that group.

Formulating Research Questions and Problems

1. With help, identifies things she or he wonders about in relation to a topic.
2. Expresses curiosity about topics; with help, translates this into specific questions.
3. Poses an interesting problem or question for research; with help, refines it into a researchable question.
4. Identifies something she or he genuinely wonders about and translates it into a researchable question.

Making Conjectures

1. Offers conjectures that are mainly expressions of fact or opinion. ("I think the Anasazi lived a long time ago." "I think tigers should be protected.")
2. Offers conjectures that partially address the research question. ("I think germs make you sick because they get your body upset." "I think germs make you sick because they multiply really fast.")
3. Offers conjectures that address the research question with guesses. ("I think the Anasazi were wiped out by a meteor.")
4. Offers reasonable conjectures that address the question and that can be improved through further research.

Recognizing Information Needs

1. Identifies topics about which more needs to be learned. ("I need to learn more about the brain.")
2. Identifies information needs that are relevant though not essential to the research question. ("To understand how Leeuwenhoek invented the microscope, I need to know what size germs are.")
3. Identifies questions that are deeper than the one originally asked. (Original question: "How does the heart work?" Deeper question: "Why does blood need to circulate?")

Finding Needed Information

1. Collects information loosely related to topic.
2. Collects information clearly related to topic.
3. Collects information helpful in advancing on a research problem.

4 Collects problem-relevant information from varied sources and notices inconsistencies and missing pieces.
5 Collects useful information, paying attention to the reliability of sources and reviewing information critically.

Revising Problems and Conjectures
1 No revision.
2 Produces new problems or conjectures with little relation to earlier ones.
3 Tends to lift problems and conjectures directly from reference material.
4 Progresses to deeper, more refined problems and conjectures.

Communicating Research Progress and Results
(This rubric may apply to oral, written, or multimedia reports.)
1 Reporting is sparse and fragmentary.
2 Report is factual; communicates findings but not the thinking behind them.
3 Report provides a good picture of the research problem, of how original conjectures were modified in light of new information, and of difficulties and unresolved issues.
4 Report not only interests and informs the audience but also draws helpful commentary from them.

Overall Assessment of Research
1 A collection of facts related in miscellaneous ways to a topic.
2 An organized collection of facts relevant to the research problem.
3 A thoughtful effort to tackle a research problem, with some indication of progress toward solving it.
4 Significant progress on a challenging problem of understanding.

Collaborative Group Work
(This rubric is applied to groups, not individuals.)
1 Group members work on separate tasks with little interaction.
2 Work-related decisions are made by the group, but there is little interaction related to ideas.
3 Information and ideas are shared, but there is little discussion concerned with advancing understanding.
4 The group clearly progresses in its thinking beyond where individual students could have gone.

Participation in Collaborative Inquiry
(This rubric is applied to individual students.)
1 Does not contribute ideas or information to team or class.
2 Makes contributions to class discussions when specifically called upon to do so.
3 Occasionally contributes ideas or information to other students' inquiries.
4 Takes an active interest in the success of the whole class's knowledge-building efforts.

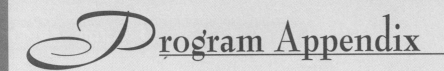

Open Court Classics Scope and Sequence

Grade Levels	Level 2	Level 3	Level 4	Level 5	Level 6
Comprehension					
Asking Questions	X	X	X	X	X
Making Connections	X	X	X	X	X
Monitoring and Adjusting Reading Speed	X	X	X	X	
Monitoring and Clarifying	X	X	X	X	X
Predicting	X	X	X	X	X
Summarizing	X	X	X	X	X
Visualizing	X	X	X	X	X
Thinking Skills					
Adapting					X
Adding to		X	X	X	X
Analyzing Information	X	X	X	X	X
Author's Purpose	X	X	X	X	X
Cause and Effect	X	X	X	X	X
Categorizing	X	X	X	X	X
Classifying	X	X	X	X	X
Comparing	X	X	X	X	X
Comprehending/ Understanding	X	X	X	X	X
Contrasting	X	X	X	X	X
Defining		X	X	X	X
Describing	X	X	X	X	X
Designing					X
Determining	X	X	X	X	X
Distinguishing	X	X	X	X	X
Drawing Conclusions	X	X	X	X	X
Elaborating	X	X	X	X	
Evaluating/Judging	X	X	X	X	X
Extrapolating Information	X	X	X	X	X
Focusing		X		X	
Forming Opinions			X		
Formulating Questions	X	X	X	X	X
Generating Ideas		X	X	X	
Identifying	X	X	X	X	X
Interpreting	X	X	X	X	X
Making Connections	X	X	X	X	X
Making Inferences	X	X	X	X	X
Organizing	X	X	X	X	
Paraphrasing/ Summarizing		X	X	X	X

Planning	X	X	X	X	X
Prioritizing	X	X	X	X	X
Proving with Evidence	X	X	X	X	X
Recalling Details	X	X	X	X	X
Redesigning	X	X	X	X	X
Sequencing Events	X	X	X	X	X
Substituting	X	X	X		
Vocabulary					
Adjectives	X		X		
Adverbs		X			
Affixes			X		
Colloquialisms			X		
Connotation					X
Context Clues		X	X		X
Denotation					X
Multiple-Meaning Words		X			
Synonyms/ Antonyms	X		X	X	
Word Histories		X	X	X	
Writing					
Descriptive Writing	X	X	X	X	X
Expository Writing	X	X	X	X	X
Narrative Writing	X	X	X	X	X
Personal Writing	X	X	X	X	X
Persuasive Writing	X	X	X	X	X
Poetry	X	X	X	X	X
Writing Process	X	X	X	X	X
Literary Analysis					
Character		X	X	X	X
Genre		X	X	X	X
Literary Criticism					X
Literary Devices					X
Plot		X	X	X	X
Setting		X		X	X
Symbolism					X
Tone			X		X
Traits of Writing					
Author's Style		X	X	X	
Word Choice		X	X		X
Writer's Craft					
Audience/Purpose			X		
Dialogue		X	X	X	
Figurative Language	X	X	X	X	X

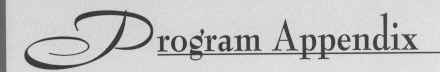

Humor			X	X	
Logical Order			X		
Poetic Devices			X	X	X
Point of View			X	X	
Sensory Details			X	X	
Similes		X	X	X	
Sound of Language	X		X		X
Supporting Details			X		
Listening/Speaking/Viewing					
Acting/Role-Playing		X	X	X	
Analyzing Fine Art			X		X
Debates		X	X	X	X
Delivering a Presentation			X		X
Delivering a Speech		X	X	X	X
Dramatic Reading		X	X		
Listening				X	
Participate in Discussion	X	X	X	X	X
Picture Essay/Photo-Essay			X	X	X
Sharing Personal Writing			X	X	
Storytelling					X
Inquiry and Research					
Collaboration	X	X	X	X	X
Communicating Research Progress and Results	X	X	X	X	X
Conducting an Interview	X		X		X
Determining Relevant Sources of Information	X	X	X		
Finding Needed Information	X	X	X	X	
Graphic Organizers	X	X	X	X	X
Making Conjectures	X	X	X	X	X
Note Taking	X	X	X	X	X
Peer Review			X		X
Recognizing Information Needs	X	X	X	X	X
Revising Problems and Conjectures	X	X	X	X	X
Summarizing/Organizing Information	X	X	X	X	X
Using a Dictionary or Glossary	X	X	X	X	X
Utilizing Appropriate Resources	X	X	X	X	
Verifying Information					X

Index